GW00863603

Raising Teenagers, The Ultimate Guide

Or

How to build teenagers who are rounded, resilient and responsible

(and try to stay cool, calm and collected)

Gianna and Kevin Lee

A comprehensive guide to successfully raising teenagers and dealing with teenage issues.

This book is dedicated to all the SENCOs, Support staff and Counsellors working in schools and supporting teenagers who are in distress or just struggling to cope.

"Give the ones you love wings to fly, roots to come back
and reasons to stay" Dalai Lama

Preface

When our children are ten, we are legally responsible for their safety and wellbeing and they are more or less totally dependent upon us. We make all the significant decisions for them and expect them to do what we tell them. Ten years later, we expect them to be more or less independent adults, responsible for themselves and making their own carefully thought out decisions. This is a huge transition for them, but it is also a huge transition for parents. Parents need to slowly loosen the reins, even though they will naturally have all sorts of fears about the extra risks that their teenagers will be exposed to. This is a delicate balancing act, with parents having to judge what responsibilities their teenagers are ready to accept, while their teenagers may well be clamouring for more independence. No parent really enjoys giving up their control, but this is the way that successful adults are built.

We don't believe there is a single perfect way to parent, nor do we claim to be the experts. Only you can be the expert for your family. Every teenager is different and the relationship between every teenager and parent is different, so there is no single solution, but this book has been written to give you advice and information to help you find the right solutions to apply to your own personal situation.

Our book will help you to transform your teenager into a happy and independent adult and help you to have an easier time in the process. It is based on our years of working with young people, but also on the latest research. It will show you the avenues to creating happy adults, as well as giving you practical steps on your journey. As you turn the pages, the keys to reaching these goals will become clearer, leaving you more confident, more prepared, and more knowledgeable, and in possession of a whole set of tools to allow you to move your family toward the future that you always hoped for.

Introduction

Usually, when people introduce themselves to you at this stage, they will try to convince you that they are the experts because they know just how to do it right and they have shown it. Well, we are not sure there are any real experts on raising your family except you and there is certainly no easy way that works for everybody.

By the time you reach our age as parents and grandparents, you have a wealth of experience. They say people learn from their mistakes and let me tell you that in raising our own family, we have made plenty of them, but we have learnt from them too.

During the last forty years together, we have always tried to get away for a few days here and there just to reconnect and to escape the strain of everyday family life. On one such occasion, on our wedding anniversary, we went away to Moreton-in-the-Marsh, which is a lovely little village in the Cotswolds. It was early autumn and it was a lovely sunny afternoon, so we decided to walk to the nearby arboretum which was about an hour's walk away. We ambled around the arboretum for a few hours, which is a beautiful peaceful place, and decided to head home. We had finished our walk in a part of the arboretum that was only about 100 meters from the main road, with just a small field in between. Crossing the field would save us about 30 minutes from the walk back, so it seemed a no brainer, but about 20 metres across the field, we realised our mistake! The ground became increasingly wet and squelchy, and by sixty metres, Gianna lost her first shoe in the mud. By now we had come too far to go back so we ploughed on until we got to the other side. We then realised that there was no gate or stile, so no easy way out, and so we had to fight our way through a hedge. We eventually emerged onto the road intact, but only just! By now we were completely bedraggled, covered with mud and scratched from the hedge thorns. We were battle scarred!

This was also the story of our journey through parenting. We set off on our journey full of hope. When our children were at primary school, we had a few ups and downs but mostly we had an easy time. We thought we were doing a good job and that we were great parents. We were walking in the sunshine.

Hitting the teenage years, we were totally unprepared, and walked straight into the mud! Things seemed to go wrong quite quickly and without warning. We floundered and panicked and lost all confidence in our parenting skills. We seemed to be doing everything wrong. We started to fight, blaming each other for things that were going wrong, and lost connection as a family.

As two professional people, both working with families and young people, our failures were not only hard to admit to ourselves, but even harder to admit to other people. After all, we were supposed to be the experts and to know how to do it properly!

Just like in that muddy field, we eventually made it through to the other side, but it left us bruised and worn out. The only good thing is that we were certainly wiser, with many of our original ideas about parenting challenged and reconsidered.

When we were preparing this book, we researched the arboretum on the internet to make sure that our memories were accurate. We discovered that there was a much quicker footpath to get to the arboretum from the village that we didn't know about, because we hadn't looked at the map before setting off on our journey.

So, we have written this book for two main reasons:

Firstly, if you have teenagers and you are still walking in the sun, we hope this will prepare you for the future possibility that it may all go wrong. Even if you have already been through all this once we can assure you that a younger brother or sister may be totally different. We hope to show you the easier footpath in advance so to speak!

Secondly, if you are already in the mud, to offer you a helping hand, to pull you out and find you a shortcut to the exit gate,

So, are you in the sunshine or the mud?

Sunshine or mud Quiz **Look at this list of questions, how strongly do you agree with the following statements?**	YES	NO	Maybe
Teenager			
My teenager is doing well at school			
My teenager is coping well at school			
My teenager is coping well with life			
My teenager is happy			
Parent			
I am doing a great job as a parent			
I am coping well with life			
I am happy			
Family			
My family life with my teenager is harmonious			
My teenager gets on with his brothers/sisters			
My teenager gets on with other household members			
As a family, we are happy			

If you answered yes for all these statements, you are most definitely in that sunny stroll in the country. If you have some or most of them where you answered no, then you are probably stuck in the mud. You might just be in the maybe column or swing between the three! Now the fact that you picked up this book suggests that either you are already in the mud, or you know someone who is, so let's try to get you out of it.

When we talk to young people about Facebook and social media, we tell them not to take what they see too literally. People only put on Facebook what they want you to see that portrays them in the best possible way. It is like viewing a West End show where we see two hours of perfectly rehearsed and choreographed performance. We forget about the six months of rehearsals, the arguments, the rewrites and the shows that never made it this far. When we look at other families on Facebook or talk to people at the school gate, we often face the same issue. Other families often seem to be totally harmonious and behave like some of those perfect families we used to see on American TV. Of course, this is all nonsense. Most families have problems, particularly in the teenage years. They don't want to let the rest of us know that for two reasons. Firstly, they don't want to 'wash their dirty laundry' in public, they want to keep these things private. That's perfectly understandable. Secondly, they think if people see that their family has problems it shows them up as failing parents. Again, this is understandable. Unfortunately, the effect of this is that struggling teenagers and their families feel very isolated. They think it's only them and that they are failing. Just as the path to true love is not always smooth, so too, bringing up a child comes with a health warning!

Let's look at some research. A survey published by the Bauer Media News and Young Minds in 2014 revealed the following:

1 in 3 parents with a teenager have visited a GP or A&E with concerns over their child's mental health

Think about that! If one in three parents has been to a doctor that's nearly two million teenagers.

The same survey showed that about the same level of parents, one in three, said they found it difficult to get help with their teenager. So what do we conclude? You are not alone. Not only are there lots of families out there who are struggling, but if we include those who have never been to a doctor it may well be the majority.

Through this book, we are hoping to help you with these struggles, but the fact is that there are lots of other parents out there in a very similar situation. We do encourage you to try to find them. We don't expect you to stand at the school gate and tell people your daughter has stolen from you or your son is swearing at you or your teenager is drinking too much, but a simple statement like "I never realised that dealing with teenagers would be so difficult" might open up a conversation. If you can find other parents, you may be able to offer each other some advice. Even if you can't, you can at least give each other some moral support and sympathy. You might also consider the many helpful parent fora on the internet where you can access advice and support from all over the world.

Our book is simple to navigate. **Part One,** the first five chapters form **The Guide Book,** which is designed to improve your understanding of teenagers and to help you develop the best possible parenting strategy.

The first chapter will give you a chance to explore parenting styles. You can identify which style you are using and decide whether you could make useful changes to be more effective. We will show you which style, based on research, is proven to be the most successful in bringing up children

In Chapter Two, we will tell you what teenagers today are worrying about, how this is affecting their mental health and wellbeing and how to spot if things are going wrong.

Chapter Three will take you through the way in which teenagers develop and why this can cause them, and you, problems. You may already have noticed that teenagers are not the same as younger children, but we will explain why they are not like adults either. We will look at what happens during puberty, particularly the hidden effects that cause the most difficulties.

Chapter Four discusses happiness. We will let you into the secret of how people achieve it and how to maximise your family's chances of capturing it.

Hopefully, by this stage you will know a lot more than you did and certainly a lot more than we knew when we were raising our family. Sadly, even that is not enough without learning the final skill.

Chapter 5 explains to you how to set yourself, and your family, positive and realistic targets and how to achieve them. We will tell you how to agree on targets for yourself and your teenager that are designed to maximise your happiness and improve your family's mental health and wellbeing.

Part Two of the book forms **The Basic Toolkit**. These are the really important issues that all parents need to get right in order to create strong and enduring relationships with their teenager and to pass the right messages on to their children so that they can, in turn, become autonomous and independent. We will talk about the parent's role and the teenager's rights and responsibilities. We will also cover the critical area of communication as well as setting boundaries, building self-esteem and confidence.

Part Three is **The Emergency Toolkit**. The more we researched and talked to parents and teenagers, the larger this section grew! This is our 'My Teenager and.......' section, and it covers a myriad of issues affecting families today. Here we provide some important tips and current information about how to manage teenage behaviour. Even if we know the longer-term targets and strategies that we need to adopt in parenting our teenagers, we still need to manage the day to day stresses and strains of dealing with teenagers who can be highly emotional, very unpredictable, difficult and sometimes very hard to live with. If you are already having a very hard time with your teenager, if you are already stuck in the mud, this might be where you choose to start.

This book is designed to be the ultimate guide for parents, both a reference book and a training manual in one. Left in a prominent place, we hope that the whole family, including your teenagers, will read it, sparking conversation, debate and openness.

Our overall aim is to make life easier for families, to reduce stress and anxiety for parents and carers of teenagers and to reduce the impact and incidence of mental ill health on our young people. We hope you find it a useful resource.

Gianna & Kevin Lee
Avenues4Life
2019

PART ONE

THE GUIDE BOOK

Chapter 1

The 'Good Enough' Parent

Old Habits Die Hard

How do we learn to parent?

"You used to be a great parent what happened to you?"

When I first saw this phrase it rather shocked me. We tend to spend so much time looking at our teenagers that we forget to think about how they see us. But we need to keep this in mind, while we look at parenting styles. These are things that we tend not to think about but are crucially important.

We know that adolescence can be a time when teenagers attempt to assert their own needs and wants in the quest for independence. For some teenagers, this is an easy ride, but for others, it can be a time fraught with confusion, conflict and frustration. And it can be the same for their parents!

When you first think about having a child, very few of you will have a conversation about how you will parent. You might have shared hopes and dreams for your child or even your views on morality or values, but when two people come together and create a life, at least two, often very different experiences of parenting are brought into the equation. Your own style of parenting reflects how you were raised, and it is shaped by morals and values handed down by your own upbringing.
How you were parented yourself might have led to you deciding "I'll never do that with my child", or "I hope I make decisions like my folks did", but usually, in the rosy glow of creating a life, most parents cross their fingers and hope for the best!

When the teenage years hit, and you try to balance the desires and needs of your adolescent with your own, difficulties often arise. It is an especially trying time in a family, but if you and your partner can understand and adjust your parenting styles to better fit a teenager's development, it can help to make life and relationships much more bearable.

So, what have we brought with us from our own experiences? You will have your own stories and memories that have shaped your parenting style but for me, this is how it worked for us

Kevin's story

Let me tell you what it was like for me, and I think most of my generation, who grew up in the fifties. My parents were strict and my school like most schools then was also very strict. So that was how most of us were raised. My older cousins had to join the army as conscription was still in place and that was an even stricter regime. Physical punishment in primary and secondary schools was considered normal and I experienced both. I was only caned once at secondary school and it made quite a mark on me – in fact, several as I am about to tell you.

It was the last day of the Autumn term. The school was going to break up at lunch-time for the Christmas holidays and spirits were running high. I was in my tutor room with the rest of my class waiting for morning registration. Now, at my school, we all had caps. These caps were compulsory. If you were seen coming or going to school without one it was an instant punishment. On this morning though, several of my classmates made a great scientific discovery. If you threw a cap across the room with a subtle flick of the wrist it would behave just like a Frisbee. Of course, at that time real Frisbees had not even arrived in England. There we were with most of the class sitting and chatting but with two or three people experimenting with their Frisbees. This was the time the Deputy Headmaster chose to come through the door. A cap flew past his nose and he was not amused. An hour later 36 boys were lined up outside his office and one by one we received three strokes of the cane. I was about in the middle of the class list alphabetically and so

11

I held out some hope that he might have tired by the time he got to me, but I was sadly disappointed. Years of experience and the caning of hundreds and possibly thousands of boys had honed his caning into a fine art. Of course, like all the other boys I didn't show it, but it certainly hurt. Did I complain? No! Did I go home and tell my parents? No! That would only have made matters worse. It was quite a challenge making sure that they did not notice until the marks had healed.

In my family, it was the tradition to go to my Grandmother's house on Christmas day and thirty people would sleep there overnight. I would be in a single bed with my brother and my two cousins. A week later that's how it was. I must tell you that my cousins were really impressed by the three red stripes on my backside. In those days they were considered noble battle scars in the never-ending war between students and teachers.

Now hearing all that it sounds quite shocking by modern standards but let me tell you something, it taught me that life is not always fair, and you just have to get on with it!

Later, when I became a parent, I automatically adopted the strict approach. I didn't make a conscious decision to do it, it was just my underlying working assumption. It had been the model of parenting that I had seen and grown up with, and it seemed to work, so why wouldn't I do it like that? I was of the 'It didn't do me any harm' brigade!

Built in to that assumption was that when I set rules they would be obeyed, but I soon found out that wasn't going to happen. The problem was that when my teenagers challenged my rules and they soon did, I had no idea how to deal with it. I had no model for dealing with conflict. My dad was a lovely man and a loving father, but you didn't dare defy him. He had been through poverty during the depression and had nearly been killed on several occasions in the war and he was tough! It had been the same at school. There were a few boys who challenged the authority, but I certainly wasn't one of them. Because of that, I had not seen a great deal of conflict and had no real experience of resolving conflict other than by physical punishment. In fact, if I spotted conflict I would always try to avoid it, so I found myself completely at a loss as to what to do.

The interesting thing when I look back is that not long before my kids hit their teens, I changed my career path and became a teacher. Did I adopt the strict approach in the classroom? No! Why? Because I set off with the belief that if I gave rules to thirty students the chances were that they wouldn't all just obey them. You know some teachers can walk into a room and there is instant silence, others can walk into the room and no one notices them for five minutes. When I started teaching I didn't have the skills or experience to be that first teacher, I wasn't very confident, and I knew that I didn't have natural authority. After teaching for over twenty years I have become much more confident and project a more authoritative image, but I am still not that first teacher!

So how did I maintain discipline?
I had much more support in school than I had as a parent, but nevertheless, in the classroom as a teacher, it is always just you, so I think I tried much harder to develop the relationship between me and my students. I certainly spent much more time explaining why students should behave in a certain way. Where I could, I also tried to be responsive to their needs and above all, I tried to convince them that I cared how they got on and I would try to support them in every way I could. I also believe that I was better than some of my colleagues at staying calm and being consistent.

I soon learned as a teacher, and subsequently as a parent, that if you shout at people they often shout back. And when you are both shouting neither of you is listening!

As I became more confident I relaxed a bit more. I would use humour when I could even if it meant making fun of myself, and some of my classes thought I was hilariously funny, in fact, I think for some of my students I even became their favourite teacher. I was still in charge, but I wasn't trying to dominate. In retrospect, it is clear, that I was using a much more balanced style and it worked in my favour.

Gianna's story

I am younger than Kevin and I grew up in the rather different era of the sixties.

I was always interested in young people, I used to be one!

Coming from a huge family of 10 kids, I learned a lot about care and support and the importance of good parenting. I saw first-hand what worked, and how things can go badly wrong if parents don't have a united approach or lack confidence in their parenting style.

The backgrounds of my father and mother were very different. My father, the youngest of 15 children spent most of his life in an orphanage after his father died when he was two. This created a passive man, prone to outbursts of aggression, who had learned, and believed, that children should be obedient, and follow the rules if they hope to live a life without getting into trouble. What I saw growing up, was that his strict method of upbringing just didn't work, and it became a great game to play to look as if we were obedient whilst living our life our way. He was a hard-working man, but his aspirations for us were few, and he just wanted us all in gainful employment. His mind stretched not much further than us learning 'some kind of trade'.

My mother, on the other hand, had benefitted from a good grammar school education, and for us her aspirations were broader. She brought us up to believe that we could do or achieve anything, and that most things are possible with hard work, organisation and commitment. She believed in the inherent goodness of our human race and taught us always to think well of everybody. Her approach was more tolerant and liberal, and I identified strongly with her style of parenting.

Although my mother needed to be incredibly organised, she had the knack of making boring things fun! She used very persuasive methods to bring us 10 children into line, and always emphasised fairness and equality and a sharing of responsibility. Generally, she didn't believe in punitive measures that involve physical punishment, but because of my father's passive nature, was often the one to wield the slipper. Yes, we were hit. Did it do us any harm? Yes! It taught me that the bigger and stronger you are the more powerful, and the more control you have! I learned to be fearful and I felt the need to please greatly and to keep the peace at all costs. It affected my life in many ways, some negative and some positive, but it also made me realise that physical violence often stems from a feeling of acute frustration and powerlessness and fear.

When my own children were small, I remember taking them to preschool and seeing so many of the kids having trouble settling in and separating from their parents. I also noticed how parents found it difficult to cope, especially with discipline, and it made me interested, so that I started training in early years care and education and even managed the preschool for several years. This naturally led on to me tutoring childcare and education as part of my professional development

Working, studying and training childcare development courses had a massive influence on the evolution of my parenting. I developed an enabling, or authoritative approach, alongside assertiveness and the belief that children deserved treatment equal to that of adults. Looking back, I realised that this sometimes slipped into being indulgent or permissive, and that was not wholly a comfortable fit with Kevin's more authoritarian style. Although not consciously aware, I over-compensated for his strict and sometimes even Uninvolved approach.

Over the years I have come to believe that parents usually want the best for their children and the fear that their child, whom they have emotionally invested in, might not achieve their fullest potential, creates great anxiety, none more so than when your child is becoming more independent and out of your control during the teenage years.

Whatever stage you are at with growing your teenager, it might be helpful to consider that how both parents manage their own relationship at this time will have a crucial impact on the development of your teenager's self-esteem and life-satisfaction. Young people capitalise on a situation, to get the answer that they want to hear, and if they are not presented with a united front from those in authority, then playing one parent against the other is just using good common sense as far as your teenager is concerned. When boundaries are not clear or consistently enforced, a situation is created that has a negative impact for both you and your teenager.

"Even as kids reach adolescence, they need more than ever for us to watch over them. Adolescence is not about letting go. It's about hanging on during a very bumpy ride." - Ron Taffel, Ph.D.

Teenagers are at a stage in their development where they need to develop their independence and self-will. This is necessary to ensure healthy growth, both emotionally and physically. Parents attempting to exert too much control over their teenager may cause them to suffer since they are not being allowed to assert themselves to the extent that they need. Conversely, without much parental support and guidance, your teenager is much more likely to make unhealthy or unsafe decisions, that impact on their future life choices and opportunities.

So where do you start? How do you create the healthiest type of relationship with your teenager and help them grow up to become independent, responsible and happy adults?
First, we will give you some useful background. Then we will give you a quiz to try to identify your parenting style. If you are sharing your parenting with a partner you can see if you are on the same page. Be aware that your answers might fall into more than one style, but the hope is that you will find the style from which you operate as a parent most of the time.

What is your parenting style and your partners?
If you were asked what your parenting style is, or that of your partner, what would you say? Most of us have no idea and have

never even thought about it. However, recognising your predominant parenting style, is an essential tool in managing your teenager to avoid conflict and smooth out those teenage years. It is also critical in finding ways to understand each other and manage teenage changes to produce the best outcomes.

Over the years, psychologists have identified four distinctive types of parenting

Enabling (Authoritative) - This style blends a caring tone with structure and consistent limit-setting. Parents who fall under this category are more likely to place limits and enforce consequences, but at the same time are able to administer fair and consistent discipline.

Strict (Authoritarian) - A parents-know-best approach that emphasises obedience

Indulgent (Permissive) –Parents provides few behavioural guidelines because they don't want to upset their children and want to be liked. Indulgent parents often seem more like a friend to the child and less like a parent.

Uninvolved (Neglectful) - Parents expect little out of their child and offer little to no supervision. Uninvolved parents sometimes do have rules, but they are loosely enforced with little to no repercussions if they are broken.

Over the next few pages, you have a chance to take this short quiz, to help you identify your own personal parenting style and to see where you fit in.

UNDERSTANDING YOUR PARENTING STYLE

Instructions: *This quiz is designed to help you better understand your parenting style. Circle A, B, C or D. Then have a look at the scoring section.*

1. Parents often have different ideas about how to monitor their teenagers. Which of the following is most like your approach?

A. I limit unsupervised time. I also routinely check up on my teen unannounced to make sure she is where she said she'd be.

B. Teens can't ever be trusted, so I really lay down the law when it comes to what my teen is permitted to do. It's not up for discussion.

C. Teens need their privacy. I would never eavesdrop or check up on my daughter because I wouldn't want her to be upset with me.

D. I don't have time to keep tabs on my teen. My feeling is that teens need to learn how to take care of themselves, so I leave it up to them to make the right decisions.

2. Which of these, best describes your role as a parent?

A. I concentrate on being a parent first and a friend second. Creating connection and openness is important to me.

B. I'm sometimes quite severe with my teenager, but he knows I love him.

C. I think my teenager sees me as a laid back and cool parent.

D. I don't see my teenage son as much as I would like, because of my commitments. He just gets on with it himself.

18

3. Which of the following best describes your beliefs about rules and discipline?

A. I usually praise my teen for good behaviour and try to ignore bad behaviour.

B. Teenagers are rebellious by nature. If they break the rules, the consequences should be severe enough to teach them a lesson.

C. I spend more time threatening my teen with punishment than actually giving it.

D. I don't think discipline works very well. I expect my teen to monitor his own behaviour and face the consequences if he makes a bad decision

4. The main goal of parenting and discipline is to...

A. Teach your children why your rules are important and help them learn to make good choices on their own

B. Get your kids to listen to you no matter what

C. Let children grow up without too many rules so that they remember it as a fun time.

D. Make sure everyone is happy and doing whatever they want

5. Which of the following reflects your beliefs about loving and nurturing your teen?

A. I show my love by spending quality time with my teenager, I try being involved, showing affection, listening, giving him positive reinforcement, and providing firm structure.

B. I always expect my teenager to behave properly and sanction him when he doesn't. He may not always like it now, but eventually he will know we were demanding because we loved him.

C. I believe loving parents try to provide for their teen opportunities and things that they didn't have when they were growing up. My teen makes more demands on me than I do on him.

D. My teen knows I love him. We provide for his needs and comforts.

6. When your kids don't help with jobs around the house you...

A. Give them a helpful reminder that they need to be responsible and remind them of their agreed responsibilities. I apply sanctions if they fail to do so.

B.   Get mad, yell and make them do them right away

C. Try again to renegotiate the agreements but accept that most kids don't like to help out!

D.   Do them yourself, it's no good making a fuss

A. Which of the following describes your relationship with your teenager?

A. Our relationship is warm and mostly positive but I'm not afraid to lay down the law when I must.

B. Like most kids her age, my teen is rebellious and acts out. I feel like I spend a lot of time and energy lecturing and issuing threats to try to keep her in line.

C. We're like best friends. My teen tells me everything.

D. Kids will be kids. No matter what I do, she will have to learn her own lessons.

B. When my teenager and I argue about something, I generally:

A.   Try to calm myself and show respect for his opinion by listening to him.

B.   Get upset and frustrated. Too many kids today talk back to their parents.

C.   Feel guilty. We are very close, and I hate when there's conflict between us.

D.   Let it go. If you let your teen have freedom, eventually they'll figure it out.

C. Your 14year old son borrows an 18 rated Playstation game, you would...

A.   Explain that the material is unsuitable, and why he is not able to play the game. Ask him to return it without using it.

B.   Get angry and tell him he is not allowed to bring any borrowed games into the house again.

C.   Let him play the game, he'll only do it secretly anyway.

D.   I don't know anything about gaming, so leave it up to him.

D. You and your teenager have a disagreement about his plans for summer break. You:

A.   Listen to your teen's opinion and try to work together to come up with a compromise.

B.   Stand firm and tell your teen that your word is final.

C. Decide to back down. It's easier to give a little ground to keep the peace

D. Let your teen do what he wants – after all, you are only a kid once.

E. What would you do if you didn't approve of your teen's new friends?

A. Try to get to know his friends better, and their parents, and then decide what to do.

B. Forbid him to spend any more time with them.

C. Feel conflicted about interfering with his friendships and being too controlling.

D. Assume he'll make the right choices and not get into too much trouble.

12. Which of these reflects your thinking about teens and drug use?

A. Any drug use is forbidden, and I've shared with my teen what the consequences will be if she breaks our rule.

B. I would severely punish my teen if I caught her using any drugs, including pot and alcohol.

C. Teens are going to try it at some point, so if I found out my teen tried pot or alcohol, I'd probably just tell her not to do it again.

D. It doesn't matter what I say or do. If teenagers want to try it, they will.

F. **Your 16-year old son wants to go to a party at a friend's house and the parents will not be home most of the evening. He keeps nagging you about it so you:**

A. Hear him out, and then explain the reasons why you won't let him go.

B. Tell him no and say "end of discussion."

(C.) Allow him to go because you trust him and his friends are all going.

D. Let him go because he will just continue to argue about it.

G. **Your teenage daughter is delaying her bedtime because she wants to Facetime her friends for a chat?**

A. Ask her to finish her call and encourage her to make her calls earlier in the evening in future

B. Get mad and confiscate her phone

(C.) Just be glad that she has a good social life with her friends

D. Let her talk for as long as she wants, it's not your problem if she is tired tomorrow.

You may have noticed a pattern in the questions as you went through.
If you circled predominantly As, then you mostly have an Enabling parenting style.
If you circled predominantly Bs, then you mostly have a <u>Strict</u> parenting style.
If you circled predominantly Cs, then you mostly have an <u>Indulgent</u> parenting style.
If you circled predominantly Ds, then you mostly have an <u>Uninvolved</u> parenting style.

It is worth looking back over your childhood and adolescence and thinking about the styles of those who raised you. This may include other close relatives or neighbours as well as your parents. How did their styles differ and whom do you remember most fondly? Schools are also important in our development. Teachers also adopt similar styles to parents and indeed schools themselves differ in style. Did you have a good time at school? Who were your favourite teachers and why?

Many of us, if we are lucky enough to have a choice of secondary schools, don't consider the style of the school, but this can have a significant impact on our children's happiness. When we join those crowds of parents and children at school open evenings, we get carried away by the brand-new gym or the rows of computers. Talk to the students, who are showing you round the school. Are they happy? Do they have any criticisms of the school? If you know other parents who already have students there, talk to them about their experiences.

When we made these choices, our children gained places at our local grammar schools, which had some of the best academic results in the country. We thought our job was done, but neither of them thrived and both ultimately achieved success in the comprehensive system. This challenged our preconceived ideas about finding the best school and fitting our children in, we realised that you need to ensure that the school is a good fit for the child. Had we had more children, I have no doubt that they would all have had differing needs and may have found their feet in either the grammar, comprehensive or independent school systems.

Parent Power
What does research suggest works best?
Let's look at what the research tells us. The following results are from a 2006 survey[1] of students aged around 15. The students responded to very similar, in depth, questionnaires, but answered from their perspective, as to how their own parents behaved. They also completed standard questions designed to measure their self-

esteem, life-satisfaction and importantly their likelihood of suffering with depression in later years. Although this is only one set of results the results that we will see have been repeated in lots of other studies. This study also looked at both maternal and paternal styles. The high scores represent a stronger relationship to the characteristic.

Maternal and Paternal Parenting Styles in Adolescents
Associations with Self-Esteem, Depression and Life-Satisfaction

Maternal parenting style

Style	Self-esteem	Depression	Life satisfaction
Enabling	4.20	1.70	5.97
Strict	3.71	1.97	4.96
Indulgent	3.87	2.00	5.23
Uninvolved	3.51	2.09	4.78

Paternal parenting style

Style	Self-esteem	Depression	Life satisfaction
Enabling	4.13	1.67	5.94
Strict	3.77	1.91	5.32
Indulgent	4.14	1.89	5.59
Uninvolved	3.56	2.07	4.80

These results give us two key lessons. Firstly, the Enabling style is best at developing people with higher satisfaction rates and with a lower chance of depression. The Uninvolved style performs the worst in all categories. Secondly, that high self-esteem is closely linked to life satisfaction and with the avoidance of depression. It is also worth noting that there was broad agreement on the effects of maternal and paternal style, although as we will see in a moment these were not always the same in individual families.

The number of parents who fell into each category in this survey surprised me. Although this may not be representative parents of teenagers in general, the numbers are quite surprising.

Style	Maternal	Paternal
Enabling	99	71
Strict	60	34
Indulgent	31	47
Uninvolved	79	108

I suspect that not that many parents would admit to being in the Uninvolved category, but in this research, based on probing questions asked of the teenagers, this was the largest category for fathers and the second highest for mothers. Now parents may be uninvolved for many reasons. They may have deliberately chosen to be so, believing that children do best if they find their feet without interference or 'just get on with it'. There are certainly some psychologists and schools in the past that have advocated this view. They may be physically or emotionally absent from their children's' lives due to other commitments such as work, bad health or other caring responsibilities. Or they may just have got to a point where they were finding parenting a teenager so difficult, they just gave up. We must admit there were times whilst we were dealing with our teenagers that we just wanted to run and hide.

In an ideal world, both parents would have an enabling style, because psychological research strongly suggests that works best, but we can see from our survey that it is not often the case. We also know that in many cultures the traditional method of parenting was the strict one. Added to this, today's financial pressure allows for very few full-time stay at home parents. Many parents, nowadays, are trying to balance all sorts of personal and work-related pressures themselves, and, in some cases, they have mental health issues themselves including anxiety and stress.

Now although the Enabling style is thought to be the ideal, both the Strict and Indulgent styles have some good points. The style to be avoided at all costs if possible is the Uninvolved style and we suspect because you are reading this book, that you don't wish to fit into that category. It is important to keep in mind that every parent/child relationship is different, so there is not one correct way to go about parenting. A sudden major change may also be somewhat unsettling and confusing for both you and your teenager, so if you are not already an enabling parent, we suggest that you slowly try to integrate some of the Enabling characteristics into your household.

What do we know about each style that might help us to make changes?

Enabling (Authoritative)
Congratulations! If you mostly use an Enabling parenting style.

What you already do well:
    Nurture, discipline and respect your teen.
    Show love, warmth and interest.
    Communicate openly and listen well.
    Set standards and clear, reasonable limits.
    Keep track of your teen's behaviour and whereabouts.
    Enforce limits and consequences on behaviour firmly and consistently.
    Allow freedom of thought and expression.

The children of enabling parents are generally more confident in themselves and have a greater sense of independence. They tend to be good decision makers and responsible adults who are happier and more successful than the other categories. They are good at cooperating with others and are achievement focused. They have high levels of self-esteem and lower levels of depression.

What you can work on:
    Keep doing what you are doing!

Be mindful that one-size does not fit all, and as your teenager gets older, continuously assess the situation.

You are the best gauge of your teenager's needs and sometimes those needs include more boundaries rather than more freedom.

Discuss your boundaries with other parents to make sure that they are still appropriate. If they are, try to make sure that the other adults in their life are aware of them.

Also, continue to build awareness of what is going on in your teenager's life by talking to other parents, family and friends.

The best parenting balances love with limits and awareness.

Strict (Authoritarian)

You mostly use a Strict parenting style. While you are very good at setting limits, your relationship with your teenager may include conflict and power struggles. You might also get frustrated trying to control your teenager's behaviour. Still, these are the things you are probably doing well.

What you already do well:
Know the importance of setting limits and expectations.

Your willingness to discipline your child shows how much you love and care.

Keep track of your teenager's behaviour and whereabouts.

Work hard to protect your teenager from problem behaviours and getting into trouble.

The children of strict parents generally obey the rules, but they can become hostile and aggressive. They are often timid and lack self-esteem and initiative. They have fewer social skills, less spontaneity and can have a tendency towards depression in later life. They often lack initiative as they are used to others making decisions for them and are often not very happy with their lives.

What you can work on:
Create a more nurturing, and warm atmosphere by verbally expressing your love for your teen through praise and affection.

Listen and respect your teenager's opinions, even though you may not agree with them. This will help keep the lines of communication open.

When a rule is broken, make sure the discipline is consistent with the consequences you've established with your teen. It is important that you focus on the consequences and not the punishment, so that your teenager understands the purpose of the rule.

When appropriate, provide opportunities when your teenager can discuss and negotiate certain rules. Take time to explain to your teenager why non-negotiable rules are in place, and then reinforce this by explaining that you love them and want them to be safe.

Shift your focus from what your teenager is doing wrong to what they are doing right. Spend more time reinforcing good behaviour than punishing bad behaviour.

Be curious rather than judgmental. Help your teenager develop the ability to think and express their own ideas and opinions.

Indulgent (Permissive)

You mostly use a lenient parenting style. While you communicate well with your teenager, you value your close relationship and may be reluctant to set limits or discipline. You might feel frustrated at times trying to get your teenager to obey rules, and fearful that you will lose his love if you try to set limits.

What you already do well:

Give your teen a lot of love and warmth.

Provide a nurturing environment, full of respect.

Communicate openly.

Allow freedom of thought and expression.

These children often struggle at school. They are not good at obeying rules and often have conduct issues. They have a tendency towards high self- esteem and good social skills but can have problems fitting in and are liable to depression

What you can work on:
Actively provide more discipline and be firm.
Be consistent and avoid making empty threats.
Set and enforce clear limits and rules and consequences for breaking them in advance.
Routinely keep track of your teenager's whereabouts and activities and check up on them unannounced.
Clearly communicate your expectations.
Network with other parents to make it easier to set and enforce rules.
Think about the values and abilities you want for your child as they mature and set expectations that will encourage that development.

Uninvolved (Neglectful)

You mostly use a hands-off parenting style. While you give your teen a lot of independence, you probably don't feel very connected to him or her. You may feel too busy or overwhelmed with other obligations to be very involved in your teenager's life.

What you already do well:
You love your teenager.
Place a high value on independence and self-regulation.

These children have low self-esteem. They often have behavioural issues and are the least happy. They can find it difficult to fit in, rebel at rules and often have aggression and anger issues.

What you can work on:
Express interest and get involved in your teen's life.
Actively set and enforce clear rules and consequences.
Consistently keep track of your teenager's activities and whereabouts and check up unannounced.

References in this chapter

1 Milevsky A, Schlechter M, Netter S and Keehn D, Maternal and Paternal Parenting Styles in Adolescents: Associations with Self-Esteem, Depression and Life-Satisfaction ,JOURNAL OF CHILD AND FAMILY STUDIES; 16, 1; 39-47Springer Science + Business Media ; 2007

Chapter 2

Worrying times

A world of worry

Teenagers are worriers, partly due to their brain development, as we will see in the next chapter, and partly because growing up in our westernised society is fraught with hazards so getting through adolescence is tough!

This chapter looks at what teenagers are worrying about and how this could be affecting their mental health and wellbeing.

The top six areas that teenagers worry about are:

School and work-related issues

Friends, relationships, sex and love

Family-related issues

The future, university and career

Appearance and fitting in

Drug and alcohol issues

School and work-related issues

In an international survey published last year by the Organisation for Economic Co-operation and Development [1], 67% of British 15year olds said that they worry about getting poor grades, while 72% said that even if they were well prepared for a test they felt very anxious. This was confirming an earlier survey [2] in 2014, that found that 49% would be devastated if they did not achieve the grades that they wanted. This is no surprise to those of us who have been at schools on results day. The happy students are ecstatic and the disappointed ones, heartbroken.

The first major issue is time management. Many teenagers feel overwhelmed by the pressures on their time from school work. They are often poorly skilled in setting priorities for themselves and just see lots of things they feel they should be doing but are not. A further problem is that other people put pressure on teenagers and they feel torn between the demands of parents, friends and teachers.

Many teenagers nowadays also have part-time jobs. This gives them a sense of independence, responsibility and the real world of work, but it can just add more pressure to the lack of time, particularly if they are working well above 10 hours a week. This is also true of extra-curricular activities such as sport. Although this is widely encouraged for fitness it only adds to the pressures on time.

The second major issue is expectations both from families and schools and from the students themselves. This is a really important issue and we will return to it in Chapter 5. The pressure on teenagers from public examinations seems to be increasing and causes a great deal of stress and anxiety among students of all abilities. (See Chapter 20 for help in dealing with examinations).

Friends, relationships sex and love
Friendship issues are causing enormous problems with teenagers and this problem has undoubtedly been made worse by social media. In the 2014 survey [2] mentioned above, 28% said that they had sent a nasty message and 46% said that they regretted something that they had said on social media. Having the right friends during teenage years is really important for mutual support, but there is often a fight going on within social groups to establish a pecking order and this can be very nasty, with various forms of bullying including belittling and isolating. This competition is often founded on a mentality that we can only be successful at another person's expense and by pushing someone else down, we push ourselves up. Of course, this mentality is not unique to teenagers, but perhaps it is more prevalent among students who have not yet developed a complete sense of who they are or how they fit in to society. In the 2014 survey, 61% of parents of teenagers said that their teenager had been bullied. (See Chapter 15 for more information about bullying)

This is also a time when teenagers are establishing their own sexuality, which can be a very confusing time. It may well also be when they first form coupling relationships with the many stresses and strains that dealing with the intensity of these relationships and all of the sexually related issues brings. Most of these relationships are unlikely to survive and both parties will then have to deal with the trauma of the breakup. (See Chapters 21 and 32 for more information about sex and sexuality).

Family-related issues
Although teenagers become far less reliant on the family and tend to spend much more time with friends, issues at home are still very important. There can often be a clash of values in the home environment about academic expectations, attitudes to sex, attitudes to drugs and alcohol and use of social media. These can all lead to stress. In addition, teenagers must deal with any tensions that may exist between their parents or between other members of the household, as well as their own relationships with other family members. Many households are also coping with the complexities of divorce and separation and often have relationships with step siblings. There may also be mental ill health or physical health problems in the family, which can be very upsetting, as well as issues relating to money, housing or bereavement etc.

Their future education, university and career
If there is an expectation to go to university, or to pursue a specific career path, this places enormous significance on exam results. In contrast, students who have no pre-conceived idea of their future careers, sometimes lack direction, and this itself is stressful. Young people worry about, how they will cope financially, how they will pay back student debts and whether they will be able to afford to leave home. They also worry about their own prospects for owning a home, finding a partner and possibly having children.

Appearance and fitting in
As children reach their teenage years, they become far better at seeing the world through other peoples' eyes and this, in turn, makes them much more self-conscious and concerned with fitting in. If they perceive their own worth by how others see them rather than how they see themselves, they are often desperate to look and behave in a fashion that they think is cool. In the 2014 survey[1] 81% of young

people said they felt under pressure to have a perfect body, mainly driven by the images seen on social media. Teenagers at this stage will also adopt clothes that project the group they wish to be identified with. In some situations, this mentality can also lead to membership of local gangs which, if it happens, is a major cause for concern for parents. We often think of this as peer pressure, but this can be misleading as there may be no pressure involved, just a desire to mimic others and to achieve a sense of belonging.

Drug and alcohol issues
Teenagers' attitudes to drugs and alcohol will start to be built up in their family environment, but there is no doubt that these can be radically changed by the behaviour of the young people around them. Many parents will be unfamiliar with the drug and alcohol culture of young people which may be completely different from their own experience. Also, as we will see later in Chapter 3 about brain development and hormones, teenagers are not very good at assessing risk and may be tempted to develop addictive behaviours. (See Chapters 11, 18 and 34 for more information about alcohol, drugs and smoking)

Teenagers on the edge
The mental health of teenagers is very important, since research [3] suggests that half of all lifetime mental disorders appear by the age of 14 and three quarters by the age of 18. Psychiatrists have spent years identifying, classifying and diagnosing conditions that affect mental wellbeing. You might have heard of some of the following:
Anxiety
    GAD General Anxiety Disorder
    OCD Obsessive Compulsive Disorder
    PTSD Post Traumatic Stress Disorder

Depression
    PND Post Natal Depression
    SAD Seasonal Affective Disorder

Eating Disorders
  Anorexia
  Bulimia
  Binge Eating Disorder

Bipolar Disorder
Schizophrenia
Personality Disorders
  BPD Borderline personality disorder
  Antisocial personality Disorder

The following four conditions are not considered to be mental disorders, but are closely associated with the above disorders.

Panic attacks
Self-Harm
Suicidal feelings
Psychotic experiences
Statistics for teenage mental health in this country are often not very accurate or up to date. Data quoted is often based on a major study [4] that is well over 10 years old. Let's look at some of those results. In 2015 the Department of Health published a report called Future in Mind [5]. This report quoted the following statistic:

11.5% of young people aged 11-16 have a mental disorder.
This meant that in the average secondary school class there were three children struggling with mental ill health and in the whole country over half a million teenage sufferers. The most common diagnostic categories were described in the report as conduct disorders, anxiety, depression and hyperkinetic disorders. Generally, girls tended to have more emotional difficulties, while boys had more behavioural problems. In fact, boys had a higher rate than girls with I in 8 teenage boys and 1 in 10 teenage girls having a diagnosable mental health problem. These rates increase throughout the teenage years and reach about I in 4, the adult rate, soon after. However, many more recent indicators suggest that teenage girls have overtaken boys for mental health disorders as we shall see below.

The latest report published by the NHS [6] in November 2018 reported higher rates of mental disorders for 11-16 year olds at over 14%. Even more worryingly it showed rates of 23.9% for girls aged 17–19 years, over twice the rate for boys. It is also believed that 70% of these young people do not get appropriate interventions early enough. Those of us who have worked in schools know that the CAMHS mental health services for young people are seriously overstretched. A recent report by the Children's Commissioner [7] covering England, stated "Less than 3% of children in England accessed CAMHS last year, a small fraction of those who need help." Of the children referred to CAMHS "Less than a third received treatment in a year."

So, as you can see, even if we identify a young person who needs help, that help is often not available for many months and, even then, may seem to be quite superficial. We also know that children with mental health problems are at greater risk of physical health problems. They are more likely to smoke than children who are mentally healthy. Children and young people with eating disorders and early onset psychosis are particularly at risk.

We can also look a little at some of the effects of these mental health problems.

Suicide rates
Although overall suicide rates have not changed much over the last twenty years the recent trends are rather worrying, particularly for girls. The rates per 100,000 for the 15-19 age group for the last five years which are available are as follows:

	All	Male	Female
2013	4.4	7.0	1.6
2014	4.9	7.0	2.7
2015	5.8	8.3	3.1
2016	5.3	7.5	2.9
2017	5.6	7.6	3.5

Source: Office for National Statistics (United Kingdom)
As you can see males are much more likely to commit suicide and this is true across the whole age range, but females are showing a

worrying trend upwards. Suicide is the leading cause of death for both males and females under 20.

Self-harming.
Self-harming statistics are not very reliable, but admissions to Accident and Emergency are increasing significantly as shown below:

Hospital Admissions for self-harm for 11-17 year olds

	Male	Female
2011/12	**2262**	**10794**
2012/13	**2357**	**12220**
2013/14	**2824**	**16533**
2014/15	**2843**	**16571**

Source:NHS

Of course, these only represent the tip of a very large iceberg as most self-harming does not result in hospital admissions. The UK is believed to have the highest rate of self-harm in Europe and one study in 2015 [8] estimated that among 15-year olds, 32% of girls and 11% of boys had self-harmed. The most common form of self-harm in the community is cutting. This is usually linked to other mental health disorders. Most frequently this is recognised as a coping mechanism for dealing with other issues, and only rarely and usually by accident, does it result in suicide. (See Chapter 30 for more information about self-harm)

Although these official statistics in themselves are worrying enough, they do not tell the whole story. There may only be three or four students with a diagnosable mental condition in each class, but a great many of the others are not coping very well either. Those of us who have been working in secondary schools see youngsters every day who are in distress. Some of them have very individual problems. They may be coping with a bereavement or serious illness in the family. They may be caring for a parent or sibling and finding it very difficult. Many are just not coping with the strains of everyday school and family life. They are literally being overwhelmed by life and do not have the resilience to deal with their problems in a confident manner.

A recent large-scale survey [9] of 14year-olds found that 12 % of boys and 18% of girls were suffering from emotional problems, while 9% of boys and 24% of girls were suffering from high symptoms of depression. These are very worrying figures supported by an international comparison of the life satisfaction of 12 year olds [10] which placed UK youngsters near the bottom in 14th place out of 15 countries.

In the report that we mentioned earlier *'Future in Mind'* the government says:
"...too often, children and young people's emotional wellbeing and mental health is not given the attention it needs."

and states that it wants them
"...to achieve their goals and ambitions by growing up to be confident and resilient so they can develop and fulfil these goals and make a contribution to society."

It also sets out some objectives to achieve this.
"Improve access for parents to evidence-based programmes of intervention and support to strengthen attachment between parent and child, avoid early trauma, build resilience and improve behaviour."
"With additional funding, this would be delivered by enhancing parenting programmes."
"Improving access to effective support with additional funding, we could also empower young people to self-care through increased availability of new quality assured apps and digital tools"
"In every part of the country, children and young people having timely access to clinically effective mental health support when they need it."

We have to say that most schools would say that they have seen little evidence of these changes and that is one of the reasons that we have written this book.

The warning signs

We know that most young people with mental health needs do not get treatment early enough, so what should parents look out for? These are some of the early warning signs that your teenager might not be coping with day to day life:

Frequent symptoms such as headaches and stomach aches
Increased irritability
Moodiness
Increased anxiety
Sleep problems
Concentration issues
Low energy or tiredness
Loss of interest in old activities
Increasingly pessimistic/negative approach to life
Problems relaxing
Constant worrying
Appetite problems
Increased behavioural problems at school or at home
Increased academic problems at school
School avoidance or refusal
Increasingly lonely/bored
Self-isolation

Of course, some of these issues can relate to normal teenage development, but be on the lookout for sudden changes, a cluster of symptoms or a situation which appears to be getting steadily worse.

These are some of the more serious warning signs that are likely to require professional intervention. At the very least, you should be talking to your GP and seeking advice.

Increasingly erratic or unpredictable behaviour
Increasingly agitated and anxious
Displaying signs of hopelessness/helplessness
Social withdrawal / avoidance of social interaction or contact
Unexplained or prolonged crying

Change or disturbance in eating patterns
Change in sleeping patterns
Starting to use Incoherent speech
Displaying Paranoid characteristics
Physical ill-health
Hearing voices
Behaviour inappropriate to the social context
Any verbalised thoughts of suicide or self-harm
Any actual acts of self-harm
Significant weight gain or loss

It is important for others to try to spot these signs because in the 2014 survey 42% of young people said that even if the stress or pressure became too much for them, they would not talk to anyone.

Where to get help
If you notice that your teenager is showing signs of failing to cope, where and how do you get help?

School – school counsellors; special needs departments; school nurse; school Pastoral Team.

Private – Counsellors, therapists, on-line information and self-help resources

Local council – Youth Services

Charitable organisations – counsellors, information, help - lines

Doctors – GPs, Accident & Emergency

Family support workers – Social workers, Health Visitors

CAMHS – multidisciplinary teams dealing with mental health of under 18s.

As you can see there are a lot of organisations and individuals that can help you, but the actual level, availability and quality of these services will depend on where you live, and in some cases whether you can afford to pay for immediate services.

You will need to assess the urgency and seriousness of your teenager's problems. The most urgent need for help is for teenagers showing real suicidal tendencies. In these situations, an urgent appointment should be made with your GP or you can try to self-refer to your local CAMHS team. However, be aware that CAMHS services may not be capable of providing any immediate response.

In desperate circumstances, you may need to go to Accident & Emergency provided your teenager is compliant. There are also telephone help lines run by several charities including The Samaritans 116 123 (24 hour) and Papyrus 0800 068 4141 (not 24 hour). In extreme cases you might have to enlist the help of the police especially if your teenager refuses help but remains at serious risk of self-harm or harm to others.

For less urgent, but serious mental health concerns a visit to your GP is probably the best course. They may decide to refer you to the CAMHS service themselves or they may have some other approaches to offer including directing you to other local services or in some cases they may offer medication.

If your teenager's concerns seem to be related to school-based issues, you should contact the appropriate person at the school. This may be a form tutor, a head of year or someone who deals with pastoral affairs. They may not only be able to give you more information about how your teenager is coping, but they may also have access to some support services of their own.

References in this chapter

1 OECD (2017), PISA 2015 Results (Volume III):Students' Well-Being, PISA, OECD Publishing, Paris
2 The Bauer Media News and YoungMinds State of Mind Survey 2014
3 Green H, McGinnity H, Ford T and Goodman R (2005) Mental health of children and young people in Great Britain, 2004. London ONS
4 Kessler RC, Berglund P, Demler O, Jin R, Merikangas KR, Walters EE. Lifetime prevalence and age-of-onset distributions of DSM-IV disorders in the National Comorbidity Survey Replication. Arc Gen Psychiatry 62: 593-602

5 Children and Young People's Mental Health Taskforce (March 2015) Future in mind: Promoting, protecting and improving our children and young people's mental health and wellbeing

6 NHS Digital:Mental Health of Children and Young People in England 2017 (November 2018)

7 Children's Commissioner:Children's Mental Health Briefing (November 2018)

8 Brooks, F., Magnusson, J., Klemera, E., Spencer, N. and Morgan, A. (2011). HBSC England National Report: Health Behaviour in School-aged Children: World Health Organization Collaborative Cross National Study. Hatfield: University of Hertfordshire, CRIPACC

9 Patalay P & Fitzsimons E. Mental ill-health among children of the new century: trends across childhood with a focus on age 14. September 2017. Centre for Longitudinal Studies: London.

10 Rees, G. & Main, G. (eds) (2015) Children's views on their lives and well-being in 15 countries: An initial report on the Children's Worlds survey, 2013-14. York, UK: Children's Worlds Project (ISCWeB)

Chapter 3

All change -How teenagers develop and why that can cause them (and you) problems

"You used to be a great kid what happened to you?"

You might remember that we started Chapter 1 with a similar phrase, but this time we are presenting it from your point of view. We often feel like that. As they reach the teenage years, our compliant, cuddly, often fun-loving, excitable and energetic young children seem to transform at times into difficult and challenging teenagers (and in the most extreme cases from angels to monsters!), and then back again! So, we need to understand why this might be happening, learn how best to react and know what to say and do, and it's much more complicated than we imagine!

Puberty - the visible signs
We might all have a general understanding of the sorts of things that we see change as teenagers go through adolescence. This chapter provides much more detail.

At the start of puberty, several hormones are released, which trigger a complex process that lasts about four years. The chemical processes are now well understood

Hypothalamus sends Gonadotropin Releasing Hormone (GnRH) to the pituitary gland
Pituitary gland sends Lutenising hormone (LH) and Follicle Stimulating Hormone (FSH) to the ovaries and testes
Ovaries release Oestrogen and Progesterone
Testes release Testosterone

However, the process that decides exactly when this will happen remains somewhat of a mystery, although the following factors are all thought to play a part in this:

Genetic factors
Diet and nutrition
Obesity
Exercise
Stress
Social factors
Environmental chemicals

Whatever the exact factors involved, the age at which puberty begins seems to have fallen by several years over the last century. For girls, the average is about 11 although any age between 8 and 14 is quite normal. For boys, the average age is about 12 with a range between 9 and 14. For individuals, these variations have a significant impact on their early teenage years. The early developing girls are likely to look much older than their age, which makes them attractive to much older boys and men at a time when they have not developed the mental maturity that may be needed to deal with this. The late-developing girls may feel a bit left behind, but they are at least maturing at about the same time as their male classmates. The early developing boys gain a lot of status from their physical size, muscular bodies and athletic capabilities, but may be encouraged to mix with much older boys and this has been linked to risk-taking behaviours. Late maturing boys can be the targets for some mockery and bullying and this can have long term effects on their self-esteem.

The following provides a summary of the obvious changes that we typically expect to see.

Girls

Early puberty
Breast buds develop
Pubic and body hair begins to grow

Middle puberty
Breasts become fuller
Periods begin
Pubic hair becomes coarser and curlier
Underarm hair grows
Start to sweat more
Increased rate of growth
Increased weight
Change of body shape

Late puberty
Breasts like adults
Pubic hair more widespread
Growth stops

Boys

Early puberty
Testicles get bigger
Scrotum thins and gets redder
Pubic hair begins to grow

Middle puberty
Penis and testicles grow
Pubic hair becomes coarser and curlier
Underarm hair grows
Start to sweat more
Increased rate of growth
Body becomes more muscular
Voice deepens

Late puberty
Penis and testicles like adults
Pubic hair more widespread
Growth rate slows
Develop facial hair

For teenagers, and indeed for parents, these physical changes can be difficult to adapt to. There are both emotional and practical issues to deal with. Emotionally teenagers start leaving their childhood behind and must come to terms with a transformation in their physical self-image which they may or may not like. Parents have an important role to play here in attitudes towards self-image. Parents who constantly worry about their own physical features and looks are likely to pass this message on to their teenagers, who may well have similar physical characteristics.

This is also the beginning of exploring their sexuality, which can be confusing and difficult for some teenagers. (See Chapters 21 and 32 for more information about sex and sexuality). In practical terms teenagers quickly need to learn new skills for dealing with periods, unwanted body hair, body odour and possibly acne. Of course, this whole process is easier if parents have prepared the ground in advance, with explanations of these likely changes and how to deal with them.

At the end of this process, both the boys and the girls will have developed adult bodies with all the appearance and capabilities of their parents. However, even before this stage adolescents may look much like adults physically. By the age of 14, the average girl is 159cm compared to the adult women's average of 162cm, so there is hardly any difference in height. The average 14year old boy is 163cm so although still much shorter than the average adult man at 175cm, he may well be taller than his mother.

It is easy for parents, and even more for teenagers themselves, to believe that because they look like adults, they will think and behave like adults, but as we will see in the next section this is far from the truth. There are invisible changes taking place which will not be complete until well into their twenties.

Brain development - the unfinished Brain

"I just don't get what's going on in your head"

Hopefully, we can begin to explain exactly that.

"The human brain has 100 billion neurons each neuron is connected to 10,000 other neurons. Sitting on our shoulders is the most complicated object in the known universe." Michio Kaku (US physicist)

As you can see from this quote, many people believe that the human brain is the most complicated structure in the natural world. Now I know many parents looking at their teenagers will find this hard to understand, but the reason teenagers behave in the ways that they do is exactly because their brains are so complicated! So, let's look at how the brain develops up to and during the teenage years.

Most of the key brain cells – the neurons- are generated in the middle months of pregnancy and despite a considerable proportion dying, it is true that new born infants have around 100 billion neurons. Although neurons continue to be generated throughout life, these occur in very small numbers and so we are largely dependent on those with which we are born.

At birth, it is estimated that each neuron is connected to about 2,500 others by what are known as synapses, but by the age of 3 this has risen to as many as 15,000. The brain is now at its most complex with all the fundamental structures that we will need for our whole adult life, so the physical and mental wellbeing of our young infants is vitally important for their future development.

"Everybody's plastic, but I love plastic. I want to be plastic." Andy Warhol (US Artist)

Andy wanted to be plastic and in fact, his brain, like everyone else's was plastic. One of the most important features of the brain is its ability to adapt to its environment and to the individual's experiences. This is known as plasticity. The process begins in the womb, but it is still carrying on to a significant degree well into our twenties. The way in which the brain adapts to its experiences is by strengthening and weakening the huge number of connections between the neurons. This process is particularly important during the teenage years.

By the time teenagers reach puberty their brains are just about fully developed in size, but they are about to undergo major changes in structure. During childhood, we accumulate lots of knowledge, which we store in the folders in our brain's filing cabinet. By puberty, this filing cabinet has got very full up and confused and so nature decides to do a thorough sorting exercise. Folders that don't seem to be used much are hidden or thrown away, while the most useful ones are brought to the front of the cabinet.

During puberty the brain reduces the connections or grey matter by as much as 40%, This pruning process is supposed to concentrate brain power, where it is needed most.
At the same time, the brain strengthens those parts that seem the most useful and increases the white matter by insulating the connections with myelin. This process supercharges the brain function and is thought to speed up brain signals by up to a hundred times.

This whole process of pruning and strengthening is thought to make the brain function much more efficient within the limited skull space that it has available. It also saves energy. A four-year old uses nearly half of their energy in brain functions and even after the reshaping that occurs in our teens and twenties, the adult brain still uses around a fifth of all our energy.

So, on the face of it, this whole process should make teenagers' brains perform better and make teenagers more able to make sensible decisions, but unfortunately the part of the brain that is responsible for these higher-level thinking processes is the last to be rewired and supercharged.

Let us look at the main structures of the brain. The brain develops from the inside out with the core functions being the basic mechanisms for the body to operate and the outer area much more concerned with more complex decision making.

The two main areas which have the most impact on the way in which teenagers behave are the amygdala and the cerebral cortex.

The Amygdala is quite a small part of the brain, but it is highly involved in human emotions including the negative responses relating to fear, anxiety, stress, and the positive responses relating to food and sex. In teenagers, this area plays a vital role and whenever they are faced with a challenging situation they tend to use this part of the brain first. As a result, teenagers tend to make decisions based more on emotional factors than rational decisions. Although they may be just as aware of the rational information as adults, their first response tends to be based on their emotions and might often be impulsive and unwise.

The cerebral cortex is the largest part of the brain and is the wrinkled outside that we see in pictures of the brain. It consists of four lobes and is the most recently evolved part of the human brain concerned with the most complex thinking. The front of one of the lobes, the frontal lobe, is particularly important in these processes. It is concerned with what psychologists call executive function. This is the ability to perform key mental processes such as:

Retaining and using information
Maintaining concentration and resisting distractions
Forward planning and setting goals
Being patient
Prioritising tasks
Multitasking
Problem-solving
Controlling emotions
Resisting impulses and temptations
Adjusting to changing demands and priorities
Coping with frustration

As you can see these are exactly the sort of attributes that many teenagers struggle with. This is because the frontal lobe is the last area of the brain to fully develop. In addition, sensible decisions clearly require a balance between cold logic and emotions and the links between the amygdala and the frontal lobe are not fully developed in teenagers. In fact, there is a considerable amount of brain development between the ages of 15 and 25, after which most physical development is mostly complete. It is believed that the peak age for human performance is between the ages of 25 and 30, and this slowly declines after that. This might explain why in the natural order of things, parents generally have their children early in life when their energy is at its greatest!

The lack of maturity in the cerebral cortex can clearly contribute to teenagers making unwise decisions and indulging in excessive risk taking. We shall discuss this further at the end of the next section.

The role of hormones
Another key area of invisible changes is the influence of hormones and neurotransmitters on teenagers. These are chemicals that are released in very small quantities in the brain and through the Endocrine System. They have a major impact not just on the way our bodies function, but also on the way we feel and the way we behave. Having the wrong levels of these chemicals can have serious short and long-term effects on both our physical and mental health. Although this is true of all ages, teenagers are particularly vulnerable due to the plasticity of their brains and the rapid changes that are going on within their bodies.

The way in which hormones and neurotransmitters work is very complicated and often inter-related. Research results are often not clear-cut but some general patterns have emerged. In the following sections, we discuss some of the main hormones and neurotransmitters which are most likely to have an impact on behaviour and mood.

The three sex hormones

Testosterone

As we outlined earlier, when puberty begins in boys, testosterone is released from the testes. Although levels of the hormone vary considerably from one person to another and even over the course of the day, the levels of testosterone will be at a lifetime high by the late teens and early twenties before steadily falling. High levels of testosterone have been linked to more aggressive and angry behaviour, although these effects are by no means consistent across all individuals. However, there does appear to be a consistent trend towards risk taking behaviours and the need for instant gratification.

Although the levels of testosterone remains significantly lower in girls, the levels peak again in the late teens and show a similar trend towards risk-taking.

Oestrogen and Progesterone

As puberty begins in girls, both oestrogen and progesterone are released by the ovaries and the levels rapidly increase and remain high until middle age, being linked to fertility. During each menstrual cycle, the levels of the two hormones fluctuate with oestrogen levels being higher in the first half and middle of the cycle and progesterone levels higher in the latter part. In many ways these two hormones act in opposing directions and these fluctuations are highly likely to affect mood and even behaviour.

Higher oestrogen levels are linked to anxiety, fatigue, memory problems and low sex drive. Lower oestrogen levels are linked to depression, concentration and sleep problems. In general, progesterone is viewed as an important hormone in maintaining the proper balance in many of the bodies' systems. It also appears to combat both depression and anxiety and has an anti-inflammatory effect.

The three fear hormones

Adrenaline and Noradrenaline

These two hormones which are also known as epinephrine and norepinephrine are very similar in their function. When we feel threatened, stressed or fearful these hormones prepare us for "flight or fight". They increase blood flow and lung function as well as increasing our awareness of our surroundings. This allows our bodies a sudden burst of energy and strength if we need it. At the same time, they reduce the levels of activity in other systems which lowers sex drive and reduces digestion and growth. These are very rapid acting hormones. When a threat is detected the levels increase enormously, but once the threat has passed, levels will begin to fall back quite quickly. These hormones are also believed to affect memories, particularly of stressful events.

Cortisol

Cortisol is often called the stress hormone. Normal levels of cortisol are higher in the morning and very low by night-time which is not entirely surprising as the hormone is linked to alertness. When we are under threat, cortisol levels increase and perform similar functions to the other two hormones but may take much longer to return to normal levels. If we continually feel under stress, cortisol levels can stay at high levels for long periods, causing problems with mental health as well as blood pressure, increased weight, memory and sleep. Stress tends to suppress higher order thinking as our stress responses favour more simple reactions. Cortisol levels are raised by alcohol and by caffeine.

It is believed that prolonged high cortisol levels can eventually cause significant changes in the body's reaction to stress which turns much of this mechanism off. This is thought to be a self-preservation measure to protect from the long-term physical effects. This can also cause problems, as it reduces alertness and can trigger fatigue and depression.

In teenagers, the cortisol response to stress becomes much greater than in younger children, which may be nature's way of preparing teenagers for greater independence and more risk taking.

The two calming neurotransmitters

GABA
GABA (gamma-aminobutyric acid) serves a major calming role within the brain and is thought to control excessive reactions to fear and anxiety. It is an anti-convulsive, helps us relax and is closely linked with our sleep function. Lower GABA levels appear to be linked to Autism and ADHD and play a role in Bipolar Disorder, mania and seizures. High levels of GABA can lead to us being over relaxed and sedated. There is some evidence that teenagers have low GABA levels particularly in the frontal lobe and this may well contribute to over impulsive behaviour.

Serotonin
Serotonin is produced mainly in the gut, but it plays a key role in regulating mood. At normal levels, it helps promote healthy body functions relating to temperature, sleep and sexual drive. Although slightly raised levels of serotonin give feelings of well-being and bliss, significantly raised levels lead to trembling, agitation and aggressiveness. On the other hand, low levels of serotonin, which is a much more common occurrence are linked to depression, poor concentration and fatigue. At very low levels, emotional reactions can be overwhelming. Lower levels of serotonin are linked to OCD, eating disorders, phobias and some anxiety disorders. Teenagers have lower serotonin levels which may make them particularly susceptible to some of these conditions and is generally linked to poor impulse control.

The sleep-wake hormone

Melatonin
Melatonin is the hormone which controls our internal clock and tells us when to stay awake and when to go to sleep. It is important to cope with disruptive events such as shift working and jet lag. In teenagers there is a shift in the pattern of melatonin production which pushes the sleep time back several hours. Since teenagers are believed to need at least 8 hours sleep this can cause problems the following morning. Melatonin patterns have developed broadly to

keep pace with day and night cycles and are affected particularly by blue light. For teenagers who tend to look at phone, computer and tablet screens late at night, this may be part of the problem in getting to sleep.

The two bonding hormones

Vasopressin and Oxytocin
These are two similar hormones that are both involved in sexual arousal and bonding. Oxytocin evokes feelings of calm and contentment. It has important roles in women relating to maternal behaviour and to building relationships and trust with partners and other close associates. However, it also appears to have a similar though less significant effect on men. Physical contact seems to play an important part of this process and some have named it the "love" hormone. Oxytocin generally has an antidepressant effect, reduces fear and anxiety and appears to be linked with empathy. A lack of these oxytocin responses has been linked to autistic behaviours particularly in males.

Vasopressin controls retention of water and blood flow but it also plays a significant role in male bonding behaviours and to a lesser extent with women. In men, it is implicated in both recognising sexual cues and responding in general to strangers. Vasopressin seems to make men more defensive and aggressive and view strangers in a more negative way, but this response is not found in women. It is thought to increase the loyalty to a partner but may also lead to jealous behaviours. Unlike oxytocin, vasopressin seems to be linked to depression and anxiety, particularly in higher levels. Another major difference between the two is that whereas vasopressin improves memory and concentration, oxytocin seems to have the reverse effect.

In teenagers, often experiencing intimate relationships for the first time, the effects of these two hormones may be greater than for adults. In addition, increases in these hormones are linked to increases in dopamine levels which as we will see below has a major impact on many areas of behaviour.

The two stimulants

Glutamate and Dopamine

These are two neurotransmitters that provoke and accelerate responses. Glutamate is involved in many body functions and works in close co-ordination with the calming neurotransmitter GABA. Glutamate is the accelerator and GABA the brake. Glutamate appears to be important in learning especially relating to memory. Raised levels of glutamate are linked to mental disorders such as schizophrenia and severely raised levels lead to seizures and brain damage. Low levels of glutamate also lead to mental disorders. In recent times the function of glutamate has also begun to be associated with maintaining addictions. In teenagers, many of the brain connections that are pruned are involved with glutamate activity,

Dopamine is a very important neurotransmitter, which is important for correct movement, maintaining attention and alertness, and processing information to problem solve. Low levels of dopamine cause Parkinson's disease and are linked to difficulties with movement and balance. Low levels also cause attention difficulties and are linked to ADHD as well as depression and lack of motivation. High levels cause suspicion and paranoia. They may enhance sensory feelings but may cause a loss of sense of reality. They are linked to schizophrenia and bipolar disorder.

Dopamine is also closely linked to the pleasure reward system, which should function to motivate behaviours such as eating, drinking and reproduction, probably by memorising cues that are associated with pleasurable experiences. but it also appears to have a major contribution to addictive behaviour. Cocaine and amphetamine directly increase dopamine levels and so the link to addiction seems straightforward, but there are many other addictive behaviours in which dopamine plays a role. These may include gambling, sex, pornography video gaming and even activities like shopping and social networking. With these activities, the addiction does not seem to be related to a sudden "hit", but rather to the ritual and the anticipation of the outcome. However, it does appear that there needs to be a degree of novelty or unpredictability in the outcome or the dopamine levels do not continue to respond. This may result in increasing the activity to try to maintain the effect. Alternatively, this might be the result of dopamine levels falling below normal levels after the activity is finished which may feel uncomfortable and depressing.

It has been recognised for a long time that teenagers tend to take far more risks than adults, even when they seem to fully understand the situation. The extent of this did not seem to be fully explained by brain development alone and it is now believed that dopamine levels in adolescence play a key role. Local dopamine levels in the brain of teenagers are thought to suppress the rational thinking at the front of the brain and encourage reward driven behaviour to satisfy the emotional cravings. It is believed that teenagers have a greater positive response to rewards and a greater negative response to not receiving expected rewards. They will get significant highs from thrill seeking and significant lows from disappointments. They seem to give greater weight to the possibility of a thrilling outcome than to a poor outcome.

We also know that teenagers take more risks when they are with other teenagers than when they are alone. This is usually thought of as peer pressure, but research seems to suggest that this description is misleading as just the presence of other teenagers encourages risk taking, even if they are not actively promoting it.

We are particularly interested in this tendency in teenagers towards risk taking and thrill seeking. While this might appear to be an unfortunate side effect of the way we all mature, some people believe that nature deliberately made teenagers this way. When humans used to live on the Savannah in Africa in small family groups, it is suggested that nature decided that, like lions in the wild, young human adults should leave their own tribe and go off into the wild to seek new mates from a different gene pool. By creating thrill seeking adolescents, nature was encouraging them to leave the safety and security of the family group and go off to look for better food, better mates and more space.

We love this theory. When your teenager and you are hurling abuse at each other across the dinner table you can comfort yourself with the thought that it's just nature's way of getting them to leave home!

It should also be recognised that the impulsiveness and thrill-seeking characteristics of teenagers are both a threat and an opportunity. At its worse, it can lead to dangerous behaviour and the possibility of drug and alcohol abuse. However, it does encourage and motivate teenagers to seek novel experiences, which may result in the acquisition of new skills of all sorts.

If we summarise all the effects of the hormonal and brain changes, we get a picture of how teenagers may be behaving:

Moody
Aggressive
Seeking instant gratification
Won't go to bed and won't get up!
Intensely emotional
Angry
Overconfident
Impulsive
Risk taking/Thrill seeking

Of course, these characteristics in themselves can make teenagers difficult to deal with, but there is another very important factor that comes into play. Between the age when puberty begins and the late teenage years, we expect our children to transform from children to adults. This means moving from being both legally and practically dependent upon parents to becoming almost totally independent. Parents must change from a situation where they expect to make all of the important decisions and issue instructions, to a situation where they have to sit back and let their teenagers make decisions and take responsibility for themselves. This is a difficult transition for both parents and children. Parents need to slowly let go of the reins, despite their natural fears about their teenager's abilities to make the right choices in their life. We will return to this in Chapter 4.

What to expect

"Children begin by loving their parents; as they grow older they judge them; sometimes they forgive them." Oscar Wilde, The Picture of Dorian Gray

So what changes should you expect to see in your teenager's behaviour and development? Well, these are some of the stages:
In early adolescence, there might be lots of arguments as your child starts to think about the world around them and compare their views with those of their friends and classmates. They may also be very influenced by what they see both in the traditional media of press and television, but increasingly more by social media such as Facebook and Instagram. Up until now, your teenager may have seen you as the perfect role model and the source of all wisdom, but that is likely to change quite quickly. The realisation that you might be wrong and that you can make mistakes requires your child to look at you quite differently. Although in many ways this is a great step towards maturity it can be very confusing both for you and your teenager and quite destabilising for the family.

In middle adolescence, your child may seem to be ignoring you. They are likely to be spending much more time at school and with their friends. They are also likely to develop interests and activities so that they are rarely at home and don't seem to need you. This is the stage at which they are most vulnerable to risky behaviours like drug and alcohol abuse, sex, as well as criminal and anti-social behaviour. It is very important at this stage that even though they are ignoring you, you should not ignore them. We will return to this topic later.

In late adolescence, your teenager may become more accepting of you, and may return to many of your values and views - they might even tolerate you! During this phase, teens may start thinking much more seriously about their future careers and relationships. This is the stage at which it is important to develop mutual respect and to encourage moves towards eventual independence.

Chapter 4

Getting a handle on happiness. How to set the right priorities for life

Becoming 'Good Enough'

What are you aiming for?

Chapter 1 gave you an overview of how you parent, and what changes might be of use to you, but, even if you get your parenting style right, you may still not develop healthy and happy adults unless you, and your teenager, get your priorities correct.

We are all often under enormous time pressure and it's critical that the time we do have available is used in a manner that is likely to maximize our chances of success in life. That does not mean financial or career success, it means being happy and content.

When asked about their hopes for the future, teenagers' best hopes often centred on money or fame, or having a well-paid career. In contrast, the number one long-term hope for parents is that their teenagers will develop into happy independent adults. Another word that parents mention a lot, is that they want their teenagers to become responsible. Now responsible is an interesting word, because it has two different meanings, to BE responsible, and to ACT in a responsible manner.

The dictionary definitions are quite interesting:

To be responsible is to take control and be accountable for something.
To act responsibly is to behave in a sensible and trustworthy manner.

So, if we sum up what sort of adults parents want their teenagers to become we have:

INDEPENDENT (doing their own thing)
RESPONSIBLE (making the right decisions)
And as a result **being HAPPY**

If you remember, these are also the kind of aims mentioned in the Government's Future in Mind report, where it talked about developing confidence and resilience.

Over the years, research studies have tried to establish what young people think are the key signs of reaching adulthood. The most important criteria quoted are usually:

Criteria for adulthood
Accepting responsibility for actions
Establishing a relationship with parents as an equal adult
Deciding on beliefs/values independently of parents/others' influences
Being capable of running a household, raising a family
Being financially independent

Accepting responsibility for one's actions and by implication 'doing the right thing' is usually the most important factor, followed by a changing relationship with parents, although there are cultural differences about the nature of this change. The last two criteria used to be more important, but nowadays many young people are not becoming financially independent or running a household until much later.

So, let's look at how we can foster the three goals of independence, responsibility and happiness in our young people.

Welcoming your Independent Descendent- Letting go of the lead and managing your fear

We'll start by looking at developing independence and responsibility.

Anyone who has raised a puppy knows that there are several important stages involved. In the first 2 months you keep the puppy at home so that it is not exposed to diseases or dangers, but you begin socialising him with the family. Then you slowly start taking him out on a lead to meet other dogs and people and make sure that he behaves properly. Finally, when you are confident about these things you let him off the lead to run free in the park. This is how dogs should be, they were never meant to be on a lead. But you worry about their behaviour- will they attack someone? You worry about their safety -will another dog attack my dog? Most of all you worry that if you let your dog off the lead he won't come back! Of course, if you have built the right sort of bond with the dog it will always come back, but just to make sure the clever owners usually reward the returning dog with lavish praise and usually their favourite treat.

With teenagers, it's not so different.

We know we have got to let our teenagers off the lead, but we worry about the consequences. Now some teenagers are already pulling at the lead, some seem to be chewing through it and we need to try to ensure that we build the right bonds and have the right treats to make sure that it all turns out well, so that when we let them off the lead they behave responsibly and keep out of trouble.

Certainly, an Enabling parenting style is likely to be the best way to build independence and responsibility, but it is not enough on its own. Adults who can function successfully in the world need to develop their own motivations and values. Teenagers should be encouraged to develop their own realistic goals and a vision for their future. They need a sense of direction and a plan to try to achieve it.

Clearly, one major aspect of independence will be to develop a career path and become financially independent. Parents can help their teenagers identify their strengths and weaknesses, find out what really interests them and identify what qualifications they will need. Schools and colleges obviously have a major role here and we will discuss this more later. However, teenagers also need to learn a wide range of life skills and you as the parent should be their main mentor in acquiring these. As children age, parents should be doing less and less of the practical things for them and allowing them to take over their own care. Hopefully, they'll quickly acquire a whole range of skills including how to run a household, how to manage their time and how to operate successfully outside of the home and deal with people.

Teach practical skills by giving information and guidance

Skills in the home

Handling money
Shopping and understanding food labels
Mowing lawn
Vacuuming/cleaning
Cooking and healthy eating
Washing clothes
Understanding medicines and labels
Safety in the home – using machinery, electrics, internet

Skills outside the home

Safety out of the home – dealing with drugs and alcohol, identifying risks, planning routes, using taxis etc
Travel skills
Dealing with emergencies
Dealing with people and situations outside home

Teach general coping and life skills by role modelling and discussion

Body self-care
Sleep
Diet
Cleanliness/hygiene
Exercise
Grooming

Time management

Setting priorities
Achieving balance work/leisure
Assessing how long tasks take
Creating schedule/timetable

Social skills – practice if possible/seek new experiences with new people

Making and keep friends
Dealing with peer pressure and bullying
Assertiveness
Speaking out and public speaking
Resolving conflicts
Co-operating

The next two are particularly important areas for development:

Problem solving skills
Your teenager will learn by example how to problem solve and survive when things go wrong. Show them the blueprint, but don't solve everything for them.

They need to learn to:

Identify the exact problem by questioning
Identify what they can and can't affect

Identify options/choices
Identify if they need to get help/advice from someone else
Weigh pros cons and consequences
Be realistic, rational, optimistic
Identify smart/safe choices
Have contingency plan for failure
Review the outcome later
Learn from success or failure

Emotional resilience to problems

Recognise most problems/adversity are not personal unless they are the direct result of your decisions/choices
They are usually not random and accidental, but are based on decisions of other people or organisations and may be predictable
Accept life has pain/hardship/consequences
Don't expect instant easy solutions
Have perspective
Learn from experience/failure
Be willing to seek help from others, listen to advice

That's a long list, how can I help my teenager?

As we saw earlier responsibility has two aspects – doing things for oneself whilst being accountable and making sensible decisions with the best outcomes.

If you can, steadily reduce doing things for your teenager or giving them the things that they want unconditionally. They should begin to understand the cost of items and be prepared to save or wait for them. They should not only be taught the household skills described above, but also be expected to take over those ones which relate to them and to contribute to performing general household chores. It is reasonable to allow your teenager more privacy, particularly regarding their bedrooms, if they are the sole occupant, but they will have to learn to become responsible for cleaning and sorting out their laundry.

Over time they should take responsibility for getting up, travelling to and from school and keeping up with their school work. As they spend more time away from home and unsupervised, they will be at greater risk than ever before. These can be worrying times for you, but teenagers need the space to grow.

Whatever your doubts, cross your fingers, develop trust in them and show them that you have confidence in their ability to cope. This will take patience, and a huge amount of personal willpower to stop rescuing them and let them take the consequences of their actions. If your child has not done their homework don't do it for them. If they want something clean to wear, don't rush to provide it, just make sure that they know the laundry routine in the household, or even how to do it for themselves! And if their general disorganisation has meant a forgotten piece of gym kit, don't rush up to the school with it, they need to learn from their mistakes and accept the consequences. Don't hover over them and don't rush to give advice unless it is asked for. When your teenager takes positive risks and finds their own solutions to their problems, encourage and praise them. Let the successes and failures be theirs, not yours, but applaud their achievements and give them honest feedback. When they fail, try to help them learn from their mistakes and encourage them not to be put off trying new challenges.

The happy adult

So, what makes adults happy?

There is no doubt that happiness is a complicated issue. There is an old quote about happiness the origins of which are a little unclear and we have adapted it slightly:

"Happiness is like a butterfly, if you chase it, it will fly away but if you create the right garden it may come back and land on your shoulder"

So, the question is how do we create the right garden?

This is the holy grail that everyone has been searching for forever-the secret to happiness. It isn't simple, because happiness is intensely personal and what makes us happy is subjective, but decades of research have identified some key factors that many people agree on.

The two biggest myths about happiness concern money and worries. Firstly, that money brings happiness. Clearly poverty is very stressful, but in the western world where most people have adequate housing and food and possessions, even if they may not be as good as they would like, research suggests that having more money makes very little difference to happiness. If you look in your newspapers every day you will see wealthy celebrities who are far from happy and in the worst cases come to very tragic ends. Secondly, that happiness is the absence of worries. Let us tell you that everyone has worries. Worrying is hard wired into the human brain and so we will never get away from it. The key to happiness is how we cope with our worries.

What are the things that truly matter, and what do the happiest people do, that others don't?

There has been lots of research on this over the years, and the key areas seem to be, that to be truly happy you will:

Relate well to others
Give to others
Appreciate what you have
Change and develop
Exercise

We are going to think about what these five key areas might mean, not just for your teenager, but also for you. The most important people at home are parents, and as we used to tell our trainee teachers, the most important people in school are teachers. That's not a value judgement about the worth of different people- it's a practical approach. Parents and teachers are the ones in charge and if they are not functioning properly the whole class or family suffers. So, let's look at the list.

Relate well to others

Top of the list is having secure, reliable relationships. This includes relationships with partners and family, relationships with friends and with the wider community. Harvard University has spent a lifetime studying a group of people, starting around 1940 and carrying on to the present day.[1] They have tracked a group of physically, financially and mentally healthy students as well as a group of individuals with greater challenges. The study is considered to be the best long-term study of its type, and its conclusions are simple. The study has shown that the dominant factor in creating happy lifetimes is having good relationships. They lead to individuals who are healthier physically and mentally and who live longer! (See Chapter 21 for more about Healthy Relationships)

So, for you as a parent, it is very important to maintain and nourish good relationships. Try to find time for these relationships with your partner and close friends somewhere in your busy schedule, and if you can find an enjoyable pastime to share even better. Of course, with your teenager, this may be the most challenging task. One idea that can work well is to set five minutes aside in the evening every day to talk to your teenager. Tell them one challenge and one success that you had that day. In turn, they need to try to tell you the same thing. Remember to avoid the thing many parents do with their teenagers, that is to tell them how they should have managed the situation better, or in other words, to speak too much and listen too little. (See Chapter 7 for more about Communication)

For your teenagers, you may not always like their friends, but don't try telling them that! If you see a good healthy relationship with a friend, or an aunt or a neighbour or grandparent that you trust, encourage it. Try to ensure that the trusted adult feeds any critical information about your teenager back to you, but do not confront your teenager with anything you learn as this will completely undermine the relationship. These relationships can leave you feeling left out, but don't be jealous, teenagers often confide more in other people, not to exclude their parents from their lives but because they don't want to disappoint them.

Giving to others

Research shows that people who help others are happier.[2] Whether they give their time their energy or their empathy, they feel better about themselves. Most parents probably feel that they are giving plenty of these things already and we agree. So, when you are rushing about like a headless chicken, trying to ferry your children to their hobbies and trying to shop and thinking about work or an elderly relative or neighbour, just console yourself with the thought that it's good for you!

One thing that can be a powerful giving tool is forgiveness. We often carry lots of old wounds from past experiences with those around us, and the resentment from these hurts can cause us a lot of stress, which can spoil our current relationships. It is often useful to try to see things from the other party's point of view, rather than as intended attacks on you or your character. This especially includes your teenage children.

For your teenager, encourage any giving behaviour.
It might be visiting an old person or neighbour who needs some assistance.
It might be looking after a younger child or mentoring a pupil at school.
It might involve taking a leadership role in a group of scouts or guides.
Many schools encourage volunteering, but unfortunately often the volunteers are the most confident students and those who would probably benefit most stay quiet.

It is also useful to remember that however anti-social our teenagers behave at home they are often warm caring individuals when they are away from us.

Appreciate what they have

Next, research suggests that the happiest people appreciate the world around them and what they have. [3] In the past, it was common for people to say grace before meals to give thanks for their food. They knew that the quality of their lives could depend on whether they had a good harvest or not and bad weather or pests could cause famine.

Nowadays we take our food supply for granted. In fact, we take a great many of the things around us for granted and it is only when we look at news items about war or famine around the world that we realise how lucky we are.

As parents, we tend to take having our kids for granted. We forget how many people never had the children that they wanted, or had children with life limiting conditions or severe mental or physical disabilities. It is also easy to forget with difficult teenagers, the joy we had when we first saw them or the pride that we felt watching them on their first day at school. Hold on to those optimistic feelings and hopes and remind yourself of them when you are having a bad day or week with your teenager. Remember that the slightly confused anxious five year-old waiting at the school gates for their first day at school is the same slightly confused anxious teenager who is waiting at the gates of adulthood.

Just a word about gratitude, sometimes it seems as if we are always giving to our teenagers, and they appear ungrateful or just take it all for granted. Remember you are modelling to them the ideal behaviour and they are watching your approach to being kind and considerate. Lessons they will hopefully adopt as they mature.

Most teenagers are allergic to gratitude, at least as far as we are concerned. They do not appreciate anything you do either as a parent or as a provider. And as an older person, and grandparent, I can tell you that they won't until they start taking on those roles.

When your teenager goes off to college or sets up in a flat with some mates, he or she will come home one weekend and say to you.

"Mum you'd never believe how expensive toilet rolls are!"
And you'll think but won't say....
"Funnily enough I know that because I was paying for the ones you have been using for the last twenty years"

Or when they have their first child and say
"Mum It's not fair how much childcare costs and what am I going to do if my child is sick while I am at work"
And you'll think but won't say....
"Welcome to the world of parenting"

And finally, when they say to you
"My teenagers in trouble at school again, I was never like that"
And you'll think but won't say....
"Oh yes you were"

Let me assure you that you will have the last laugh when this happens. And eventually your teenager, in the fullness of time, will realise that you may not have always got it right, but parenting is damned difficult and at least you did your best.

"If you want your children to turn out well, spend twice as much time with them and half as much money!" Abigail Van Buren

Change and develop

We can all get stuck in a rut and we need new challenges to give our lives variety and to learn new skills. Sadly, many of us lack the self-belief and confidence to stray far out of our comfort zones and we miss out on some great opportunities. For us, trying to write this book was incredibly frightening. We didn't think we had the skills to do it. But it has been exciting and rewarding and you know what – as we got into it we realised not only that we could do it, and enjoy it, but that we felt quite good at it. Also, although we have raised a family together, this is the first time we have ever been partnered in a business venture and we have both been surprised by how well we co-operated.

For your healthy state of mind try to take on some new challenges or experiences if you can. You will always have time and money constraints, but see what is possible - even if it's just doing an evening course for an hour or two a week.

This is also true of your relationship with your teenager. If it's causing you lots of grief see if there are any way of changing it. You are not a tree. If you don't like where you are, move!

For your teenager, it's great to encourage them to experience new things. There are just a couple of warnings. One, we know teenagers can take too many risks, so you may not want them to take up mountain climbing or rally driving. Secondly, in the years when your teenager is sitting public examinations, they will be under severe time pressure. Do not commit them to something that will absorb all their time. Nevertheless, an activity that gets them out and away from studying for a while is great. You might even discover that you share a passion or interest in a similar activity that you can do together.

Exercise
Lastly exercising is very important, not just for your physical health, but it also has a major impact on mental health. It really helps with stress and anxiety. It is great for you and your teenager. And It doesn't have to be super intense. You don't have to go to the gym for hours or try to run a half marathon. Walking is great and hobbies like gardening are good too. Being outside can be very helpful both for the exercise and for appreciating the beauty of the world around us. It may even be something else you and your teenager can enjoy together. The Scandinavians, who are often considered to be the happiest people in the world are very good at outdoor pursuits where they are close to nature.

What are the characteristics of happy people?

So that's what some happy people do, but what sort of people are they? These seem to be key characteristics:

Principled- they have a set of values
Resilient -they bounce back from adversity
Optimistic - they take a positive view of people and life
Unique - they recognise their own worth
Directed- they have a sense of where they are going in life

Before we look at these characteristics individually, which are all challenging things for teenagers to acquire, we need to think about role modelling. Teenagers develop their own values and characteristics based on their experiences of life and the people around them. Whether you like it or not and whether it is deliberate or not a significant part of this will be observing their role models within the family. Parents need to be good role models for their teenagers and demonstrate as far as possible their own versions of these characteristics. (See Chapter 6 for more on Parent's Roles)

Principled - they have a set of values
Principled people have values and know what they are. They may be based on religion or ethics or just on experience, but they help them to make choices. They try to act in a conscientious manner. Teenagers are likely to develop values based on observation of parents, teachers and other significant adults in their lives. Good role models should demonstrate characteristics such as honesty, fairness and kindness.

Resilient - they bounce back from adversity
Resilient people can bounce back from setbacks. They have found ways of overcoming adversity and are confident in their ability to ride out troubles. They don't give up easily and are persistent and determined when faced with problems. Teenagers are generally not very resilient and seem to be getting less so with time. Of course, they lack experience and often lack skills, but they are also under

increasing pressures of all sorts. In fairness, even with our experience, there are many modern-day issues involving rapid changes in technology and society that even we can't deal with. Learning early that they can find solutions or cope when things go wrong, helps to build a 'can do' attitude that continues throughout life and certainly helps when bigger or more important problems come along.

Optimistic - they take a positive view of people and life

Optimistic people take a positive view of life and expect things to turn out well. They see life as full of opportunities rather than problems and tend to focus on the good aspects of life and of people, rather than the bad.

Many teenagers find it difficult to take an optimistic and positive view of their situation and this is a major factor in depression. They concentrate too much on their problems without seeing enough opportunities. You'll need to help your teenager to build optimism.

Here are a few strategies that might help:

Get them to listen to that little voice inside their head that says they can't do it and challenge any self-talk that is negative.

Slow down and think through the options-you can help by making a list together

Optimistic people can find positive aspects in negative situations, we call this positive reframing. A useful skill for your teenager.

Help them to look for the lesson when something goes wrong, so that they are not always looking for someone else to blame.

Get them to practice perspective taking so that they can develop a sense of proportion, instead of catastrophising when things look like they might go wrong.

Challenge your teenager's extreme language, it leads to extreme thinking, are they furious or just annoyed? do they really' hate' someone? Is it really a 'disaster'?

Get them to set realistic goals (More in the next Chapter).

Encourage them to count their blessings and let them see you doing it too!

Winston Churchill said

"The pessimist sees difficulty in every opportunity. The optimist sees the opportunity in every difficulty."

Unique - they recognize their own worth
Unique people recognise that they have their own worth. They are different to everyone else and that's a good thing. Many teenagers struggle to see the value of their unique worth. Firstly, they are trying very hard to fit in to the groups around them, rather than trying to stand out as individuals. Secondly, they often don't feel very good at anything and this sense may be reinforced by a lack of praise and recognition from others. Honest praise will not make your child 'full of themselves'.

Directed - they have a sense of where they are going in life
Directed people feel a sense of purpose in their lives and importantly have at least some control over achieving it. Teenagers often lack direction as they have not yet worked out the path they intend to follow. They also often feel that they have little control in the way things are going as they see their future as being dictated by others, including parents, schools or society in general.

Avenues to happiness - Ways to make it happen
We now know the elements that we need to pursue and encourage. These should be our long-term goals, and we need to keep them in the forefront of our mind.

Now some of you may have come across the Eisenhower Principle if you have ever been on a time management course. This defines Important and Urgent tasks as follows:

Important activities have an outcome that leads to us achieving **our goals**.
Urgent activities demand immediate attention but are often associated with **other peoples' goals**.

The principle gives priority to the important over the urgent - in other words, we should be focusing on developing independence, responsibility and happiness in our teenager and not spending too much of our time and energy on this weeks' crisis unless it really matters.

If we prioritise the things that make us happy we are more likely to be successful.
If we prioritise those things which appear to make people successful, we may well not achieve happiness.

So, what are likely to be the urgent short-term issues? Well, of course, every household has all sorts of issues and problems, but the number one short term goal that parents often focus on is that they want their teenager to do well at school.

At first sight, this seems to be entirely consistent with the long-term goals, but this needs to be looked at closely. The key question is what does "doing well at school mean"?
Increasingly Government has focused on school performance tables and examination grades as the key factor determining a successful school and it is easy for parents to look at success for their children solely in terms of examination results. The problem is that for more and more teenagers this obsession with results is causing tremendous anxiety and stress problems. Around three-quarters of teenagers say that they are stressed about their school grades and we know that teenagers who have mental health problems at school are much more likely to have problems in their adult lives.

We have identified the major factors that encourage happiness, so the question is to what extent schools are supporting and encouraging the development of those activities and characteristics?

We are sure many schools think they deliver these elements, and it is certainly true that they play an important role. They can certainly assist in encouraging good relationships, new experiences and exercise and by promoting acts of giving and selflessness. The ethos of a school and perhaps more importantly its students will also play a major part in developing values. However, the obsession with examination results particularly in the core subjects, creates enormous pressures on teenagers and imposes a one size fits all model. It emphasises narrow academic achievements as the yardstick of success and does not recognise the value of diversity.

Today, we have come to recognise the value of people of different genders, ethnic groups, sexualities, religions and disabilities, but we completely fail to recognise the value of people with diverse academic ability. If a GCSE exam is truly challenging, why should everyone be capable of getting a C grade or above? We are all different! The current system places far too much value on a few subjects, with little recognition or development of more creative and practical talents, at which many, less academic students can excel. It ignores the needs of large sectors of the workforce such as the creative, caring and catering sectors. Even more worrying, the focus on narrow academic ability does little to encourage the most important human traits.

Since we know that the essential route to happiness is through relationships with other people, it is useful to look at the personality traits that are most important to friendships and intimate relationships. Research suggests that intelligence is not a major factor in choosing a friend, and only a small factor in choosing partners. [4] [5] The most important things that people value are:

Being trustworthy – honest, dependable, loyal, sincere, moral

Being co-operative – fair, supportive, trusting, sharing, open-minded

Being congenial – friendly, funny, sense of humour

Being caring – empathetic, kind, warm, good listener, compassionate

Being emotionally consistent – self-confident, calm, happy, optimistic

There is a big danger that nearly every major effort at school is about demonstrating intelligence and the other key personal characteristics get ignored. Sadly, this obsession with grades has spread to the workplace where many of our most caring and empathetic youngsters are prevented from taking on roles in childcare or nursing because they can't get a grade C or equivalent in Maths or English!

Another major problem is that if we as parents and our teenagers buy into this obsession with examination performance to the exclusion of other things, there is little time left in the week to ensure that our teenagers are developing the other life skills that they will need as adults. We should steadily be integrating them into the skills of running a household, of managing their finances, of relating to a wide range of people and all the other skills they will need as adults, including an appreciation of the world at large. An adolescence dedicated solely to study will never achieve this. It is also worth bearing in mind that as we have seen in Chapter 3, the teenage brain is developing according to the demands that are being placed upon it. If those demands are primarily academic, they will develop brain functions that are great for academic issues, but that may not be suited for much else!

References in this chapter

[1] Harvard study of adult development: Grant study and Glueck study

[2] Post S. (2005). Altruism, Happiness, and Health: It's Good to Be Good. International journal of behavioral medicine. 12. 66-77. 10.1207/s15327558ijbm1202_4

[3] Witvliet C, Richie F & Root Luna L & Van Tongeren D. (2018). Gratitude Predicts Hope and Happiness: A Two-Study Assessment of Traits and States. The Journal of Positive Psychology. 10.1080/17439760.2018.1424924

[4] Campbell K & Holderness N & Riggs M. (2015). Friendship chemistry: An examination of underlying factors. The Social Science Journal. 52. 10.1016/j.soscij.2015.01.005

[5] Sprecher S & Regan P. (2002). Liking Some Things (in Some People) more than Others: Partner Preferences in Romantic Relationships and Friendships. Journal of Social and Personal Relationships - J SOC PERSON RELAT. 19. 463-481. 10.1177/0265407502019004048

Chapter 5

Emerging from the shadows

In this Chapter we are going to look at the expectations and goals that we give ourselves, and how these are often unrealistic and unhealthy. Some of these goals we learn from our parents and grandparents, some we learn from schools and colleges and some we just create for ourselves. Wherever they come from, we need to take a good look at them and decide whether they are really sensible and achievable, or whether we are just setting ourselves and our teenagers up to fail.

The Three Own Goals

There are a great many unrealistic goals that many of us carry with us, but these are some of the worst three.

Own goal 1   I must be the best
Own goal 2   I must get everything right
Own goal 3   I must be good at everything

As you can see we call these own goals because as in a football match, they are goals that work against us. Let's look at them one by one and we'll consider some human examples to see how they work.

Own goal 1   I must be the best

The story of Usain Bolt

If you follow athletics you will have heard of Usain Bolt. He was the most successful sprinter of the last decade. If we look at his record, we can see that he won just about every major championship over this period except when he was injured or disqualified.

Year	Championship	100m position	200m position
2008	Olympics	Gold	Gold
2009	World	Gold	Gold
2011	World	Disqualified	Gold
2012	Olympics	Gold	Gold
2013	World	Gold	Gold
2015	World	Gold	Gold
2016	Olympics	Gold	Gold

If we look at Own Goal 1, what does that tell us? Well, firstly it tells us that every other sprinter during this period was not the best. They may have been the best in their school or college, their county or country, but judged against this man they were failures. They were never THE best!

Even Usain himself wasn't the best before 2008 and, in the world championships of 2017, he came third. Like the dominant lion in the pride, who will one day be displaced by a younger stronger lion, his days of being the best were over.

It is the same if we look at any sporting knockout championship. In the end there is only one winner and everyone else is a loser.

So, we can see that none of us is likely to be the best unless we only judge ourselves among a small group or for a short period of time. Remember being the best is more of a statement about the level of your competitors than it is about your own worth.

Own goal 2 I must get everything right

The story of Henry the Eighth

Henry the Eighth is one of the most famous English kings. He is particularly known for having six wives, two of whom he executed. Like many kings before and since, Henry probably thought he was getting everything right. He thought that he had a divine right to rule and nobody would dare defy him for fear of execution. He changed the whole course of British history by breaking with the Catholic Church, so that he could divorce and remarry, and he executed anyone who refused to recognise him as the supreme head of the church.

Did he get everything right? Of course not, – he just thought he did!

We, like many of you, have had bosses rather like that who never listened to advice and would often try to penalise anyone who ever disagreed with them. Of course, not only did they not get everything right, but usually they made a lot more mistakes than they should have.

Nobody should expect to get it right all the time or try to always do it on their own.

Own goal 3   I must be good at everything

The story of Theresa May

As we write this book, Theresa May is the current British Prime Minister. Imagine her trying to be good at everything. She is trying to run the country and deal with a whole host of issues on a day to day basis. At the same time, she must cope with some completely new challenges such as Brexit and terrorism. She has 70 million people who are relying on her good judgement for their wellbeing and security and she also has to cope with opposition in Parliament and within her own party. Of course, she has a team around her, but as we all know things can still go wrong. By the time you read this, she may well be out of a job, leaving just her record for us all to decide how well she did. Even then, there will probably be considerable disagreement, as different people will have different ideas about what a good job would have looked like.

Look at this list and think about how many of these statements apply to you:

I am good at writing
I am good with numbers
I am a good singer
I can draw great pictures
I can act
I can dance
I can run fast
I am a good friend
I am a good team player

How many did you get? Most of us would do well to agree with even half of these. If you ticked most of them, you are the sort of talented allrounder who used to really annoy your classmates because you seemed to be good at everything. If you are like that you may well be having a very difficult time with parenting your teenager, partly because you usually find everything rather easy, and partly because you want your teenager to be at least half as good as you were!

Nobody can be good at everything. We all have our strengths and weaknesses and we need to recognise those areas where we are likely to need help.

Conclusion

These three own goals are all targets that are impossible to continually achieve. Psychologists call these sorts of targets perfectionism. They lead us to think of ourselves as failures, even when we are getting it right most of the time.

Most of us have self-doubts about our abilities, which is like having a little gremlin on our shoulder who feeds us messages like:
"You are never good enough"
"See you failed again"
"You will never amount to anything"

These self-doubts hang over us like a shadow and whenever we fail to achieve perfection, we beat ourselves up and our self-esteem takes a knock.

Buying into these perfectionist goals has been linked to low mood and depression. Several recent studies of suicides have also found this to be a factor with many relatives describing the victims as people who had exceedingly high expectations of themselves.

So, we need to find new more healthy goals both for the sake of our own mental health and for the sake of our children. If you have unhealthy goals even if you don't teach them to your children, they may well copy them, as you are their main role models, and they watch how you deal with life.

We also must be careful as parents that we do not say things to our children that might encourage these perfectionist ideas. Many of us are so keen to encourage our children and not to crush their dreams that we give them the message that they can be good at everything or follow any career path that they want.

We also don't like to tell them when they lack talent in a particular area. How many of us watch talent programs like the X Factor and see people who believe that they can sing brilliantly, but clearly can't. We think "Why didn't anyone ever tell them?", but often we fall into the same trap.

We need to be honest with our children, or find someone else who will be, and they should understand that they don't need to be good at everything, but that even if they are not very good at something, they can still enjoy it.

We all need some goals in life but clearly the three own goals are the wrong ones. So, let's look at how we can change them.

The Three Amigos (and also a Fourth)

We need to replace the three own goals with targets that can be achievable and that can boost our confidence and self-esteem. We prefer to call these the 'Three Amigos'. You will notice that these targets begin with I will, not I must. They are things that we will try to do, not things that we have to do – it is our choice.

Amigo 1   I will do my best

We have seen that we can rarely be the best, and even when we do it is likely to be short-lived, but we can certainly do our best. That means putting as much effort as we can into the activity and taking a pride in what we do and what we achieve, even if the progress is slow and difficult. We need to be realistic about the level that we can achieve, bearing in mind our own talents and the level of our experience and knowledge. If you want to set yourself attainment targets work in small steps and adjust them as you go. Remember the greatest musicians started at grade 1 and the greatest swimmers with a 10 metre certificate.

If you have a long-term target that seems a long way off, try not to think of it as a mountain that you are trying to climb. Think of it as a mountain that you are coming down. You still need to descend carefully one step at a time and find the best and safest route down, but the journey may get easier as you move on.

Every time we achieve one of our targets, however, small it may seem, we need to celebrate and give ourselves a pat on the back. Then we can move onto the next level in a spirit of confidence.

If we are trying our best the only things we need to think about are whether we are working in the right way with the right strategy to maximise our improvement and whether we want to carry on or choose to put our efforts into something else.

Amigo 2   I will celebrate when I get it right

None of us gets it right all the time, but when you do achieve the successes that you are hoping for, however small, celebrate them – they are your achievements and they belong to you – no one else. It can be helpful to write them down somewhere such as a diary so that when you are having a bad day you can remind yourself of your successes. Try not to dwell too long on the things that turn out badly. Yes, we can all learn from our mistakes, but we always assume that there is a perfect solution to every problem and that we must have missed it. Often there is no perfect answer only a least bad solution. Even though the one that you chose may seem to have worked out badly, the alternatives may have turned out even worse. We talked in Chapter 4 about building in a 5minute conversation with your teenager highlighting their successes and challenges during the day. We all find it so easy to criticise ourselves or others for perceived failures but recognising and affirming our achievements is much more useful in building self esteem in the short and long term.

Amigo 3   I will prioritise my time and efforts to achieve the things that are most important to me.

None of us can be good at everything and we certainly don't have the time to give every task our full attention. If we are not to be overwhelmed by all the conflicting demands upon us, we need to make a conscious effort to prioritise. If we don't prioritise the things that are the most important to us and are most likely to make us happy, we will be swept away by the pressures set by other people or organisations. In the previous Chapter we looked at the sorts of activities that encourage happiness and we need to build them into our priorities where possible. We all have financial and other practical constraints on what we can and cannot do, but we need to try to create a healthy balance in our lives.

In the next section we are going to look at trying to reinforce these positive goals so that we can transform our children's lives, but first it is worth reviewing how to change your general expectations of your parenting skills.

If you judge yourself on the three own goals you will expect to be the perfect parent, who gets everything right all the time. In fact, parenting teenagers is one of the most challenging tasks that many of us will ever have to do. Not only is there no perfect answer, but what works today may not work tomorrow. You may never be the best parent, but you can certainly try your best and take pride in your efforts, however successful they may be. You will never get it all right but when something goes well, celebrate it. You will never be good at everything but do try to make your priorities right for you and your family. In the end, we can only try to be good enough.

Lastly, there is fourth amigo, which is perhaps the most important of all.

Amigo 4   Be kind to yourself

If you are trying your hardest, you deserve success as much as anyone else.

ACT - Action Changes Things

"Act as if what you do makes a difference – it does" William James

Let's look at how this problem of having unhealthy goals is having a major effect on the mental health of many of our teenagers and what we can do about it. We need to act to change things and these actions need to be consistent and maintained year after year.

Change "I must be the best" to "I will do my best"

When teenagers feel that they must be the best, whether that means being top of their class or achieving top grades, it puts them under tremendous stress and the most badly affected students are the most able. Average and below average students soon realise that they cannot be the best, because they see people around them who are consistently beating them in test results. Sadly, in many cases, they then give up trying altogether, as they feel that all their efforts are wasted, and they are just "no good at it". As a result, they never achieve anywhere near their potential and miss out on learning valuable skills.

For the most able students, the problem can be even worse. They get closer to achieving the best position in the class or achieving top grades and may achieve it sometimes, but they inevitably struggle to do this all the time and across all subjects. This causes them a good deal of stress and anxiety. They work harder and harder, but they can never quite achieve the perfection that they seek. This severely dents their self-confidence and they can become deeply unhappy about their perceived "failures".

So, what can I do for my teenager?

Firstly, you need to accept that your teenagers can only do their best, and you must convince your teenager to adopt this goal as well. Focus on praising your teenager for their efforts, rather than their grades or achievements and try to help them to make sure that their efforts are well directed and thought out to maximise their effect. Praise is vitally important and those of us who did not receive much praise in our childhoods are often not very good at giving it.

Secondly, don't compare your child to other brothers or sisters or other people at school. Everyone is unique, they are a person in their own right, with their own strengths and weaknesses. Nobody can help being the person they are rather than someone else. Valid criticisms of behaviour or effort do not require adverse comparisons with others, which only lead to frustration and resentment.

Finally, do not set them, or allow them to set themselves, unrealistic grade targets. We are told, and it is supported by some evidence, that teenagers whose parents and teachers have high expectations of them achieve better results, but if we set these goals too high, the pressures on our teenagers can be overwhelming or they can give up altogether. We must find the right balance, bearing in mind their current level of performance and effort. Not all students are going to achieve the highest grades in their examinations. If a student is a year away from the public examination and is consistently graded at C in tests, then giving them an A* as a target is only going to give them stress and result in them feeling like a failure. Set a shorter-term target of achieving level Bs in the next three months and, if they achieve that, move the target up. Get advice on what they need to do to improve both in terms of improving their knowledge and improving their work methods. Focus on one improvement at a time. Small steps are much easier to achieve than giant ones and every step, however small, can be celebrated.

Let us show you how small steps can work:

The story of Jenny

Let me tell you about one of my students who I will call Jenny. I was a maths teacher and Jenny was in one of my classes. She would often turn up to my lessons late and then sit at the back of the class. Sometimes she fell asleep but even when she did not, she took little interest in the lessons. However, occasionally she came in with a bit more purpose and when she tried in my lessons she did quite well.

Now I asked around school what might be affecting Jenny. Although some people clearly did know I was not going to be one of them and so I never knew.

Jenny was in Year 9 and in those days the year 9 students had to take a SATS test at the end of the year. Since doing past papers is great practice for students, I started giving my students a test every Friday about two months before the exam. In the first test Jenny got 35, which was a level 3. Most of her class mates were achieving between 45 and 60 which were mostly levels 4 and 5 with a few of the bright sparks at level 6. I asked Jenny why she thought she only got 35 and she told me "I'm no good at Maths". I said to her "You know what, I think you are fine at Maths. When you try, you are as good as the rest of the class. I think you can get a 4 and maybe even a 5 by the time you do the exam." She looked at me and I wasn't convinced that she'd taken any notice. The next week we had the test and on the following Monday I gave out the marks. She was still bottom of the class, but she had gone up to 39. Not only that but 39 was a level 4. It was the bottom mark for a 4, but it was still a 4. When I told her, I caught glimpse of a smile, now that was probably the first smile I had seen all year.

In the next few weeks her marks steadily crept up and every week I would congratulate her and say to her "See I knew you could do it". Two weeks before the exam we had our last test and Jenny came out with 60, which was right in the middle of the 5s. She did her SATS and a month later we got the results. Jenny got a level 6! She had ended up in the top ten of my class of 30.

So small steps and praise really works, even with quite disinterested children.

Before we move on, let me just say a few words about the school grade targets that now appear on most reports.

Wherever these targets come from, they are usually based on average performance of all students and for a whole variety of reasons they may not be appropriate to your teenager. The main purpose of these targets is not to motivate your teenager, but to monitor schools and individual teachers. They ensure that a great many teachers get exam stress every year. Having been closely involved with running public examinations over the years and seeing the difficulties that many students have, we can tell you that everyone is different. Every teenager has their own story with their own individual stresses both at school and at home.

Last year we posted this poem on our Facebook page on the day that the examination results were published to encourage students not to feel labelled by their examination grades, which may tell very little of their personal story.

Making the grade

It's not really the A star
That makes me proud of who you are
It's the way you go and visit Gran
And rub her back and hold her hand

I'm so impressed with that grade A
With all that time you've been away
The chemo and the loss of hair
They didn't stop you getting there.

Fantastic that you got your B
I think that stands for bravery
For days you struggled from your bed
And fought the demons in your head

OK you missed your target C
But they cannot know you, quite like me
I've seen the sister that you've raised
While your mum has been away

It may only have been a D
But you're much better I can see
The scars upon your arms have healed
Your eyes, new happiness reveal

Some will say you scraped an E
But that's just great from where you've been
You've helped your family survive
The trauma of the one who died

Although you ended with a U
You helped your mum to fight the blues
You struggled with her inner fears
And you're the reason she's still here

Everyone has an individual story. Don't let your children be defined by their grades. Let them be defined by who they are and how they live their life.

In this section we have tended to concentrate on school grades, but of course, this approach of focusing on and praising effort rather than achievements covers every aspect of a teenager's life. Whether you are talking to them about how well they carried out some household job, how well they dealt with a friend who had a problem or how well they are getting on with their siblings the same thing is true. If their motives are good and they are trying their hardest, then they are doing their best, and they deserve praise, whatever the outcome!

Change "I must get everything right" to "I will celebrate when I get it right"

If your teenager believes that they should be getting everything right, they will judge every result by how far away from perfection they are, and they will constantly feel like they are falling short. Always try to focus on their successes and not on their shortcomings, on their achievements not their failures. Constant nagging about their shortcomings, even if it appears justified, merely implants in them a sense of not being good enough and it can become a self-fulfilling prophecy.

At school, the desire to get it all right seriously affects students' attitudes towards their achievements. Even if they get 90% in a test their first thought will be "what did I do wrong in the 10%?" and often parents reinforce this attitude by doing the same thing. We are so intent in looking for ways for them to improve, that this becomes our first thought, rather than recognising what they did well. We must turn this thinking upside down. If your teenager gets 90%, say "that's great well done", try not to even talk about the 10%. There may well be a time to focus on improvement and what they have learnt from their mistakes but leave it for another time such as when they are preparing for their next test. If they got a much lower mark, see if you can turn it into a positive:

"Hey, that's 5 marks better than last time"
"At least you got the question on that topic right this time"
"Well you know that's often your worst subject, so I think that's pretty good"

Look for signs of progress that you can praise.

Try to be sensitive to what your teenager sees as their talents and achievements and what areas they think matter to them. Listen out for mentions of things that have gone well during their day or examples of where they think that their actions have made a positive difference and encourage them to talk about them. It is easy for parents to ignore these things, either because they seem rather trivial or because they do not relate to the areas of their life to which we may give priority, like school grades in academic subjects, but noticing these successes is really important both in developing your teenager's self-confidence and finding out what they are good at and what they enjoy. These are areas that can not only be celebrated but should be built into the priorities we discuss in the next section.

Change "I must be good at everything" to "I will prioritise my time and efforts to achieve the things that are important to me"

At school, our teenagers are probably doing exams in at least 7 and possibly up to 10 subjects and are trying to balance the demands of all those different teachers. At the same time, they are juggling the demands from home, friends and possibly other activities such as sport, music, dance, drama etc. Nobody can spread their time across all these things, and try to do them all well, without feeling overwhelmed.

Overwhelm tends to lead to a feeling of helplessness, and our natural response is to opt out. You might see this when your teenager has numerous commitments and is short of time, yet just appears to be doing anything rather than what is required. Being immersed in YouTube and closing their eyes to what needs doing is an effective coping mechanism. Fear of not meeting deadlines stimulates their 'fight and flight' brain response and feels hugely uncomfortable, so it is not surprising that they want to avoid those physical feelings.

One of the key skills that teenagers need to learn is time management and they can only do that by developing a sense of priorities. You'll need to encourage your teenager to pace themselves and to focus on those demands which are likely to have the most beneficial effect on their future wellbeing. Try to identify your teenager's strengths and weaknesses, because encouraging the strengths is likely to have the greatest benefit for their self-confidence. More importantly, find out what they enjoy and encourage it. let them follow their dreams and priorities, not yours! Parents should not impose their ambitions and career goals on their children. Children need to find their own paths if they are not to risk being trapped in a future career or lifestyle that they may hate.

The story of Picasso

"I took me four years to paint like Raphael but a lifetime to paint like a child" -Pablo Picasso
Pablo Picasso is believed by some to be the greatest artist of modern times. Picasso's father was an artist who trained his young son to paint. He was a classical artist and he taught his son so well that by the age of 14 or15 he painted pictures such as the "Bust of a young man", which shows that he had already mastered these skills.

His father continued to push Picasso and at the age of 16 he was accepted at the most prestigious art academy in Spain. His father must have been delighted but Picasso hated it and soon dropped out. He had become somewhat disillusioned with classical art forms and later said "I paint objects as I think them, not as I see them".

Before he was 30, Picasso was painting in his own distinctive style as shown by pictures such as 'Portrait of Ambrose Vollard', an art dealer who Picasso knew.

By then, his father had died but we suspect that he would never have approved. Picasso had effectively rejected all his father's ideas about art and developed his own. He had not only changed his own ideas about art but had effectively changed the whole world's!

Much of the focus in schools today is on the core subjects of English and Maths, but these may well not be the subjects that give your teenager the most pleasure or fulfilment. Find out what subjects they have the most interest in and encourage them. Students who end up choosing options for other people's sake, not their own, are not only likely to find it harder to motivate themselves but are also likely to achieve worse results. Don't condemn your teenager or yourself to a career with which there is no emotional connection unless they really do not have any other choices.

When they come home, ask them what they enjoyed most at school today and why. Have conversations that focus on the future

"When the exams are over, we'll be able to ………."
"Let's look at this brochure after you've done your French homework and then we can plan…"
"You really are on the way to being successful and I can see how motivated you are"

Introducing your child to the idea that for every action there is a consequence is fine and giving them "objective" advice on the implications of their choices can be helpful, but hold back on the 'doom and gloom' about how awful things will be if they make the wrong choices now. In this changing world, it is very difficult for anyone to predict the best career choices and their ideas may be just as valid as yours. We hope that our children will be self-motivated and want to work towards their own best hopes, becoming independent along the way. If their chosen path does not seem to be working out, encourage them to have a rethink, but don't nag them and don't tell them how right you were!

Try to foster a balanced approach to work and play within your household and encourage them to pursue activities that release happy feelings or help relaxation. Proper sleep, good nutrition and exercise can all play a role in this, but so can having fun and creativity of all sorts. They may choose things you hate such as music styles or dress styles, but that is all part of them developing their individuality. You may also be able to find activities that all or part of the family can share in and you should look for those opportunities.

Celebrating success
We have tried in the first five Chapters to give you information about how teenagers develop and why they may be struggling to cope. We have looked at different parenting styles and which ones are likely to achieve the best results. As we have seen, most parent's primary aim for their children is "to be happy" and we have introduced you to The Avenues to Happiness and The Three Amigos, and suggested ways in which you, your family and your teenager can change their attitudes and priorities to achieve a happier future and better mental wellbeing. Hopefully, by now you will have some good ideas about changing your overall parenting strategy, if things are not going well, or adapting it to produce even better results if things are currently all right.

In the following chapters, we have provided a tool kit to give you much more detailed information about how to improve in specific areas and how to deal with some difficult issues. Whether or not you are currently experiencing these issues or even if your children are not quite teenagers, these tips can be very useful, and it is never too early to start making changes, even if they are small ones at first. From the time that our children are seven or eight until they are in their late teens we expect them to transform from totally dependent individuals into independent, responsible adults and that will only happen if we are constantly adapting our parenting to suit their level of maturity. This is not only a challenging balancing act for parents, but also involves moving from being the most important people in their lives to taking something of a back seat. This can feel very difficult. However well we handle this task, our teenagers will probably still be infuriating, exhausting, costly and egocentric, but we should see some real signs of improvement. We have seen how important it is for all of us to celebrate our successes, so how will we recognise the successes that we achieve with our teenager?

Well hopefully we will see our teenagers smiling more and when they do, the smile may reach well above the mouth to the eyes!

You will notice an increase in your teenager's self-esteem and confidence.

You will observe them developing self-growth and stepping outside of their comfort zone to take a few risks with life, not just doing the things they like, but developing a sense of accomplishment that comes from being curious about life and learning to solve new problems, work with others and push beyond existing boundaries.

You will see them overcoming life's challenges with courage and picking themselves up after dealing with the consequences of their own poor decisions. Surviving failures with determination and persistence to do it differently next time.

You will witness a burgeoning resilience and self-confidence as they start to believe in their own ability to do new things and to be successful.

You will allow them more freedom, with the removal of some of the restrictions of early childhood, and they will see that they are being trusted and respected and are being taken seriously as an individual. Their confidence in their own ability will come from your confidence in them.

Then they will begin to develop a sense of purpose and value, independently of you their parent, bravely creating new relationships and experiencing the rewards that come with being part of a wider community, taking part in social activities and developing consciousness of the world around them with their own views, ideals and attitudes.

You will have achieved your main aim as a parent.

To develop happy and independent young people with 'Roots and Wings'

You will have given them the roots to know who they are and where they have come from and given them the wings to fly through life's challenges with confidence.

PART TWO

THE BASIC TOOLKIT

Introduction

If you go into any major bookshop, you are likely to find a whole shelf full of books advising you how to parent babies and infants, but if you look for books about parenting teenagers you will be lucky if you find one. This is despite the fact, that in many ways parenting teenagers is much more challenging and difficult and when things go wrong the impacts for both parents and teenagers can be long-term. Of course, there are books on parenting teenagers and there are lots of sites online that touch on the subject, but these are often hard to find, especially if you want advice on resolving an immediate problem.

So where do we learn how to parent our teenagers. Well most of us have memories of our own upbringing, but of course we can only remember these from our own point of view, which is probably very different from our parents' recollection. Whether, or not, we think our parents did a good job, the truth is that the world has changed. Many forms of chastisement which were used in the past are no longer acceptable and the world in which teenagers are growing up is very different than for past generations.

The Toolkit below has been written to give parents ready help and advice. As with any toolkit, if your household is running smoothly, you might not need it, although the Basic Toolkit is designed to reduce the chances of things going wrong in the future and many of the suggestions are best begun before the teenage years. It contains general advice about how to maintain a relationship with your teenager that will promote the development of a happy and competent adult. The Emergency Toolkit which follows is advice on dealing with some particularly difficult problems that may occur.

There is no single correct way of raising teenagers as every parent and teenager is different, and every relationship is unique – so use the Toolkit in the way that you find most useful.

Chapter 6

The parent's role and responsibilities

As a parent, you have a responsibility to house, feed and clothe your child in a safe and loving environment. Your role is to raise your child so that they can function successfully in adult life. This means being able to interact socially with other people in a wide variety of situations and being able to sustain close relationships with friends and partners. It means being able to support themselves and maintain a household, and most importantly being able to problem solve and cope with all the pressures that life throws at them. It is not your role to be their best friend, rather, you should be their guardian and mentor, whose main focus is on training and directing them towards achieving the ability to be responsible and independent adults.

Whether you like it or not and whether you notice it or not, your child will study your behaviour and copy many aspects of it. You are their most important role model and as such, you need to try to ensure that you are giving them the right messages. Of course, none of us is perfect and our behaviour often falls below the ideal, but we need to be very aware of the image that we are projecting. We need to try to be at our best in front of our children and, if we know we are going to be involved in something that will set them a bad example, we should do it elsewhere.

The importance of role modelling has already been mentioned in earlier chapters and will appear later under several specific topics. However, the following are some of the most important general areas to consider. Of course, some of them are much easier than others depending on your personal circumstances.

Promoting a healthy lifestyle
The basics of maintaining optimum physical and mental health come from ensuring that we eat and drink healthily, that we get enough exercise, and that we get adequate good quality sleep. Developing these good habits both for ourselves and for our children is important. Aim to set a positive example in prioritising fitness over looks, and accepting our bodies the way that they are. Be aware of the model you set for your children in your use of cigarettes, alcohol and drugs and how that is likely to be reflected in your children's attitudes.

Be grateful for what you have
Showing your children that you are grateful for things that you have and not focusing on what you are missing, celebrating having good health, good friends and family and adequate food and shelter and being aware of those who are much worse off. This shifts the emphasis away from merely material gain.

Respect and help other people
The way in which you are seen to interact with other people is extremely important to your children. Of course, you won't always get on with everybody, but you can show respect for other people's rights and a willingness to try to understand them. Demonstrate how to be a loyal and reliable friend or partner and be someone who is prepared to help and support others in need.

Be honest
Honesty matters, but you need to be age appropriate with your children. Owning up to your mistakes and sharing your successes and failures with your teenagers gives them the freedom to also be less than perfect some of the time.

Show emotional control
The way in which you are seen to cope with everyday frustrations and distress is extremely important. Demonstrate the ability to deal with life in a calm, collected and rational fashion as much as possible. Of course, we will all get angry and distressed from time to time and this may be totally justified, but try to ensure that your

children understand when this is appropriate, and that it should never be an excuse for anti-social or violent behaviour.

Show coping and problem-solving skills
Your teenager will develop their own coping skills when they observe you demonstrating a positive and confident approach to life and your ability to deal with it. Showing that you can successfully manage your money, and run a household, and find ways of solving your problems as they arise will provide them with the knowledge that for every problem there is a solution.

Find other good role models
Parenting is often a very tough job and the more help we can find the better. Be prepared to share some of your responsibilities with other adults, provided that you trust them, and believe that they are also setting a good example. This may well include relatives, friends or neighbours, but may also include teachers and coaches.
Discussion of what is good or poor behaviour in public figures such as politicians, sportspeople and entertainers can be very valuable. Older siblings and other relatives can be good role-models but beware of constantly comparing your child with these and celebrate individuality.

Show an interest in your children's life
Finally, it is essential that however busy and difficult your life may be, you stay involved and interested in your children's lives. If you are to give them the support that they need and to encourage them to overcome obstacles, you need to be fully aware of their successes and failures and to recognise when they are having problems.

Chapter 7

Getting communication right

In Chapter 4 we identified that successful relationships are the most important element in maintaining happiness throughout life and of course the relationships between parents and their children are a very important part of this. For many parents, the relationships with their teenage children seem to become increasingly difficult. Some of this is a natural breaking of the bonds of dependency that teenagers need to go through before they reach adulthood, but many of the problems are made worse by poor communication between parents and teens. Parents see their teenage children as poor communicators, who don't listen, show little interest in having meaningful conversations with their parents and often seem incapable of expressing more than a few words or grunts in response to questions. In fact, it is often we the parents, who are the poor communicators and need help to learn more effective communication skills and not just our children.

When we are dealing with our younger children, even if we feel like we are giving them encouragement and support, much of the time we are issuing instructions to ensure that they behave in the way we want them to and to keep them safe. We take for granted that we know best and that we will always have the final say on what they can and can't do. Unfortunately, we find it very difficult to change this style of communication, even though our children are changing dramatically as we discussed in Chapter 3. Our teenagers therefore often come to see us as people who don't listen to them, don't respect their opinions and as being unresponsive to whatever they say.

So, if we are to improve our communications with our teenagers, we have to start to change our ways to ensure that our communication is a two-way process. It is worth looking back on your communication with your teenager over the course of the day and considering how much was shared conversation and how much was instruction or advice giving.

Plan opportunities to communicate

Start by recognising that having meaningful conversations with teenagers is not easy and you'll have to do a bit of planning. It can be helpful if you create some windows of opportunity when both parties are not likely to be distracted by other things. This will depend entirely on the schedules of the individuals themselves and how the family functions. It may be when they first return from school; it may be during a shared meal at home or elsewhere or it may be during a regular car journey. Your attempts may not always be very successful but keep trying. Make sure that you know as much as possible about what is going on in your teenager's life both inside and outside of the home and show a consistent interest in their affairs, even if they don't seem to want you to!

Be a good questioner

Learn to be a good questioner. This means finding out more about what your teenager thinks by gently, calmly and tactfully asking them. It is much better with teenagers to always try to use "open" questions, that is questions that cannot be answered with a simple yes or no such as:

How do you feel school went today?
What do you think you can do to improve things?
Why do you feel like that?
What do you suggest we should do?
What will happen if you do that?
How can we best support you?
How will you know if you made the right decision?
How will you notice if things get better?

Be a good listener

It's vital that you learn to be a good listener. That means giving the conversation your complete attention and looking at your teenager. Letting them talk and take as long as possible to say it. Not interrupting or trying to add to or finish what they are saying. Showing that you are listening with appropriate nods and body language and whatever is said trying not to take it personally and keeping calm. Remember that you have two ears and one mouth, and good listening comes from using those in proportion!

Be a good responder

Learning to be a good responder is another very useful skill. That means showing that you have heard and understood what has been said. If necessary, repeat back what you think has been said or try to summarise and make sure that is what was meant. Take stock, by looking and listening, and consider the emotional state of mind of your teenager and try to respond to that.

You don't have to agree with your teenager, but by validating their position, you show that you accept what they are saying and are trying to understand it. If you dismiss or ignore what they are saying or try to minimise something which may be very important to them at this moment, it will not promote good communication. Try not to judge them and do not call them silly or stupid or wrong.

Sometimes the only response that a teenager may need is a bit of empathy, but, on other occasions, you may need to help them identify solutions to their own problems. Go through the options with them and get them to identify the pros and cons of the various approaches. You may need to discuss issues that involve moral judgements and ethics and you need to recognise that they probably live in a world with different ideas of what is normal or acceptable than you. It is important that you justify your position by explaining it, even though they may not accept it. Try to be as honest and open as possible. Remember the aim is to encourage independent solution finding and not necessarily to fix their problems.

Involve your teenager in household problem solving

Sometimes you could involve teenagers in helping you find solutions to your own, or household problems and seek their advice and contributions whenever there is an opportunity. Teenagers are often great at giving advice about computers and technical issues. They may not appreciate all the financial implications of what they say, but this is a good opportunity to encourage their involvement. They are also likely to have a view on family holiday locations, what cars to buy and many other issues in the home. Listen to them and don't ignore their ideas. If you accept them say so, and if you don't say why not. Try not to instantly dismiss ideas with a "yes but." and don't be overcommitted to your own pre-conceived ideas.

Hopefully, by following the above guidance, you will find that over time your level of communication with your teenager improves. You will notice that the above guidelines are about conversations, which are not argumentative or confrontational, but where the emphasis is on identifying possible solutions together. We will deal with these later, but you will find if you improve the lines of communication in general, that arguments and conflicts may be reduced.

Don't be a bad boss

As a final thought, think about all the bad bosses that you might have had. Bad bosses are usually categorised by three main faults:

They tell you to do things without explaining why
They never praise or give you credit for what you do right
They never listen to your point of view

As parents, we need to try to make sure that we do not treat our teenagers like this!

Chapter 8

Setting boundaries and consequences

Every child needs boundaries to ensure that they behave in a safe and appropriate fashion, but for teenagers, these are especially important. Adolescence is a time when teenagers are trying to build their independence by testing out new experiences and behaviours and they need a firm framework in which do this in a responsible manner. Unlike the boundaries that we set for youngsters, the boundaries that we have with teenagers need to be flexible and adaptable to suit their level of competence as they grow older. They also need to be open to discussion and negotiation. So how do we establish sensible boundaries and what should they cover.

Well firstly, we don't need boundaries for everything. If you overregulate your teenager, they will complain that they feel like they are living in a barracks or prison! This is likely to stifle their ability to develop their independence and lead to resentment and probably rebellion. Choose those areas, which you will regulate carefully, to avoid as many major conflicts as possible, without constantly impinging on your teenager's development as a unique and emerging adult. Teenagers can be allowed their own space as much as possible and arguments about their preferred styles of dress, hair or music are largely a waste of time and unnecessary. If your teenager has their own room, they should also be allowed a good deal of freedom about the state in which it is maintained, provided nobody else is expected to clean it and you haven't run out of cups! So, you should restrict your regulations to the major issues.

These may depend on your own household circumstances, but are likely to include rules about the following:

Responsibility for doing household duties
Behaviour towards others in the house, particularly siblings
Bedtimes
Doing homework or revision
When and where they go out to
When they must be home
Use of social media, phones, computers
Bringing friends/partners home
Use of alcohol, cigarettes, drugs
Swearing and other inappropriate language

As far as possible boundaries and consequences should be discussed and agreed in a calm environment, before they are likely to be fully tested. As we have already mentioned, developing good communication with your teenager is important, and this involves listening carefully to their arguments and point of view. Being prepared to negotiate, where possible, is also a useful skill to have up your sleeve! Boundaries should be open to re-discussion in the future if you or your teenager thinks that they are no longer appropriate. As a parent, one of your key responsibilities is to loosen the reins on your teenager as they demonstrate the ability to act independently and responsibly. If they have been behaving well and operating within all the existing boundaries, be prepared to take the initiative in relaxing some of them. There may also be special occasions, holidays etc. when it is appropriate to temporarily relax boundaries.

When setting boundaries and consequences everybody must be entirely clear about what has been said and agreed. You'll have a responsibility to ensure that you have exactly the same understanding as your teenager. To avoid misunderstandings, you may wish to write something down that you can refer to later and it is always useful to ask your teenager to repeat back to you, what they think you have agreed. It is essential that your teenager is clear what they are and what they are not allowed to do and what the consequences will be if they disregard the rules.

With younger children, it is common to use rewards to encourage good behaviour and it is tempting to use rewards or financial incentives to encourage our teenagers along the same lines. However, this needs to be done with care. If we are to encourage teenagers to make their own choices and behave in a responsible fashion, we should not have to bribe them to do so. Nevertheless, it may well be reasonable to link certain privileges to duties and responsibilities so that the consequences of teenage behaviour are good as well as bad.

"When you have finished your homework each night, you can have 30 minutes playing computer games".
"If you wash the car once a week, I will collect you from your friend's house."

However well boundaries have been discussed and agreed there will be times when they are not obeyed and then the consequences will have to be imposed. These consequences should, as far as possible, reflect the seriousness of the lapse although some flexibility is appropriate for more minor issues. They should also be appropriate to the nature of the offence. Try not to get angry and overreact. All teenagers get things wrong and try to bend and avoid rules and you should be prepared for this. If your teenager thinks there is a good reason for what has happened, hear them out, even if you disagree. Remember the main purpose of the consequence is not to be punitive or hurtful, but to encourage good behaviour in the future. So, what are the best consequences?

The best consequences take effect either immediately or in the very near future. They may be allowing the natural outcome to take place. If your teenager hasn't done homework the school may well impose a penalty. If your teenager hasn't given you their sports kit to wash, they will have to wear it dirty or find an alternative. If the consequence is one that you need to deliver make sure that you do impose it, but don't threaten a consequence that you cannot deliver or that will cause you or other people difficulties. Consequences should generally be time limited as longer or indefinite sanctions become less effective over time and teenagers will try to find ways around them.

Some of the more common consequences are:

Loss of privileges - This is often a very good way of finding a sanction which fits the problem. If your teenager didn't do homework because they were playing computer games, withdraw the computer access for a period or remove the game from the device.

Tightening of the rules - If your teenager keeps missing a 10 o' clock curfew, move it back to 9 o' clock or stop them going out for a period.

Withdrawal of parental co-operation - Teenagers usually rely on parents to help them in all sorts of ways including acting as a taxi service, laundering/ironing clothes, lending them jewellery, clothes, equipment. These are all things that can be stopped if appropriate.

Grounding - Grounding needs to be used with some caution. Long periods of grounding are difficult to enforce and often there are desirable activities that we would like our teenager to continue.

Financial penalties - In general money should not be used as a consequence as this only complicates the whole issue of sensible money management. However, if the transgression involves money it may then be appropriate to make your teenager pay someone back out of pocket money or have them "earn" some money to recompense them.

Restitution - If your teenager has caused damage or messed something up they should be expected to do whatever is needed to repair or clean up either directly or by using their time or money to help to reverse the situation.

Negotiation - It is also sometimes worth discussing with your teenager what sanction that they think is appropriate. You don't have to agree with them and sometimes they are more punitive than you would have been.

Before we finish this section, we will add a few strategies for encouraging good behaviour in teenagers so that we need to impose consequences as little as possible. The four main strategies are:

Role modelling - In every part of teenage life, the example that they are given by the adults that they grow up with is crucial. If you want your teenager to behave in a calm, collected and responsible manner, that is the way that you need to try to behave. Similarly, if you want them to be respectful of other people and to deal with alcohol, drugs and other temptations then you must show them the way.

Communication - Take every opportunity to explain to your teenager why certain behaviours are good or acceptable while others are not. Explain the social consequences of bad behaviour and make sure that they fully understand what is legal and what is not.

Praise - Recognise and praise good behaviour whenever possible. Not only does this reinforce the standards that you are setting, but it will boost your teenager's self-esteem, which is a very important aspect for their future happiness and for keeping them out of trouble.

Supporting autonomy - Give your teenager the message that they are important individuals with their own ideas and attitudes, who deserve to be heard and respected. They are entitled to challenge our views and those of the society around us, provided they respect other peoples' rights.

Chapter 9

Establishing teenage rights, privileges and responsibilities

The culture of entitlement among teenagers is widespread and can be extremely damaging in later life and so it is essential that parents can distinguish between their teenager's rights and privileges. In fact, the rights that teenagers should expect are quite limited:

The right to live in a safe physical and emotional space
The right to adequate food, clothing, shelter
The right to be loved, valued and treated with respect

Teenagers do not generally have the right to any of the following privileges, although they may sometimes be necessary for safety or health purposes:

Expensive clothes
Special diets or meal times
Parental taxi service
Money for non-essentials
Access or ownership of phones/computers

Even more importantly, as we shall discuss shortly, teenagers should not expect to be protected from disappointments and hardships, or to not having to contribute towards the functioning of the household.

Teenagers are very egocentric and often find it hard to see other peoples' point of view. The logic of a teenager's sense of entitlement goes something like this. If I want something badly enough it is a parent's duty to give it to me as otherwise, I will be really upset. Unfortunately, many parents and other involved adults collude with this approach. They indulge their teenagers to demonstrate how much they love them, and to avoid arguments and disappointments, and convince themselves that they are maximising their children's opportunities and happiness. They overpraise and over-reward normal behaviour and overprotect them from the consequences of their actions. As a result, they achieve the exact opposite of what they intend. Rather than developing successful and happy adults, they create self-centred people who have unrealistic expectations and are likely to meet considerable disappointment. They are embedding attitudes that most adults struggle with including:

Poor impulse and emotional control
Poor coping skills
Lack of perseverance
Poor resilience
Lack of self-discipline
Low self esteem

So, what should I be doing instead?

The following are strategies that might be employed. As usual, it is better if these begin before the teenage years, but it is never too late to start.

Be prepared to reject, postpone or negotiate your teenager's demands

No matter how much anger it may cause, you should always be prepared to reject a demand if you think it is undeserved, unnecessary or unaffordable. Your teenager needs to learn that in life you do not always get what you want. As far as possible, you should explain your reasoning, even if they don't accept it.

It is often a good idea to delay or postpone a demand. Teenagers need to realise that they can't always have instant gratification. You might say they can have it for their birthday or Christmas present, or that they can have it when the old one is no longer suitable.

Lastly, you may wish to try to negotiate a solution with your teenager. This may involve saving up or doing paid jobs for you or someone else or possibly selling something that they already have. These are good opportunities to develop problem solving techniques as well as the skills of money management.

Give your teenager responsibility for themselves

As far as possible you should encourage your teenager to take responsibility for looking after themselves. They should be responsible for their own hygiene, cleaning their room and sorting out their laundry. They need to steadily take over organising themselves both for their school and domestic requirements, so that they become skilled in time management and setting priorities. They also need to develop money management skills. Giving them an allowance is a good idea, but it must be clear what it is or is not meant to pay for. It should also be clear that once it is spent, it will not normally be topped up.

Give your teenager responsibility to the household and to others

Your teenager needs to learn early that the world won't revolve around them and that families and society in general, are two-way processes of give and take. Provide as many opportunities as you can for them to take responsibility for some general household duties, so that they can make their contribution to the running of the household. This is also a good opportunity to teach them domestic skills such as doing the vacuuming, doing the laundry, cleaning bathrooms etc.

Encourage your teenager to help other people. Volunteering to help children with disabilities, deprived families or old neighbours helps teenagers develop empathy and a better understanding of other people. It reduces the obsession with themselves and can lead to greater gratitude of their own circumstances.

Stop rescuing your teenager

Your teenager ought to learn to be responsible for their own actions and to take the consequences. They should be made to pay for damages caused to other people's property and to apologise for bad behaviour. Hard as it might be, for you and for them, they need to learn from their mistakes. If this seems unkind, just consider how long you want to wear that superhero cape! They will learn from experience, but if you keep rescuing your child from the consequences of his decisions, or lack of thinking ahead, you are robbing him of valuable lessons that will stick with him for the rest of his life.

Stop shielding your teenager

Think about the moment that you first discovered that life is tough and often unfair! It was a hard lesson, but a necessary one. Your teenager must be allowed to make mistakes and deal with their own failures. They also should be allowed to take more risks and move out of their comfort zones, if they are to develop independence. Where appropriate, include and let them be involved in discussions about family problems including work, health or financial challenges.

Enforce boundaries and expectations

If your teenager misbehaves or ignores boundaries, there need to be consequences. Once you are clear in your mind (and theirs) what their privileges are, it is much easier to impose sanctions or instigate rewards. Your teenager will continue to make bad choices and persist in negative behaviour until the pain that comes from those decisions outweighs the perceived benefits.

Praise appropriately

Too many parents overpraise their children in a bid to boost their self-confidence. Praise is good, but only when it is linked to the right activities. Activities that involve hard work and perseverance are certainly praiseworthy, as are helping others or making a valuable contribution to the household. Try to encourage your teenager to feel pride in their own behaviour, rather than just responding to your reaction. Rather than saying "I'm proud of you for that", try to encourage them to reflect on their own feelings about their achievements:

"How did you feel knowing that you had achieved that?"
"You should feel really proud of that"

We need to develop teenagers who achieve and behave well for their own sake and not for the approval of other individuals. Reliance on other peoples' approval can lead to problems as it assumes that other peoples' expectations are justified and correct. It may also make it difficult for teenagers to say no to others when they should.

Be consistent

All the adults who are closely involved with your teenager need to be working in a co-ordinated and consistent fashion. This includes parents, step-parents, grandparents and others. It is no good for teenagers having requests refused if they just go elsewhere for them. This becomes difficult in families where divorce or marital breakdown leads to one or the other parent point scoring. In the ideal scenario, both parents would agree to abide by the same ground rules, talk, reason and negotiate for a solution that works. But the emphasis here is on agreeing what course of action to take to ensure that your teenager is very clear about sanctions and consequences.

Chapter 10

Building self-esteem and confidence

People who have low self-esteem can have significant problems as adults. They often focus on their shortcomings and mistakes and can have a pessimistic and negative approach to life, causing them to avoid new challenges and be prone to depression. So, what contributes to low self-esteem and what can parents do about it?

The two main strands of low self-esteem are a feeling of not being worthy and loveable and a sense of inadequacy and incompetence, and both strands need to be addressed. As we stated earlier in our list of children's rights, they have a right to be loved, valued and respected. This is not just about how parents feel about their children, but about how their children interpret their behaviour. We also talked about parents as role models and if parents themselves have low self-esteem and confidence, this can be inadvertently modelled to their children. The following are important ways to help your child feel loved and valued.

Model respect for others in the family and unconditional love

The way in which every member of the family is treated should demonstrate a positive and caring attitude. Avoid screaming and shouting and avoid insults, ridiculing, name calling or labelling others. Demonstrate empathy with other people's situations and attitudes, this is a learned behaviour. In general, discussion, explanation and negotiation are more productive, than constantly directing or commanding. If you respect individuality and avoid comparisons with other "better" siblings or other people, your teenager will feel valued and unique in their own right. Showing your children that you love and accept them and that this is not dependent on their behaviour will prevent labelling as the 'bad' child or 'black sheep of the family'. This doesn't mean that you will not need to criticise unacceptable behaviour, but if it is constructive, it will be done without undermining the child's sense of worth. Being prepared to forgive and forget and accept that we all make mistakes, will help to get the relationship back on track. When you can, demonstrate warmth and affection for your teenager, and if possible, sometimes provide treats that are not necessarily linked with some perceived action or achievement, but are a reward for 'just being'.

Use praise wisely

Whenever a child does something that you believe deserves highlighting as an achievement or success, or does something that shows personal growth or development of positive attitude, be quick to praise, and explain why it was a praiseworthy act. It's important though that the praise be genuine, and constantly praising for the sake of it is self-defeating. Although achievements and successes should be celebrated, praise for effort and perseverance is very important, even if this has not led to a favourable outcome. Praise may be for things that have been done or things that have not been done, as well as for actions themselves or deeds that illustrate good personal qualities.

Use criticism constructively

Criticism should always be constructive and always be about the behaviour not the person. Explanation of why the behaviour is unacceptable and how to do things better in the future is needed. Criticism needs to be fair and used in moderation and should be done in private to avoid public humiliation.

Focus on strengths

Focus on emphasising your child's strengths, inner resources and achievements and not on their failings and shortcomings. Challenge any negative opinions that they have about themselves. These are often incorrect or exaggerated and based on opinion rather than evidence. Use past examples of when they used a certain strength to overcome a difficult situation or deal with an issue well.

Encourage your teenager to start a strengths list and put it on the back of their bedroom door. Here is an exercise designed to build self-esteem and the following areas are suggested for compiling the lists:

1. People who love me (e.g. Family, friends, colleagues)

2. Things I'm good at (e.g. Things I have learned how to do well)

3. Personal Qualities (e.g. Things that are a part of me, or make me who I am)

4. Hopes and dreams (e.g. Aspirations, desires, what I want to achieve now and in the future)

5. Things I do for fun (e.g. Hobbies, activities that make me happy)

6. Compliments to myself (e.g. Things I could say about myself that helps to recognise my own value)

For some teenagers with low self-esteem, it's hard to think of even 5 words to add to each list, so this is an ongoing exercise, get them to start at 5 and work up to 50!

Reading through the lists when things are tough, can restore a sense of proportion and positive self-esteem.

Listen to their views

Children feel valued if they are consulted for their views and where appropriate for their advice. Teenagers need to be increasingly treated like adults and involved in decisions within the household. Whenever possible, demonstrate that your teenager's comments have made a difference and thank them for their input.

Take an interest in their lives

One of the worst things for self-esteem is to feel ignored and overlooked. Spending individual time and sharing joint experiences whenever possible can help to cement the relationship between you and your teenager. In larger families it is especially important to try to find one to one time. Be available to listen and talk to them about their issues and lend emotional and practical support whenever it is needed. It is very useful to get to know the people in your child's life including friends and teachers as well as getting to know who their role models are. Where possible encourage any positive role models and try to diminish the influence of poor or negative role models, although this needs to be done in a subtle way.

Encourage respect for their body

Many teenagers are very concerned about their appearance and dissatisfaction with their own bodies is a major problem. You have two key roles in managing this. Firstly, as already discussed, to encourage a lifestyle that promotes good health and fitness. This includes teaching and modelling the values of healthy eating, exercise and good sleep practices. Secondly, to emphasise the value of diversity and uniqueness in appearance, as well as a level of gratitude for the physical abilities that we have. Of course, many parents are not happy with their appearance and if they treat this as a serious problem, their children are likely to copy them, particularly as they may well have inherited the same features.

The second strand of building self-esteem is creating a sense of adequacy and competence and this requires a careful balancing act from parents to give teenagers as much independence and responsibility as they can successfully deal with.

Do you overprotect?

When children are young, parents correctly see one of their main responsibilities as protecting their children from the real and perceived dangers in the world around them, but with teenagers, this becomes much less appropriate and many parents find it very difficult to change this mentality. Teenagers need to learn to cope with life's dangers and difficulties on their own before they reach adulthood and it is essential that they are allowed the freedom to develop their own ability to do this. Of course, it is your responsibility to teach them safe behaviour, but teenagers need to be exposed to the normal risks that they will be meeting as adults and to learn the skills to deal with moderately risky activities. Managing appropriate risks is an important skill that needs to be learnt, especially in this thrill-seeking phase of life. The media tells us that we are developing a risk-averse generation, and this has the potential to create young people who might live closed and unadventurous lives. In addition, try not to over protect them from situations where they may fail. Teenagers need to learn to be self-sufficient and to deal with setbacks and failures. As already mentioned, it isn't helpful to constantly rescue your children from the outcomes of their own actions.

Encourage and stretch, but watch those expectations

You need to have sensible expectations for your children, not only at school, but in life in general. Whilst it is natural to want your children to achieve their fullest potential, expectations should be based on your children's abilities, not on your aspirations. These should generally be modest, shorter term targets based on their current levels of competence and ability. Having a target which seems too distant or difficult is very demotivating. It is much more achievable to move forward in small steps one step at a time and to praise the attainment of each target in turn. Having some longer-term aims is fine, but adolescence is a time of developing individuality and teenagers may end up going in an entirely different direction to the one anticipated. You also need to be aware of the time commitments of your teenager, who may well be under pressure from parents, relatives, friends and school as to how to spend their time and this can be very difficult to deal with. If you can help your teenager manage their time and teach them how to set priorities, life will become easier and less stressful overall.

Encourage activities in which they can excel

It is important for everyone that they find activities, where they can feel that they have ability and can be confident. For many teenagers, this will not be in their academic work, but is far more likely to be in a physical or creative sphere such as sport, music, drama, dance or art. Many teenagers also benefit from volunteering to help other people including younger students or people with disabilities or who just need help.

Encourage new experiences

It is important that teenagers learn to leave their comfort zone and try out new activities without fear of humiliation or failure. This provides both the opportunity to identify new activities in which they might excel, but also the chance to identify their current strengths and weaknesses. These may be activities which are available at school, at home or on holiday. Sometimes these activities can be whole family activities, but often it is better to give your teenager some privacy to see how they get on without supervision or judgement. However, you will need to be aware of how much real risk each activity carries. Taking a weekend job can also be a very valuable and confidence building activity, as well as encouraging time keeping, teamwork and money management skills, but make sure that your teenager has enough time to devote to other essential roles and duties.

Give responsibilities

It is important that teenagers are increasingly given greater responsibility as covered earlier. They need to develop the confidence that they can care for their own physical needs and live independently as adults.

Look for teaching opportunities

Keep looking for opportunities to teach your teenagers skills, whenever possible by letting them get involved. Cooking meals, doing DIY, gardening and even driving are all practical skills, where teenagers can be encouraged to take part and develop competence. Opportunities to teach more subtle skills like study skills, assertiveness skills, decision-making and time management should also be taken. We have already touched on some of these in chapter 4, but it is worth saying more about assertiveness.

Teach assertiveness skills

The skill of assertiveness ensures that we learn how to express our views in a calm and clear manner and to listen to and be heard by others. It stops other people from dominating or ignoring us and is an essential skill for us to exercise our own free will and independence within social situations. If you consider your own childhood rules, you might have learned that saying "No" was rude, and that "I want" doesn't get. Is it any wonder then, that in the name of 'manners', we have become a nation unable to recognise what we want out of life, or to ask for it without guilt? And how many of us mentally kick ourselves for not saying no when we really want to, and end up over stretched, over committed and resentful?

To teach your teenager the difference between being selfish and having a sense of self is not something we always think is important. After all, we keep hearing that teenagers are egocentric and demanding and very aware of their 'rights'. However, these are valuable skills, alongside making requests respectfully, understanding that responsibilities go with rights, and learning how to receive constructive criticism and treat people as equal to

125

themselves. This last area of equality is sometimes difficult for parents to take on board and can require a major shift in their thinking with a large dollop of trust thrown in for good measure. Assertiveness skills can be learned, in the same way that we learned to swim or ride a bike, through practice and repetition. For effective parenting, learning basic assertiveness is a vital measure for both you and your child to have in your skills bank, to facilitate communication, manage feelings and equip you both to cope with current and future relationships.

Spot signs of trouble

Sometimes children's self-esteem can change from high to low over a relatively short period of time. This is usually due to some significant change in their lives. This might be a divorce or some other change in their environment, or it may be caused by moving home or changing school. It can also be caused by some form of abuse, by being the victim of bullying or the breakdown of a close or intimate relationship. Some signs to watch out for if you are concerned about your teenager's low self-esteem are the following:

Avoiding new situations and challenges
Fear of failure and humiliation
Poor motivation and interest
Negative descriptions of themselves
Inability to accept compliments
Constantly apologising
Submissive body language, head down, eyes down
Often demonstrates frustration
Does not persevere, gives up easily
Makes excuses or blames others
Some teenagers with low self-esteem may also behave in an overly aggressive, loud and even bullying fashion.

Part 2 has outlined the kinds of issues relevant to all young people as they move into adult life from being a teenager.

Part 3 offers you in-depth help and support for a variety of life circumstances that may or may not affect you and your teenager.

Use it as a resource when you need to access the information covered in this section of the book.

Your teenager might also find the information and advice useful.

PART THREE

THE EMERGENCY TOOLKIT

The Emergency Toolkit part of our book gives you information advice about dealing with a wide range of specific problems. Some of them you are almost bound to encounter, some of them you may be lucky enough to avoid. You can use this section as a rapid source of help if you have a problem or as a useful source of information to prepare you for the possibility of future issues. In general, statistics and laws quoted relate to the United Kingdom. Of course, many of the United Kingdom trends are reflected in other countries and the general advice and guidance provided can be applied to parenting anywhere in the world.

My Teenager and............

Chapter 11

Alcohol

Some young people are experimenting with alcohol at earlier ages than ever before. However, your influence can set the path to better drinking patterns and reduced rates of alcohol dependence as your teenager grows up, so you can have more of a positive influence on your teenagers' relationship with alcohol than you realise.

What you say, how you behave and the messages you send to your teenager can help delay when they start drinking, which is critical if they are to avoid the harmful and life-long effects of alcohol on the developing brain.

Adult attitudes to alcohol

For many parents, dealing with alcohol can be quite a challenging issue because alcohol use is so common and they themselves may be drinkers. In most countries in the world, its use is entirely legal, at least with adults, although there are often restrictions on where and when it can be purchased. In Europe and America, its use is widespread with most adults indulging to varying degrees. Following the apparent failure of prohibition in the United States in the period between the two world wars, prohibition is no longer discussed, but many people argue for further restrictions based on price or availability, due the perceived risks associated with alcohol. These include:

Short and long-term health risks

Short term health risks include acute alcoholic poisoning and unconsciousness caused by binge-drinking, as well as susceptibility to accidents and injury and to criminal assaults. There are also longer-term chronic effects. Heavy drinking is associated with liver disease, cardiovascular disease, some cancers and some brain deficits and disorders. It is also linked to general poor nutrition and health, dementia, depression and suicide.

Antisocial and violent behaviours

Alcohol is often linked both to vandalism and violence often in group situations in pubs, clubs and on the streets. It is also often a factor in sexual assaults. It also plays a role in domestic abuse, which can be physical, sexual or emotional and in the neglect and abuse of children.

Risky and endangering behaviours

Alcohol is a contributory factor in many road injuries caused by intoxication of drivers and pedestrians. Intoxicated people are also vulnerable to physical and sexual assaults as well as robberies.

Risk of addiction

Like many drugs, alcohol can become an addiction and a small, but significant number of heavy drinkers become alcoholics. For teenagers, there are additional risks which will be discussed later.

Why adults drink

Having outlined above all the negative impacts of excessive alcohol intake, you might wonder why people drink at all, or why alcohol hasn't been banned. Of course, many people see the above problems as relating to heavy and irresponsible drinking and not to them and they believe alcohol has some desirable benefits including:

Getting a sense of wellbeing
Alcohol produces, at least in the short term, a high, with a sense of euphoria. The effects of alcohol on the brain will be covered in more detail later.

Relieving stress

Alcohol has a sedative effect that can relieve tensions and provide an escape mechanism from worries.

Improves socialising

Alcohol reduces inhibitions and is used by some people to make them more outgoing and extravert. It is also a significant factor in parties and other group gatherings and provides a shared experience.

Health reasons

Alcohol is used on occasions to dull pain or as a medication for common ailments such as colds. Some research also suggests that moderate drinking may partly alleviate the risks of cardiovascular disease, strokes and diabetes in older people. Although this is unlikely to be the reason that people drink, it may provide a reason or an excuse for them not abstaining altogether.

How many adults drink?

It is not always easy to get accurate information about levels of alcohol consumption but the overall picture in America and Europe appears to be similar, with about 20% never drinking, around 60-70% drinking regularly, and about 10-15% considered heavy drinkers.[1]

In the UK the proportion of people drinking has been slowly falling, with the largest falls among younger adults. The heaviest drinkers are men who are higher earners.

The physiological effects of alcohol on adults

Alcohol affects a great many parts of the brain, but its major effects appear to be in three areas.

The pre-frontal cortex
This is the area that is concerned with rational thinking and decision making. Alcohol reduces the activity in this area, which affects judgement and the ability to make sound and sensible decisions.

The hippocampus
This is an important area for memory formation and learning. Alcohol seems to interfere with memory formations and this may be why binge drinkers often experience blackouts where they can't remember what has happened.

The Cerebellum
This area controls movement. Alcohol interferes with this area and is why intoxicated people struggle to walk in a straight line.

Alcohol is an unusual drug with complex effects because it acts as both a stimulant and a sedative. Although the reasons for this are not fully understood, research suggests that these effects are mainly linked to two distinct neurotransmitters

Dopamine
Alcohol increases the release of dopamine, which is the "feel good" neurotransmitter. Dopamine can create a feeling of elation and euphoria but is also capable of playing a role in addictive behaviours.

GABA
GABA is the main inhibitory neurotransmitter and controls many neurological systems. Alcohol seems to interfere with GABA processes and this seems to be responsible for the sedative effects of alcohol, which cause the slowing down of thoughts, speech and difficulty concentrating.

133

The stimulatory and sedative effects of alcohol on individuals depend on how much alcohol is consumed and over what period, but broadly the initial response seems to be as a stimulant which is gradually followed by the sedative response.

The effects of alcohol are mostly short-term, but long-term heavy drinking can result in structural changes in the brain, which affect the connections between different parts of the brain. This is thought to affect the ability to concentrate and to learn and memorise.

Teenage drinking – UK Law

UK law mostly applies to buying alcohol and drinking on licensed premises. To buy alcohol you must be eighteen or over, and you must not buy alcohol on behalf of under eighteens. On licensed premises, you can only buy alcohol if you are eighteen or over. You can only consume alcohol if you are eighteen or over, or sixteen or seventeen and drinking beer, wine or cider with a meal accompanied by an adult (England).

In public places under eighteens should not drink or be in possession of alcohol. In the home, there is very little legislation, but it is illegal to give alcohol to children under five. However, the Chief Medical Officers advise an alcohol-free childhood, with no drinking until at least the age of fifteen. Even then it should be infrequent and supervised by a responsible adult. Parents and young people should be aware that drinking, even at age 15 or older, can be hazardous to health and that not drinking is the healthiest option for young people. If 15 - 17year olds do consume alcohol, they should do so infrequently and certainly on no more than one day a week. There are no longer daily alcohol guidelines, but the implication of the advice is that the drinking should be less than 3 units or about one pint of beer or one large glass of wine.

Why teenagers drink

The reasons why teenagers drink are broadly similar to those that cause adults to drink, but there are some reasons that relate specifically to teenagers. The reasons that young people think that their age group drink changes as they get older, with 12 year olds thinking the main reason is to look cool, but 15 year olds listing the main reasons for drinking as "to be more sociable" or "to give them a buzz"[2]

Other reasons that are often cited are:
To copy 'adult' behaviour modelled by parents, older siblings and other adults.
As part of the natural experimentation involved in growing up and developing their own personality
As a rebellion against rules imposed by others.
Because alcohol is so widely available, heavily advertised and considered normal.

Trends in teenage drinking

Teenagers' attitudes to alcohol in the UK have been steadily becoming less accepting. Between 2003 and 2016, the proportion of teenagers (11-15years) thinking that it was OK to drink alcohol to see what it was like has fallen from 67 to 50%. In the same period, the proportion thinking that it was okay to get drunk once a week fell from 20 to 7%. Nevertheless, alcohol remains much more acceptable to older teenagers with 76% of 15 year olds thinking that it is okay to see what it is like and 44% thinking that it is okay to get drunk to see what it is like.

Among those that drink, consumption seems have been steady over the last ten years, but wines, beers and cider have become more popular at the expense of alcopops and spirits. Teenagers are now much more likely to drink at a home or at a party with a significant decline in drinking outdoors or at licensed premises. Most drinking occurs at the weekend with Saturday being the most popular day followed by Friday.

Teenagers (11-15years) are most likely to be given alcohol by their parents, other relatives or friends, but there is a significant amount of taking alcohol from home without permission. Similarly, they are most likely to drink with their parents, but also with friends.

How many teenagers drink?

The good news is that the number of teenagers who drink is in long term decline. The proportion of 11-15year olds, who have ever drunk fell between 2003 and 2016 from around 60% to around 40%. Over the same period the proportion of 15year olds, who had drunk in the last week, halved from 49% to 24%. However, it is worth noting that by the age of 17 nearly two-thirds of boys and nearly half of girls are drinking on a weekly basis – figures that are not far from adult drinking levels. [3] Nevertheless, even among this age group hospital admissions linked to alcohol have fallen rapidly over the last ten years suggesting that the incidence of binge drinking has lessened. The reasons for this long-term decline in the number of younger teenagers who are drinking, which began around 2003, is not fully understood.

Some possible reasons that have been suggested are:

Stricter enforcement of laws: It may be that the rules preventing the purchase and consumption of alcohol by under 18s have been more rigorously enforced by pubs and shops. However, most younger teenagers obtain their alcohol from other people, rather than buying it themselves as we shall see later. There are also generally more restrictions on drinking in public places or on public transport than in the past.

New technology: The use of social media and on-line games has tended to mean that teenagers spend less time on the streets. It has also been suggested that images of drunken behaviour are quite off-putting and the possibility of having a similar image of yourself shared on social media, may lead to a greater reticence to get drunk.

Parental modelling: Adults under 45 are tending to be more health conscious and drink less than the previous generation. This may mean that teenagers grow up in an environment where alcohol has become less prevalent and binge drinking more frowned upon.

Parental monitoring: Parents, nowadays, tend to be more worried about their teenagers' safety than previous generations and probably monitor their behaviour more closely. Mobile phones have also provided the opportunity to keep a closer watch on where their teenagers are at all times.

Demographic changes: There have been significant changes in the cultural mix particularly in some of the larger cities. In some of these cultures, alcohol is not allowed at all, while in others it plays a much smaller social role than has been the case in the UK.

Cost of alcohol: The cost of alcohol has generally been increasing over the last ten years and poorer households generally consume less alcohol. However, the picture is complicated. Pub prices have become much more expensive, but cheap alcohol is available in many supermarkets and off-licences.

Decline in pubs and clubs: The number of pubs and clubs has been falling. This has particularly affected local pubs with a concentration occurring in many city centres.

Teenage culture revolves around schools/colleges: Over the last ten years more and more older teenagers have been staying in full time education with around three quarters of 16-18year olds now doing this and only about one in twenty of them at full time work. This means that the culture now revolves around school and colleges with a strong emphasis on examination results and educational achievement. This may result in less time for socialising and drinking particularly on weekdays.

The effects of alcohol on teenagers

The effects of alcohol on teenagers, although similar to that for adults, are thought to differ in a number of ways:

The sedative effect of alcohol seems to affect teenagers less with the ability to control movement less affected. This may lead to teenagers being more tempted to binge drink as there seem to be less immediate adverse effects. It may also make it more difficult for parents to notice when their teenagers have been drinking heavily.

The stimulant effect of alcohol linked to dopamine, may be more pronounced in teenagers. Dopamine has been linked to addictive behaviours and this may make them more susceptible to abusing alcohol. The earlier teenagers start to drink, the more likely they are to drink heavily. Dopamine has also been linked to higher levels of risk-taking behaviours. This is a problem for teenagers and younger adults, particularly males, where road accidents for drivers, passengers and pedestrians are a major cause of death.

The detrimental effects on memory and learning seem to be particularly noticeable with teenagers and the ability to process information is also affected. Teenagers' brains are still forming with important connections being made. These are the connections which heavy alcohol consumption seems to interfere with, and a significant amount of research suggests that teenagers' brain structures may be permanently affected by binge drinking, leading to problems with future learning, memory and decision making. [4]

The effects of alcohol on rational thinking and decision making are even more important than for adults as this part of the brain is not fully developed in teenagers. This may well lead to unwise decision making and risk-taking behaviours.

Another problem with teenage drinking is that research suggests that it can interfere with the sex hormones, which appears to delay and possibly interfere with the normal process of puberty.

Teenagers experience all the risks associated with alcohol that were covered for adults but are more vulnerable in a number of ways. Their inexperience with alcohol may lead them to overdrink with a greater risk of nausea, vomiting or even alcohol poisoning. Their susceptibility to peer pressure may lead them towards risky or even illegal activities, while they are drinking. Their impaired judgment may put them at risk of assault or abuse or lead them into unprotected or unwise sexual activities.

Teenagers are also at risk of the longer-term mental health issues associated with heavy drinking and may be even more susceptible than adults as their brains are still in a developmental stage.

Binge drinking and alcohol poisoning

Binge drinking is very common and can be described as drinking five or more drinks at one time, for males, four or more for females. The concentration of alcohol taken quickly, can cause teenagers to pass out, black out (lose memory of events that occurred while they were drunk), feel sick, miss school, or behave in ways that would otherwise be unlike them. For example, they may drive while drunk or get into arguments.

Some binge drinkers drink heavily every weekend and abstain or drink only in moderation during the week. Others binge less often— for example, during holidays, on special occasions, or at times of great stress. This kind of problem drinking may go unnoticed because people may excuse an occasional binge as a celebration that got carried away or as a response to unusual stress.

Binge drinkers are particularly at risk of alcohol poisoning, a severe and potentially fatal reaction to an alcohol overdose. Because alcohol is a central nervous system depressant, drinking too much, too fast, slows some bodily functions (such as heart rate, blood pressure, and breathing) to a dangerous level, causing the drinker to lose consciousness.

Some signs of alcohol poisoning include:

Unconscious or semiconscious state
Slow respiration—eight or fewer breaths per minute, or lapses
between breaths of more than eight seconds
Cold, clammy, pale, or bluish skin
A strong odour of alcohol on the breath and coming from the skin

If you suspect that your teenager is suffering from acute alcohol
poisoning:

Never leave them alone to "sleep it off."
Call 999 immediately.
Gently turn them onto their left side, using a pillow placed at the
small of the back to keep them in that position. This will help
prevent choking should they vomit.
Stay with them until medical help arrives.

Key factors affecting the level of teenage drinking

Although it is not always easy to prove which factors lead to
increased drinking, the following are all linked to those teenagers
who drink more alcohol:

Parental attitudes: The most important factor affecting whether
teenagers drink and how much they drink appears to be parental
attitudes. Research among teenagers suggests that about a third of
parents of 11year olds and two-thirds of parents of 15year olds
don't mind them drinking in moderation. Research suggests that
consumption is closely linked to parental attitudes with the lowest
consumption linked to parents who try to stop alcohol
consumption and the highest to those who are most tolerant of it.

Number of drinkers in the household: Consumption among
teenagers increases the higher the number of drinkers in the
household. This suggests that it is not just the role modelling of
parents that is important, but also older brothers and sisters.

Relationship with parents: Teenagers are more likely to drink if they have a poor relationship with their parents. A good relationship should involve open two-way communication with clear boundaries, but not overly strict or tolerant.

Personality traits: Teenagers who are more rebellious, less successful at school or who tend to be thrill seekers are more likely to drink and indulge in drug use. Teenagers who struggle with stress and anxiety may also become heavier drinkers.

How do you spot the signs of alcohol related problems?

Most teenagers will experiment with alcohol at some time and may well turn up at home in a drunken state. It is important that you stay calm and not to panic. This is not the time to have a sensible discussion about alcohol. If your teenager is very drunk and may be at risk, you'll need to take the appropriate steps to keep them safe (See Chapter 28 Dealing with parties etc). Otherwise it is best to let them sleep and have the conversation the next day. Talk about how and why they got drunk and reiterate the possible consequences of alcohol abuse. Try not to overreact as this can create more rebellious behaviour, the odd incident does not represent a major problem with alcohol, but repeated occasions may well do.

Many of the signs that teenagers are developing an ongoing problem with alcohol are the same as those that they may have with other drug related problems. Taken in isolation they may just be typical teenage behaviour but if you see a pattern involving a number of these issues, you need to act.

Some of the physical signs of alcohol abuse are:
Changes in sleeping patterns or being overly tired during the day
  Breath or clothes smelling of alcohol
  Slurred or garbled speech
  Lack of co-ordination
  Bloodshot eyes
  Red face or skin
  Deterioration in physical appearance or hygiene

There may also be significant changes in behaviour including:

Deterioration in performance or attendance at school
Problems with concentration or memory
Mood swings with periods of depression or anxiety
Losing interest in hobbies
Changing friends
Becoming more argumentative
Becoming more withdrawn and secretive
Lying and being deceitful

Around the house you may notice alcohol going missing, levels going down or being diluted as well as finding empty bottles or cans. If possible, alcohol should be stored somewhere that it is not readily accessible or in a manner where any unauthorised tampering can be spotted.

Sensible drinking guidelines

If you are happy with your teenager drinking or if you are not, but they are doing it anyway, you will want to minimise the potential problems. You won't be going out with them or be with them every time they drink, and in any case, this would go against what you are trying to achieve, the development of independent adults who can think for themselves and make sensible choices. Instead, like every other concern, it is sensible to instigate family discussions about alcohol in advance and get your teenager to consider the following advice, which of course also applies to you as an adult:

Limiting their intake

Set a sensible limit for your age and weight and stick to it
Don't copy or keep up with other people
Don't let others persuade you to drink above your limit
Count how much you drink
Don't pre-load before events
Drink slowly
Eat before and during drinking

Dilute drinks with non-alcoholic mixers
Drink soft drinks or water between alcoholic drinks
Choose lower alcohol alternatives where possible
Never binge drink

Minimising the risks

Be aware of what is happening around you
Do not drink alone
Drink with others and look out for each other
Don't leave drinks unattended and watch your friend's drinks
Don't accept drinks from strangers
Never mix alcohol with other drugs
Don't go home alone and don't leave friends alone
Never drive after drinking or accept a lift from someone who has
Don't swim or go near deep water after drinking
Don't do or allow your friend to do anything you will later regret
If in trouble call or seek help from a responsible adult
For medical emergencies call an ambulance
Be able to recognise and deal with drunkenness and alcohol poisoning

Where to get help

Parents can talk to their GP or seek help from local or national support groups or counsellors (See below)

Useful organisations

Addaction – www.addaction.org.uk
Provides support for individuals, families and communities to manage the effects of drug and alcohol misuse.

Action on addiction – www.actiononaddiction.org.uk
Provides residential rehab and community-based addiction treatments.

ADFAM – www.adfam.org.uk
Information and advice for families of alcohol and drug users.

Al-Anon – www.al-anonuk.org.uk
Al-Anon is worldwide and offers group support and understanding to the families and friends of problem drinkers. They have a helpline 0800 0086 811

Alcohol Concern – www.alcoholconcern.org.uk
Provides general information about alcohol, a self-assessment tool and can indicate your nearest alcohol advice centre.

Alcohol Focus Scotland – www.alcohol-focus-scotland.org.uk
Provides information and advice on responsible drinking.

Alcoholics Anonymous Great Britain – www.alcoholics-anonymous.org.uk
Part of the worldwide network of men and women who share their experience in meetings hoping to solve their problems and help others to recover from alcoholism. They have a helpline 0800 917 7650.

Drinkaware – www.drinkaware.co.uk
Provide information and advice regarding alcohol. They are linked to Drinkline, which runs a helpline 0300 123 1110 for people who are concerned about their drinking, or someone else's.

DrugFAM – www.drugfam.co.uk
Provide information and support to people affected by someone else's addiction. They have a helpline 0300 888 3853

NACOA – www.nacoa.org.uk
National Association for Children of Alcoholics providing information, advice and support to children of alcohol-dependent parents. They have a helpline 0800 358 3456

NHS – www.nhs.uk/live-well/alcohol-support
This site provides advice and information on alcohol and offers a database of support and treatment services

Turning point – www.turning-point.co.uk
Provide a wide range of support and services including rehab for those with problems, including drug and alcohol issues and their families.

References in this chapter

[1] World health Organisation (2011) : Global status report on alcohol and health
[2] NHS Smoking drinking and drug use among young people England 2016
[3] Public Health England : Data Intelligence Summary: Alcohol consumption and harm among under 18 year olds
[4] Crew F, Kuhn C, Robinson D, Wilson W, (2016) Alcohol and the adolescent brain: Immediate impairment, long term consequences.

Chapter 12

Anger

Anger is scary! Teenagers can blow for the smallest of triggers, like asking them to put their empty plate in a dishwasher, or whether they have finished their homework. The intensity of the emotional outburst can range from mild irritation, to red hot rage, and when faced with it, our bewilderment and shock can cause us to get 'hooked in' and challenge their anger with an over the top response of our own. It's easy to see how parents all over the world are struggling to cope. When we bring to the situation our own childhood experience and fears of how anger was managed, we can understand how it can contribute to the confusion and turmoil within our home. Home is where we might expect to have shelter from the pressures of the outside world and where we hope to live a peaceful and harmonious existence with those we love and care for.

We all get angry, it is an uncomfortable, but useful emotion in working out what we will accept and what we will not. The ability to manage our anger appropriately is a skill that develops with age, hormonal growth, positive role modelling and the understanding and impact of consequences. We saw in Chapter 3, that the teenage brain development, leads to teenagers often reacting in very emotional and intense ways, so they are liable to get angry with what appears little provocation. The anger is often taken out on parents although the underlying causes can be frustrations, confusion and issues with friends, school or many other things outside the home.

As parents, we want our children to be happy and we want to be approved of, so we avoid situations where conflict might arise, we allow children from a young age to have their way so that anger is infrequent. Alternatively, we get tough with them when they show anger, or punish them, so that they often fail to learn how to deal with anger in a controlled and safe family environment.

We know that young people tend to take things personally, and they see our often innocuous, comments as criticism or as our effort to exert control. The speed of escalation of the angry response and the defiance that comes back at us, is an attempt to thwart our control. It can include violent outbursts, swearing, breaking things, and in extreme cases physical assaults against us. No wonder then that we hide from our teenager, give in to their demands, keep quiet when we really want to ask questions and quite frankly, are glad of the respite when they leave the house.

In today's age, where we seem to want to label everything and everyone, we are often glad to think our own teenagers are suffering from a particular syndrome or disorder. We hear of Oppositional Defiant Disorder, or Intermittent Explosive Disorder but really, most young people will demonstrate an angry outburst at one time or another as they struggle to control those unfamiliar impulses, and ultimately, they will become well rounded and reasonable adults. How you manage those episodes will be the difference between your sanity or otherwise at the end of the experience.

These are some important strategies for dealing with anger.

Be in control of your own emotions

This is key to coping with your teenager's anger. You can't control your teenager's outbursts when they are in full flow, they will gradually learn that skill for themselves, but you can control how you act and react. As the adult, this is about <u>not</u> allowing yourself to be 'hooked in' to what is being thrown at you. This is easier said than done and takes some mental rehearsal. Try to imagine your teen as someone else's child, it will help you to respond more cautiously, and allow you to consider whether your own actions and reactions are appropriate. You are less likely to shout, threaten or hit out with a child who is not your own. Accept that you might be in 'shock'. A teenager can use highly emotive arguments and language that you may never even have heard of before, and when it is directed at you, it can completely floor you with its hurtfulness and callousness. Once the 'fight and flight' response kicks in, you will both be dealing with a surge of adrenaline that can quickly escalate an already fraught situation.

Know when to retreat

This is not about winning and losing! It is amazing how when faced with a barrage of vitriol, we can talk ourselves into a fight! A common call is "How dare she!" or "I'm the parent, he <u>will</u> listen to me"

Let me tell you now, that kind of thinking will escalate the situation! This is not a good time to start training your teenager to manage his or her anger, or to discuss who said what, when and how. Allow yourself and your teenager a degree of physical (and emotional) distance.

"You're angry, we'll talk later when we are both calmer" is a helpful statement.

Then, retreat to your own safe space. You have not given ground, or acceded to your teenager's demands, but it buys you time to consider the following:

Am I being reasonable? Is their request reasonable? Is there a compromise? Is a sanction appropriate? Does she need to be held accountable? What would be fair?

Sometimes, no is simply no, taking time out can help you to clarify your thinking and it can keep you and your teenager safe.

I am not saying that they won't follow you and continue to shout or demand or try to make themselves heard, or try to wear you down, or continue to tell you what a lousy parent you are, but I strongly suggest that you identify your 'safe space' put an internal lock on the door and have a facility to play some relaxing music on headphones as a distraction.

Space will also give your teenager an opportunity to think through the situation and calm down themselves. Whatever caused the anger, can be revisited later with a clear mind and a strategy, and often with a third person present to act as a balance or to mediate.

Watch for the signs as anger builds

Sometimes it is just like a tornado and appears to come from nowhere, but often, there are warning signs that an angry outburst is imminent. If there is time, and your teenager is receptive, you can encourage them to scale their anger between 1 and 10. This can give you a head's up and is more useful than describing the feeling in words. There is a huge gap between mildly irritated and boiling! Look for signs of physical tension, really notice if they appear stressed. Parents describe conversations with their teenager as 'walking on eggshells', so you are never going to get it right completely, and I quickly learned that no conversation could be had before my teenager was fed and watered on their return from school! Equally, keep a check on other contributing factors, like lack of sleep, exam stress, peer group issues and bullying or relationship issues. More serious anger triggers might relate to alcohol or drug related addictions, or family breakups, or more serious mental health disorders.

Teach your teenager to manage their anger

Parents need to teach teenagers to manage their own anger by:
   Recognising the main triggers e.g. friendship issues, schoolwork, invasion of privacy, sibling relationships, having to do something they don't want to, not being allowed to do something they do want to do
   Recognising physical signs e.g. sweating feeling hot, going red, breathing rapidly
   Developing cooling off mechanisms e.g. exercise, music, punch bag, diary, breathing exercises, singing

Avoid the post-mortem, but do set boundaries

Very often, a teenager will be horrified at the way they have behaved during an anger outburst. Learning to tame the anger dragon is a slow process, not achieved overnight, and your teenager can also be shocked and upset at their own behaviour, language or thoughts.

When the storm has abated, set some ground rules, and agree different ways to share concerns, and views. Some families swear by regular round table meetings, others have a comments box and write down their messages. The rule of thumb here is that you should always strive to make criticism constructive and not use it as a stick to beat each other up.

Agree how you will manage when things seem to be getting out of hand and how you will call time on a conversation that is going nowhere fast. The key here is to get the message across that no subject is out of bounds but must be discussed respectfully. When someone starts to feel that the balance of power is unfair or that they cannot be heard it is time to ask for time out. This isn't a way out for an uncomfortable subject to be dropped, because those kinds of discussions will happen throughout life, but it will allow a regrouping and an exploration of whether it has been approached in the most helpful way. Following up on anger can be very helpful in exploring feelings and learning to manage difficult emotions.

Remember to underline with your teenager that all feelings are valid and allowed, but how they are expressed is important. Separate the emotion from the behaviour. Giving your teenager the message that you have faith in them and their ability to find a compromise, or a solution to their own issues or problems safely and calmly, will equip them with the confidence to move into adult life.

When to get more help

Typically, teenagers exhibit bursts of anger as they are learning to cope with the rush of emotions associated with puberty and adolescence.
Sometimes though, it is so extreme, that you may wish to consider counselling or family therapy. Even if your teenager refuses to take part in these, you can still develop further parenting skills by undertaking face to face or on-line courses.
The important thing to remember is that it does get better!

Disarming Anger

This involves taking the energy out of a confrontation or strong emotional expression, neutralising the other person's ability to remain angry or hostile, thereby creating opportunities for more productive conversation. This 6 Step technique requires you to use assertive skills and takes practice, and you need to be willing to see past your teenagers rude or attacking demeanour.

How to do it successfully:

1. Don't take it personally, shout or get hooked in - Remain calm "I can hear how strongly you feel about this"; *"I want to listen,"; "I am listening"; "Please don't shout, we can talk about it better when we are calm"*
2. Be appreciative and genuine, sarcasm is a killer! *"Thank you for telling me how you feel"; "I had no idea that you thought that"*
3. Ask for more information if you are not clear, you might also need to ask for thinking it over time. *"I'd like to give this some thought before agreeing...."; "If you can explain ..... I can give it more consideration"*
4. Find something that your teenager is saying with which you agree, and if you can, find a common outcome that you both want. *"I can see that you have really thought about this, you have some good points, or I see that really, we both seem to want the same thing...."*
5. Begin to focus on a solution
6. Your body language is important here, how you react is important in maintaining a controlled situation, so use an even tone of voice and keep calm. Demonstrate a relaxed posture and movement and remain matter of fact. Practise empathic listening and then reflect back what you have heard for clarity. Most importantly, don't get defensive, sarcastic or superior or grill your teenager. The aim is to reach an understanding about the issues or concerns that are fuelling the anger and to resolve those where possible.

Useful organisations

**The British Association of Anger Management –
www.angermanage.co.uk**
Provides self-assessment tools and runs courses.

Chapter 13

Anxiety and panic

What is anxiety

Anxiety is a normal part of life for all of us, so it is likely that at some stage of your teenager's development you will be called on to offer support. Anxiety has a useful reason for being there. Your teenager's brain is great at protecting them and its ability to do that has evolved over millions of years.

Using brain imaging and neurochemical techniques several parts of the brain have been identified as key in the production of fear and anxiety. Memories are made of many elements and are stored in different parts of the brain. The two main components involved are the amygdala and the hippocampus

Amygdala- Emotional memories are stored here and the amygdala alerts the brain that a threat is present

Hippocampus- Encodes specific threatening events into the memory.

We all worry about things, and when we feel threatened or in a stressful situation our brain releases our 'safety hormones' (see Chapter 3). If it thinks there's something to worry about, it will instantly flood our body with adrenaline, noradrenaline, cortisol and oxygen so that we can respond immediately, and act to keep ourselves safe. This is known as the 'fight or flight response' and it is our natural way of preparing ourselves to deal with physical threats by making us more alert and giving us a sudden burst of energy and strength. The small, almond shaped glands responsible, are located at the back of our brain and are called the amygdala and they are there to protect us.

Sometimes though, our brain gets a little overprotective and it acts just the same for many situations, where there is no actual physical threat, but just a mental perception of risk or danger, or even in day to day situations that just make us feel uneasy. When our brain perceives a threat, it doesn't stop to think about whether, or not the threat is real, it just swings into action and doesn't wait to find out the facts! In fact, the part of our brain that is able to think clearly, calm things down and make decisions about what to do next, is shut down if the brain senses a threat.

Common situations where this may happen are before and during examinations, interviews, public speaking or performances, but everybody will have different triggers. Although anxiety makes us feel physically rather uncomfortable, it can help, even in these non-physical situations, by improving alertness and short-term focus.

These feelings of anxiety should be relatively short-lived and should recede once the trigger has been removed or feelings and situations have been managed. However, anxiety can become a significant mental health problem when people seem to be worrying a lot of the time, have many different triggers, or seem to have intense physical signs of anxiety which are difficult to manage and often extreme. If these problems are causing distress and interfering with the ability to carry out everyday life, such as learning and socialising, over a sustained period, then help is likely to be needed to learn techniques and coping strategies.

Teenagers are usually experiencing a lot of changes in their lives as they mature physically and mentally and will learn to deal with a whole range of new challenges. Some common situations that can cause anxiety are changing schools, moving to a new home, bereavement, parental divorce, bullying, friendship issues and examinations, but sometimes there is no obvious single cause.

Research suggests that as many as 30% of all adults will experience an anxiety disorder at some time and that over half of these have begun by the teenage years. [1]

Types of anxiety

There are many different anxiety disorders. the most common ones are described below.

General Anxiety Disorder (GAD)
In GAD, people feel anxious and fearful for long periods of time without any specific cause. They feel on edge and tense most of the time.

Obsessive Compulsive Disorder (OCD)
In OCD the anxiety causes obsessions and compulsions. The obsessions are unwelcome thoughts or images that keep entering the mind. The compulsions are mental or physical routines that have to be done to relieve the anxious state.

Panic Disorder
Panic disorder results in severe panic attacks, which can come on very suddenly and sometimes without obvious cause. Panic attacks cause intense fear or dread and can often be associated with intense physical symptoms such as heart pounding, breathing problems and nausea.

Phobias
A phobia is an intense fear of certain situations or things, which are unlikely to harm you. Some typical phobias are fears of heights, enclosed spaces, flying, thunder, spiders, insects or animals, but can be almost anything.

Post-Traumatic Stress Disorder (PTSD)
PTSD causes strong feelings of anxiety often with flashbacks or nightmares, when someone has witnessed or experienced something traumatic or frightening. It can happen soon after the event or much later.

Social Anxiety Disorder
Social Anxiety Disorder is a fear of social situations such as meeting new people or speaking in public that could cause personal embarrassment.

Why does anxiety feel the way it does?

When you don't need to fight or run, but your body has been flooded with fuel to help you deal with the imminent danger, it takes time to burn off the hormones and adrenaline that is in your system. As this builds up, it produces physical symptoms that can feel severe, and can affect your feelings and emotions. Here are some of the things you'll probably feel.

Physical symptoms
Rapid breathing - *your brain is trying to save oxygen to send to your muscles, so they can use it for energy to fight or run. Your brain organises your breathing to change from normal, strong breaths to rapid breathing to increase oxygen.*
Dizziness *-as the oxygen builds up, the carbon dioxide drops, making you feel dizzy and confused.*
Fast thumping heartbeat or chest pain - *your heart is working hard to pump the fuel around your body, so it can fight or run*
Nausea, dry mouth - *everything that's happening in your body that isn't necessary at that moment for survival will shut down. One of these is your digestive system, it's a great way to save energy, but the hormones released increase colon contractions and that can make you feel sick, or have an upset stomach or diarrhoea*
Sweating - *your body does this to cool itself down. It doesn't want to overheat if it needs to fight or run*
Hot flushes or blushing - *the blood rushes to your face and it might feel warm.*
High blood pressure or headaches - *as the stress builds, the hormones produced temporarily narrow your blood vessels and raise your blood pressure. You might also experience tension headaches.*

156

Shaking, tremors and trembling-*your brain's fight or flight response can produce hyperstimulation when it sends fuel to your arms (so they can fight) and to your legs (so they can run away).*
Aches and pains-*for as long as the stress hormones remain high in your body, you can experience tension, stiffness and tightness in one, or a group of muscles.*
Sleeping difficulties-*stress causes hyperarousal which can upset the balance between sleep and wakefulness*

You can see from this list that there are very good reasons why our body responds to anxiety in the way it does. It is meant to keep us safe. Our mood and thinking are also affected in ways that can also increase our anxiety, making it especially difficult to manage.

Mood
When the amygdala is highly active, you might get emotional or angry at all sorts of things or nothing at all, or you might experience:

Feeling tense or on edge
A sense of detachment or numbness
Inability to relax
Irritability and anger

Thinking
Difficulty concentrating
A desire to escape
Dreading or fearing the worse
Racing thoughts
Constant worrying
Avoidance of any stressful situations

How can parents help?

You will be concerned and worried yourself when you see your child trying to cope with their anxiety. Your reaction might be to get in there and remove any trigger or cause of anxiety, and to organise your child's life so that they are as worry free as possible. When you consider that the anxious feelings associated with stress are so extreme, it is natural to want to take any steps to avoid them feeling that way. This will only result in your teenager becoming overwhelmed when faced with stressful circumstances, because like it or not, life is stressful!

In childhood, our amygdala is unsophisticated, but as we mature, we can train our brain to respond more appropriately to stress, and we can learn to manage the effects better. This means though, that we do need to put ourselves repeatedly into situations where we have stress, so that we can practice coping with the anxiety it causes.
So instead of protecting your child from all stress and anxiety, what is more helpful to them, is for you to support them to take control of their anxiety and to learn how to respond when their brain reacts to things that aren't really a threat.
You will need to show empathy and support for your teenagers and take their problems with anxiety seriously whilst showing them that you have done some homework.

Here are three important messages you can give your teenager:

Anxiety is a normal part of life, and it won't kill them, even if it feels like it will. Some brains will be a lot quicker to sense threat than others and an anxious brain is just as healthy and strong and capable as a non-anxious brain. The symptoms and effects listed above, are very physical, but have a reason for being there.

Anxiety isn't their enemy, it is just the amygdala doing its job and trying to protect them, by providing the fuel to make them strong powerful and safe. As soon as your teenager puts their thinking brain (the pre-frontal cortex) back in control, the amygdalae will believe they are safe and stop the 'fight and flight' response. Once the adrenaline, oxygen and hormones are neutralised in the body, the intense physical and emotional feelings will all start to settle down and your child will begin to feel better.

The single most useful way that your teenager can send this message to their brain to tell it to stop worrying, is to trigger the relaxation response that is programmed automatically into their brain. They can do this by breathing in a controlled manner, strong, slow deep breaths that come from low down in their diaphragm. Between five and ten breaths is often enough to make a huge difference to how quickly they could begin to feel better.

Breathing in through their nose for a count of three,
Pausing for three seconds
Breathing out through their mouth for five seconds.

If anxiety is causing severe distress and affecting your child's ability to cope with everyday life, then you'll need to seek help. Schools may offer a counselling service or for ongoing situations, the GP should be consulted. Parents should offer to make the appointments and accompany them if they wish.

If your teenager is unwilling to seek help, they should be encouraged to try some of the self-help techniques described below or find suitable alternatives online. You'll need to find out as much as possible about how to relieve anxiety. Try to persuade your teenager to try some of the techniques, but don't pressurise them. Stay calm and offer to support your teenager in whatever way they want. It is useful to try to determine exactly what are the main factors causing the anxiety and to try to encourage your teenager to find ways of dealing with them, rather than avoiding them. This may involve practising how to deal with them and setting small targets.

Try to ensure that your teenager has a good, balanced diet, a sensible sleep routine and some regular exercise. It is also useful to encourage them to find activities that are relaxing and enjoyable. Maintain a calm environment at home and deal with their anxieties in as calm a way as possible.

Don't forget to look after your own wellbeing, as supporting teenagers suffering from anxiety can be quite stressful. It can be helpful to find a support group or forum.

How is anxiety treated

Anxiety can never be completely removed, but it can be reduced and controlled over time. Doctors should assess the anxiety symptoms and decide on the degree to which it is interfering with normal life. For most anxiety, doctors are likely to offer advice about self-help and may also offer talking therapies depending on what is available locally or at the school. If the initial treatments do not appear to be working, they may offer medication or refer the patient for help from specialist psychiatric services such as CAMHS. This is likely to involve further assessment and some intensive talking therapies.

Self-help

There are various books, on-line information and courses available on dealing with anxiety and one or more of these may be recommended. In some areas, there are also self-help groups. Advice on self-help usually covers dealing with the physical symptoms of anxiety by some of the following:

Breathing Techniques Anxious people often hyperventilate (over-breathe), which results in too much oxygen. Various techniques encourage slower breathing to increase Carbon Dioxide levels. This can bring some quick relief from the tense feelings.

Muscle Relaxing Techniques Anxious people tense up their muscles and these techniques help them to relax them again.

Diet - A balanced and sensible diet ensures that dietary factors are not making matters worse. It is recommended that stimulants such as caffeine, alcohol and cigarettes are avoided as these all increase tension

Exercise - Exercise is generally seen as beneficial to most mental health conditions and can be a useful way of both reducing and distracting from tension

Relaxation activities - These will depend on what the individual likes. They can also act as a distraction. Some suggestions are:
Pampering – aromatherapy baths using oils e.g. lavender; bubbles: massage; hair or nails treatment.
Entertainment –, listen to relaxing music; play music; sing
Exercise – dance; cycle; swim; skate; gym; country walk gardening.
Arts and crafts – paint; sculpt; collage.
Other – shopping; sunbathing.

Sleep - Getting regular, good quality sleep is an important factor for mental health.

Complimentary Therapies - Some people also find complimentary therapies useful. These include meditation, yoga, mindfulness, aromatherapy, acupuncture and massage. These may help to encourage relaxation and improve the emotional state.

Diaries - Maintaining a diary is a useful way of identifying both what triggers the anxiety problems and what methods seem to work best at relieving them.

Talking therapies - Talking with a counsellor is often helpful and may identify issues or situations that need to be dealt with and suggest techniques for dealing with them. It will often also try to change the way the anxious person is thinking, often using CBT (cognitive behavioural therapy). One approach is to systematically identify and challenge the negative thoughts causing the anxiety. The thoughts are identified using a daily record or diary and then analysed and challenged logically to assess whether or not they were really valid.

Another area that can be important is managing worries. When people are constantly worrying it is useful to find ways to minimise the overall level of worrying and to deal with individual worries. Again, systematic identification and analysis of the worries is useful followed by action plans to deal with those valid worries, which can be dealt with.

Talking therapies will often encourage people to deal with their anxiety by initially avoiding certain situations, then to slowly try to experience them. Avoidance leaves the anxiety unresolved, whereas often the experience can be dealt with as long as there is adequate preparation and practice. Although the situation is likely to be uncomfortable, the more often it can be experienced, the more likely anxiety levels are likely to fall or disappear altogether.

Medications - Medications can be used to treat anxiety, although some of the medications used for adults are considered to be less suitable for teenagers. These medications may have side-effects, may take some weeks to work or may not work at all. Four main drug types are used:

Anti-depressants: These are used to treat anxiety disorders including generalised anxiety disorder (GAD), panic disorder and Obsessive Compulsive Disorder (OCD).

Anti-convulsants: These are usually only used if the anti-depressants have not worked.

Benzodiazepines tranquilisers: Doctors will only prescribe benzodiazepines for short periods if the anxiety is particularly extreme to help overcome a crisis. This is because they lose their effect over time and are addictive.

Beta-blockers: These can help with the physical signs of anxiety. They can help to lower a fast heartbeat, shaking or blushing. They can be helpful for social anxiety disorder if a significant event is being undertaken or for phobias where exposure to a particular trigger is planned or unavoidable.

Useful organisations
Anxiety care UK – www.anxietycare.org.uk
Provides information and counselling services to anxiety sufferers.

Anxiety UK – www.anxietyuk.org.uk
Supports anyone with anxiety or anxiety-based depression. Provides information and paid for self-help resources and therapies.

Childline – www.childline.org.uk
Provides a free and confidential telephone service for children. Helpline: 0800 1111.

Family lives – www.familylives.org.uk
Helps parents deal with changes in family life. They also offer a free helpline at 0808 800 2222.

Mind – www.mind.org.uk/Anxiety
Provides information and support on a variety of mental health issues and has an information helpline 0300 123 3393.

NHS Choices – www.nhs.uk/conditions/anxiety
Provides information on anxiety and how to get help.

No More Panic – www.nomorepanic.co.uk
Provides information, support and advice to sufferers of anxiety and panic and their carers.

No Panic – www.nopanic.org.uk
Provides information, support and advice to sufferers of anxiety and panic and their carers. They have a helpline 0844 9674848.

OCD-UK – www.ocduk.org
Provides information, support and advice to sufferers of Obsessive Compulsive Disorder and their carers.

Overcoming – www.overcoming.co.uk
This website has information on self-help guides you can buy for a range of different conditions. They are not free resources. You can buy the books direct or you may able to get some of the books second hand on auction sites.

Rethink mental illness – www.rethink.org
Provide advice and information to anyone affected by mental illness and have over a hundred support groups.

SANE – www.sane.org.uk
Provides information and support to people affected by mental illness. They have a mental health helpline called SANELINE at 0300 304 7000.

SASH (London Social Anxiety Self-Help Groups) – www.sashgroup.org
Runs groups in the London area for sufferers of Social Anxiety Disorder.

Social Anxiety UK – www.social-anxiety.org.uk
Provides information and support for sufferers of Social Anxiety Disorder.

The Mix – www.themix.org.uk
Supports under 25s on a wide range of issues including anxiety.

Triumph over phobia (TOP UK) – www.topuk.org
Provides information and advice for sufferers of Phobias and Obsessive Compulsive Disorder.

YoungMinds – youngminds.org.uk
Provides information and advice on children's mental health issues and a parents helpline:0808 802 5544.

References in this chapter

[1] Kessler R. C., Berglund P., Demler O., Jin R., Merikangas K. R., Walters E. E. (2005). Lifetime prevalence and age-of-onset distributions of DSM-IV disorders in the national comorbidity survey replication. Arch. Gen. Psychiatry 62 593–602. 10.1001/archpsyc.62.6.593

Chapter 14

Arguments, conflict and defiance

Arguments with teenagers can be very emotionally wearing but are an almost inevitable outcome of teenage development. The most common reasons for teenagers to argue with parents are:

Developing their ability to think for themselves

As their brains become more developed teenagers begin to think in more complex ways, and are more likely to challenge you, and many of the norms around them at home, school and in the wider world.

Developing their own identity

As they experiment with their own identity adolescents are likely to try new forms of dress and music which may seem quite strange to you. The opinions of their contemporaries will be much more important than what you think, and they are likely to be drawn towards the behaviours and moralities of their peer group. As such, they may also be tempted into risky behaviours.

Developing their own independence

As teenagers crave more independence, they will want to make more decisions about their own lives and will expect existing constraints and boundaries to be eased or removed entirely. This balancing act can be very challenging for parents, when young people believe themselves to be ready to take on responsibility and decision making for themselves, and you think otherwise.

A sense of fairness

Teenagers are at a stage where they question many aspects of the world around them and they are often very concerned about what they see as fair or not. This is a good thing, but of course they are often basing their judgements on limited experience, limited information and often from only one perspective. More than one of you will have heard the cry "It's not fair!".

Conflict between being a child or an adult

Conflict will inevitably arise between you and your child in deciding how they should be treated especially as they may behave in totally different ways in different situations. In their hurry to achieve maturity, your teenager might also appear jealous of what they perceive as adult privileges with you appearing to have freedoms, choices and resources that they are not allowed.

Disillusion with parents

Add to the above that your child has often seen you as all-knowing and perfect, and generally do not question your knowledge or your behaviour, but as teenagers become more aware and perceptive they realise that you are not always right and do not always behave perfectly.

Power struggle

Teenagers want to assume power over their own lives and to reject parents controlling them.

There is nothing wrong with arguments between teenagers and their parents so long as they are constructive. Indeed, teenagers need to learn the skills involved in asserting their own opinions and influencing other people. Unfortunately, because the teenage brain is more closely attuned to the emotional rather than the rational side, arguments can easily change from passionate to angry and from respectful to insulting. Arguments need two parties to be involved and if they are to be constructive both parties need to be prepared to listen to and to be influenced by the other person.

So, when should you argue with your teenager?

Choose your arguments carefully

Arguments need two people and a wise parent should generally think carefully before getting involved in arguments with their teenagers. The best context for constructive arguments will be debates about issues that do not directly affect the home and the behaviour of those within it. Discussion and debate about ethical issues, politics and news items are good places to start. Discussions about school issues may also arise but need to be treated more carefully. It is important to allow teenagers to have their say and to acknowledge the points that they are making. It is a good opportunity to give them further relevant information, but don't sound superior and don't preach to them. If you are not prepared to modify or adapt your own position, it may not be a very worthwhile exercise, as this is dismissing your teenager's views. However, you certainly don't have to agree with them and there is nothing wrong with agreeing to disagree. If you do have a controlled and sensible discussion, give them some praise.

Stay calm and respectful

Whether you choose to have an argument or not, stay calm and be respectful. If you are going to argue it is great to be passionate, but if your teenager's passion turns to anger or if they start trying to name call or demean you, call an end or a postponement to the argument.

Avoid arguments about domestic rules and consequences

Arguments can arise when a teenager wants to bend or defy your rules. The best way to avoid this is by having clear and preferably agreed rules in the first place. These rules should be subject to negotiation from time to time, but in a cool fashion and not when they are about to be challenged. Parents should simply reiterate their rules and consequences and walk away.

Look for argument triggers and try to address them

If arguments are frequent, you might try to identify what is causing them. Sometimes this is obvious but there may be a deeper underlying problem. If there is a repeated pattern, parents need to plan their responses in advance or find a way of eliminating the issue. In some cases, it may be possible to address the issue by problem solving with our teenager. For instance, some family conflicts are caused by poor time management and a lack of priority setting.

Deal with arguments that get out of hand

If an argument descends into anger or name calling it is time to stop. The parent should call an end to the discussion or demand a break for everyone to cool down. It is usually a good idea to come back to the argument later, rather than just leave it unresolved, but this should only be done when everybody is in a calm and listening state, which may best be left for another day. Parents should be prepared to apologise if they have lost their temper or said things that they regret. Its also helpful to let your teenager know if you find that you got your facts wrong in the first place and to thank them for the opportunity to rethink certain issues.

Focus on one problem at a time

Often parents seem to be faced with a whole range of teenage behavioural issues which lead to constant nagging and disputes. This is detrimental to the whole relationship and often does little to resolve the underlying problems, causing teenagers to complain that you are "always on my back!" Parents need to prioritise which are the most important issues and either ignore the more trivial ones or leave them to another time. It is much better to focus on solving one problem at a time, before moving on. Even then, do not expect instant results. Change takes time.

Avoid power struggles

The most difficult arguments to deal with are those that involve power struggles with the teenager. You may rightly feel that you should be in charge, and that this means you must control your teenager's behaviour. This is partly because you are worried about your teenager doing risky things that are unsafe to themselves. You may also worry about irresponsible and antisocial behaviour that will affect and be judged by other people. Let's face it, you have had to be on your toes and in charge for several years when your children were younger! In fact, it soon becomes obvious with any rebellious teenager, that parents cannot control them. The best that they can hope for is to teach them and model ways of controlling themselves. Parental authority that is based on physical size or threats soon becomes irrelevant to our grown teenagers and parents will have to try to earn their respect.

Teenagers themselves are developing their own identity and a sense of their own importance and you must respond to this by giving them more freedoms and responsibility as long as they demonstrate the ability to deal with it. Nevertheless, some teenagers will demand freedoms that are unacceptable to you and will threaten to, or actually behave in ways that are defiant of your authority. Continued extreme forms of defiance can be part of a psychological condition, but in most cases, it is just part of the power struggle of who can control whom.

When dealing with outright defiance, you have to be realistic. Giving ultimatums usually only makes matters worse and encourages your teenager to carry through their defiant behaviour so as not to lose face. Rather than pushing your teenager into a corner, try to give them some time and space to consider their position. Explain the choices that your teenager has and what the consequences of each will be. After that, try to retreat. If the teenager goes through with the defiant behaviour, you need to ensure that these consequences are followed through.

In cases, where there is ongoing deliberate and often aggressive defiance, you may need to seek external help. Discussion with their school is always a good place to start as it is important to know if the defiance extends to other areas outside the home and a shared approach may be useful.

Useful organisations

Relate (Family counselling) – www.relate.org.uk
Provides family and individual counselling services

The Spark – www.thespark.org.uk
Provides family and individual counselling services in Scotland.

Chapter 15

Bullying

One huge worry for parents of teenagers is that they may experience bullying. Whilst you might worry that your child may be on the receiving end of bullying, it is important to consider that your child may themselves be doing the bullying.

Coping with your own feelings is something that needs to be under control before you can rationally think about how to manage the situation. You might feel:

Angry and want to punish the bully.
Helpless and not sure if and what you can do to manage the situation.
Isolated and think you are the only family dealing with this experience.
Confused and not sure what to do, or who to speak to.
Anxious and find that your thinking is muddled, and the problem is all-consuming.
Emotional and overwhelmed by an instinct to protect your child.
Disappointed that your child failed to stand up for himself or herself, or that they may have harmed another child.
Embarrassed to think that others know your child is bullying and that it might reflect on you or get your child a name for him/herself.

Types of bullying

In the UK, about half of teenagers say that they have been bullied at some time with about one in ten being bullied in the last week. At the same time, about one in eight teenagers admits to having bullied someone, although far more admit to having deliberately upset or excluded someone or have even physically attacked someone. More boys than girls admit to bullying and far more boys admit attacking someone. In general, disabled people and gay/lesbian and transgendered people admit to a slightly higher level of bullying others, but are also far more likely to be bullied themselves. [1]

There are many different forms of bullying. The majority are directed purely at the individual, usually based on some form of difference, while others are directed not just at the individual, but involve prejudice against a certain group of people. Types of bullying include:

Appearance bullying - including size, shape, hair colour, facial features.

Achievement bullying - based on high or low grades in school.

Style bullying - based on interests, hobbies and youth culture identity.

Association bullying - linked to the bullying or denigration of a friend or relative.

Gender bullying - purely based on being male or female or transsexual.

Sexuality bullying - based on actual or perceived sexual orientation.

Racist bullying - based on skin colour or ethnic group.

Religious bullying - usually based on a minority religion.

Disability bullying - based on physical disability, learning disorder or autism.

Of course, many forms of bullying are simply based on a sense by the person bullying that the victim is an easy target and won't be able to retaliate, which may or may not include some of the above categories.

Methods of bullying

Among people being bullied the most common problem is verbal bullying from insults, abuse, teasing or threatening. This is followed by social bullying such as being excluded/ignored having rumours spread about them or being publicly embarrassed. This may not only be happening in person, but also online (cyberbullying). A smaller number have experienced physical assaults such as punching, kicking or tripping, or had property stolen or damaged.

The impact of bullying

Bullying can have a profound effect upon the victims, which can have lifetime consequences. Victims of bullying say that they suffer from anxiety and depression, which can even lead to suicidal thoughts.[2] This anxiety can result in self-harm, eating disorders or drug and alcohol problems. Victims may also become very withdrawn, refuse to go to school, or even run away to escape the situation. The bullying adversely affects their self-esteem, confidence and optimism about the future.
Of those who are being bullied about a third don't tell anybody. This may be because they feel that they can deal with it, but it is also because they feel that it won't be taken seriously, or they think that it would only make the bullying worse.

Cyberbullying

Most teenagers are now using social media daily. Nearly three quarters say that they have been the victims of cyberbullying, with around a third suffering on a highly frequent basis.[3] The most common problem is nasty comments or rumours being spread about them, but some people have also suffered from private information being shared and from pictures and videos of them being shared that they don't like. Much of the bullying occurs on Facebook, Instagram or Snapchat. (See Chapters 22 & 35)

Bullying and the law (UK)
Some forms of bullying are directly covered by the law and should be reported to the police. These include:
Being the victim of a physical assault
Having property stolen
Being repeatedly harassed or intimidated. This includes verbal abuse and threats, unwanted emails, text messages or phone calls

and cyberbullying. Written abuse can fall under the law concerning malicious communication.

Being the victim of discrimination or a hate crime. It is an offence to discriminate against people with certain "protected characteristics". These characteristics include gender identity, sexual orientation, race, religion or disability. Any form of abuse based on these characteristics can be treated as a hate incident or hate crime.

The role of schools

By law schools have a responsibility to provide a safe and healthy environment and must have measures in place to prevent all forms of bullying. They must have a behaviour policy which includes dealing with bullying. Schools also have a legal responsibility to prevent discrimination and harassment. Schools have the right to discipline students for behaviour both within and outside of schools including on public transport or on local streets. However, they may not get involved with incidents that occur on non-school days.

Preventing your teenager bullying

Two-thirds of parents worry about their children being bullied, but equal consideration should be given to making sure that your children do not bully.

Here are five important areas for parents:

Be a good role model
Show your children how to treat other people with respect and talk to them about how the victims of ill treatment feel. Explain to them how words and forms of social isolation can be just as hurtful as physical bullying.

Do not let your child be bullied in your household
Children who are bullied are far more likely to bully other people. Parents need to prevent bullying by siblings, but even more important, they must not bully themselves. Parents don't always

realise that they are doing it, but often do it just by their strength of personality and by constantly issuing instructions rather than listening and encouraging. Teenagers need to feel that they have some say and influence in their home life or else their frustrations may be taken out on other people.

Teach them empathy
Children need to learn how to see things from the other person's point of view. Children who can put themselves in others' shoes are far less likely to mistreat them.

Discuss their social media activity
Many teenagers admit to posting nasty messages and often regret these afterwards. Talk to your teenager about the dangers of posting without thinking and posting just to follow the crowd.

Teach your child to say no
Teaching young people the difference between good and bad and between good and nasty behaviour is only half of the battle. They also need to learn the assertiveness skills needed to be able to say no even to their own friends and "gangs" so that they don't join in with bad behaviour including bullying. (See Chapter 29 for more about Peer Pressure).

If your teenager is bullying

You will often not see your teenagers bullying, unless it is with siblings, but should watch out for signs that they are disrespecting other people. They may talk about some of their classmates in a very derogatory or even insulting manner or they may have money or possessions that are not theirs. If you suspect that your teenager is bullying or are confronted with an accusation from another teenager or from school, then you need to act.

Never assume the innocence of your teenager, nor go into a rage about how badly they have behaved, but do discuss the situation with your teenager to try to establish exactly what has been happening and why. In some cases, your child will not even have realised that their behaviour is bullying. There may have been no deliberate intention to hurt or abuse the other person. In this case, a discussion about empathy and realising how the other person felt, may be sufficient to stop the behaviour. If the behaviour was deliberate, some form of appropriate discipline may be needed. For instance, if cyberbullying was involved, restrictions could be placed on the use of phones or social media. However, it is more important to try to change the behaviour by addressing its cause. This may be a lack of empathy or respect for other people's rights, which will need to be discussed. However, the situation may be a reaction to other events, which are causing them stress, insecurity or anger, including being bullied themselves, or it may involve other people who are encouraging the bullying. If the school is involved, make sure that they keep you closely informed of any future incidents.

Preventing your teenager from being bullied

Bullying is so widespread, particularly in the teenage years, that parents will never be able to totally protect their children from bullying. However, children who are resilient and assertive are less likely to be seen as easy targets by bullies and are likely to cope with bullying better. Teenagers need to be shown that their feelings are important and that they, and their friends, have the right not to be abused or maltreated by anyone. They need to be confident in expressing their views and expecting to be heard. They also need to develop good social skills and the more social situations that they experience the better.

Spotting the signs of bullying
Children, who are being bullied, often show a range of changes to their normal behaviour. These may include:
    Not wishing to go to school or to certain places
    Deterioration in school performance
    Being anxious or unhappy before or after school
    Changes in eating or sleeping patterns
    Becoming more withdrawn and isolated
    Changes in normal mood or becoming aggressive
    Lots of minor aches and pains

Of course, these may be signs of other issues and it is useful to think about whether there have been any other significant changes in their life. Bullied children may also have physical injuries and damaged or missing possessions. If your teenager is showing any of these signs, try to talk to them about what is going on in their life and why they seem to be having problems.

If your teenager is being bullied

If your teenager tells you that they are being bullied they have taken a major step. Try to stay calm and listen carefully to what is said, then explain that being bullied is not their fault and is a problem that a great many teenagers and adults need to deal with. Talk to your teenager about what help they would like rather than jumping in and getting involved straightaway. It is very rarely a good idea for parents to confront the bully or their parents directly.

If the problem is happening at school, parents may wish to involve the school, depending on how serious it is. If it is serious, it may involve a criminal offence (as discussed earlier), in which case the police should be informed. If there are injuries or malicious texts or emails take photographs and keep a record. Otherwise, it is often useful to try to deal with it by giving advice. However trivial the incident may seem, do not dismiss it or underestimate its impact. Do not tell teenagers or expect them to sort it out themselves. If they have told you, they are asking for help. Telling teenagers to ignore it is easier said than done and not very helpful, although if the bullying is happening on the street or somewhere they don't have to be, they may be able to avoid it.

Telling teenagers to retaliate or give as good as they get rarely works and will often make the situation worse. It can be helpful to role play with the teenager to try to practise appropriate responses It is also useful to try to encourage them to have a more confident demeanour by working on their posture and their voice. Even if it is too late for the current bullying, this may help prevent future problems. It is also important to try to change your teenager's response to the bullying, so that the bully does not get the response that they were looking for.

Involving the school

As discussed above, schools have a duty of care towards their students and must try to protect them from any form of abuse. If you do decide to involve the school, make sure that you have all the facts documented including when and where incidents have taken place, who is directly involved and who might have witnessed it. Make an appointment with the most suitable teacher/head of year and decide with your teenager whether they wish to be there. If they don't wish to attend, ask them what they want you to say. Whether or not they attend this meeting, the school is likely to want to re-interview them anyway. The school may well need time to investigate and so a second meeting is likely to be necessary, unless there is criminal activity involved. Once the school tells you what action they are going to take, make sure that it is documented.

If the problem persists, record the details of each incident and inform the school. If you are not happy with the school's response or think that your teenager is still at risk, write to the head or appeal directly to the Governors.

Useful organisations

Bullies Out – www.bulliesout.com
Run workshops and train peer mentors.
Bullybusters – www.bullybusters.org.uk
Run workshops, train peer mentors and provide mediation services. They have a helpline 0800 169 6928.
Bullying UK – www.bullying.co.uk
Part of Family Lives that provides advice, parents' courses and have a helpline 0808 800 2222.
CEOP – www.ceop.police.uk
Part of the National Crime Agency to which cyberbullying or online abuse can be reported.

Childline – www.childline.org.uk
Provides a free and confidential telephone service for children. They have a helpline: 0800 1111.
Ditch The Label – www.ditchthelabel.org
An international organisation providing online information and support related to bullying.
EACH – www.each.education
Works to reduce harassment and bullying of LGBTQ community and has a helpline 0808 1000 143 to report problems.
Kidscape – www.kidscape.org.uk
Provide information and run workshops for schools and bullying victims.
National Bullying Helpline – www.nationalbullyinghelpline.co.uk
Provides advice and a helpline 0845 22 55 787 for all sorts of bullying.
Red Balloon – www.redballoonlearner.org
Runs programmes for bullying victims who are not at school.
The Mix – www.themix.org.uk
Supports under 25s on a wide range of issues including bullying.
YoungMinds – youngminds.org.uk
Provides information and advice on children's mental health issues and a parents helpline:0808 802 5544.

References in this chapter

[1] Ditch the Label: The Annual Bullying Survey 2017
[2] Ditch the Label: The Annual Bullying Survey 2018
[3] Ditch the Label: The Annual Cyber Bullying Survey 2013

Chapter 16

Depression

What is depression?

Everyone has ups and downs in their lives and there will often be times when your teenager will have low moods. Although they will feel depressed for a short while, this doesn't mean that they are suffering from depression. If the feelings of sadness go on for weeks or months or keep coming back and when the depression is having a significant effect on their ability to cope with everyday life however, they may have depression. Young people can feel sad and worried about a whole range of life situations and events but sometimes there seems to be no identifiable reason.

Depression is quite a common condition with possibly as many as one in five people suffering at some point in their lives, although only a small number of people suffer from the most serious forms of depression.

A study among 14year olds found that 24% of the girls and 9% of the boys reported having high levels of depressive symptoms. [1] These are quite similar levels to a 2016 survey of British students which asked about their mental health, where 26% of women and 15% of men self-identified as suffering from depression. [2] However, the rates of depression that are identified and treated at any one time are only around 4% for adults and probably even less for teenagers. [3]

Signs of depression

Depression affects people of all ages differently, and that makes it difficult to diagnose. Sometimes it is hard to work out whether your child being silent, withdrawn and grumpy is teenage angst or something more serious, but in most cases, it affects mood and how people think and relate to other people as well as often having physical symptoms.

Mood

Low mood most of the day, every day sometimes linked to anxiety.
Frequent tearfulness.
Voicing/showing feelings of hopelessness and helplessness.
Voicing feelings of worthlessness and guilt.
Irritability and restlessness.
Feeling empty, numb and despairing.
Disinterest in life with little or no enjoyment of things that were once interesting to them.

Thinking

Showing low self-esteem and self-confidence.
Feeling inadequate and useless.
Difficulty concentrating or making decisions.
Struggling to cope with things that used to be easy.
Thoughts of self-harm.

Relationships with other people

Struggling with relationships.
Being irritable and intolerant of others.
Shy or anxious in company.
Lonely or withdrawn and increasing social isolation.

Physical symptoms
Changes to sleep patterns (for example, problems going to sleep and/or waking throughout the night).
Loss of appetite and weight.
Lack of energy.
Slowing of movements.
Loss of sex drive.

What causes depression?

Depression varies in its intensity and duration and is often categorised by doctors as mild, moderate or severe depending on how seriously it is affecting the ability to carry out normal life. At its most severe, it can cause delusions, hallucinations and suicidal thoughts. In this form, there seems to be an association to a malfunctioning of the brain signals that control mood relating to dopamine, noradrenaline and serotonin. (See Chapter 3 Hormones) There is also sometimes an inherited genetic factor, with some families having a history of depression. The most serious forms of depression seem to affect men and women similarly. Depression can also be linked to drug or alcohol abuse.

The milder forms of depression seem to affect women and girls more and can sometimes be linked to hormone levels. Depression can be triggered or associated with physical illnesses, but more often it is thought to be caused by the inability to cope with stressful events, life changes or personal circumstances. There may be an obvious cause for example:

arguments with friends and family,
relationship breakdown,
school or exams
changing social or domestic circumstances
work problems
bereavement or other loss
being bullied
abuse or neglect
long term illness

However, the cause may not be clear at all. Personality seems to be quite important in the milder types of depression with sufferers often being shy and sensitive and self-critical. In some cases, depression is linked to childbirth (post-natal depression) or is seasonal (seasonal affective disorder). It can also be a sign of bipolar disorder.

How can I support my teenager?

If you believe that your teenager is suffering from depression, you should try to persuade them to seek help and an important next step is for your child to visit their GP to learn about depression and how it is treated. If they are uncooperative, don't put pressure on them or give them advice, unless they are showing suicidal tendencies, and let them choose where to go for help, which may be another parent, a teacher, school counsellor, family member or friend.

Do keep trying to talk to your teenager without judging them and without pestering them, to see if there is an obvious cause of the problem that you can help to be addressed. You'll need to give them as much emotional support, encouragement and praise as possible. Be honest and explain that you're worried that they're going through something difficult. Don't blame yourself for any problems they are having – this won't help the situation, just tell them you'll "be there" for them when they do want to talk. It probably won't be helpful for you to try to cheer your teenager up or tell them to pull themselves together, but encourage them to be as active as possible, particularly with activities that they normally enjoy.

In many cases, the cause of the depression may not be obvious, or your teenager may be unable or unwilling to talk about it, so point them towards websites or helplines that can give them information on depression, so they can find out the facts themselves.
Caring for people with depression is stressful and difficult and you may need to seek support for yourself, do try to find out as much as you can yourself about depression and how to deal with it.

How is depression treated?

Doctors will assess your teenager's depression symptoms and decide whether the depression is mild, moderate or severe depending on the degree to which it is interfering with normal life. For milder depression, doctors are likely to offer advice about self-help and may also offer talking therapies depending on what is available locally or at the school. They may suggest a course of medication. For moderate depression, or if the initial treatments do not appear to be working, they may refer the patient for help from specialist psychiatric services such as CAMHS. This is likely to involve further detailed assessments, possibly some medication and some intensive talking therapies. For the most extreme and possible life-threatening depression, treatment may require hospital admission and may involve other kinds of therapy.

Self-help: There are various books, on-line information and courses available on dealing with depression and one or more of these may be recommended. In some areas, there are also self-help groups. Advice on self-help usually covers the following:

Exercise: Exercise is generally seen as beneficial to most mental health conditions.

Keeping active: People suffering from depression often withdraw more and more and do less and less. It is important to try to keep active and to particularly focus on activities which are enjoyable and fun or that help relaxation. It can also be helpful to have an activity with a clear sense of achievement. The activities will depend entirely on the individual, but some suggestions are:

> Pampering - bath with aromatherapy oils, bubbles, massage, hair or nail treatment
> Entertainment – go to a play, concert, film, listen to music, play music, sing
> Exercise – dance, swim, skate, gym, country walk, gardening, sport
> Arts and crafts – paint, sculpt, collage, sketching
> Other – shopping, sightseeing, sunbathing, chatting with friends, holiday

Diet: A balanced and sensible diet ensures that dietary factors are not making matters worse.

Sleep: Getting regular, good quality sleep is an important factor for mental health.

Avoid alcohol and cannabis: It is tempting to use alcohol or cannabis to relieve the depressive symptoms, but research suggests that these make matters worse or can lead to problems of substance abuse. [4][5]

Alternative Therapies

Some people also find alternative therapies useful. These include meditation, yoga, mindfulness, aromatherapy, acupuncture and massage. These may help to encourage relaxation and improve the emotional state. They are sometimes also useful in relieving the side effects of prescribed anti-depressants. Some people also find that herbal remedies can help. St John's Wort is a herbal remedy that is often suggested to relieve mild depression, but it is useful to discuss this with a doctor first.

Talking therapies: Different talking therapies may be suggested depending on whether a prime cause for the depression has been identified. Talking with a counsellor is often helpful and may identify an underlying cause. If the problems seem to stem from relationship problems, the talking therapy may cover family or interpersonal therapy. Sometimes talking therapies aimed at improving problem-solving are useful. Another important form of talking therapy is dealing with negative thoughts, often using CBT (cognitive behavioural therapy). Depressed people often dwell on the things in their lives that go wrong and fail to recognise their successes. They also overrate other people's qualities and underrate their own. They sometimes make assumptions about how other people think about them and how badly things will turn out, They can also blame themselves for things that go wrong, even when they are not really responsible. A 2016 research study demonstrated that strengths based, Solution Focused Brief Therapy (SFBT), significantly decreased depression scores and could be used as an intervention program for the general population of women with depression.[6]

Medications: Medications called anti-depressants are widely used to treat depression, although some of the medications used for adults, are considered to be less suitable for teenagers. Medications are usually prescribed for a few months and it is very important that they are taken in the dosage and timing prescribed, and also that the patient does not suddenly stop taking them. Different medications work better with different people and so it may be necessary to try several before the best one is found. Medications should reduce symptoms and help people to cope better with everyday life, but the effects may take several weeks to start working. Some medications may also have unwanted side-effects and so it is important that those people on medication are carefully monitored.

ECT (Electroconvulsive therapy): ECT is a procedure sometimes used to treat the most severe forms of depression, especially when the situation is considered to be severe enough to be life threatening. An electric current is passed through the brain, whilst the patient is under a general anaesthetic.

Useful organisations
Bipolar UK – www.bipolaruk.org.uk
Provides support and information for anyone affected by Bipolar

Breathing Space –www.breathingspace.scot
Provides a free helpline for Scotland for anyone with low mood, depression or anxiety at 0800 838587.

Childline – www.childline.org.uk
Provides a free and confidential telephone service for children. They have a helpline: 0800 1111.

Charlie Waller Memorial Trust - www.cwmt.org.uk
Provide training and information to help young people and adults recognise and deal with depression.

Depression UK – www.depressionuk.org
Is a self-help group helping people cope with depression and provides information on local self-help groups.

Family lives – www.familylives.org.uk Helps parents deal with changes in family life. They also offer a free helpline at 0808 800 2222.

Friend in Need – www.friendsinneed.co.uk
Friends in Need is a way for people affected by depression to meet online and in their local area. It's for people over 18 only.

Heads above the waves – www.hatw.co.uk
Raises awareness of depression and self-harming in young people and gives advice for dealing with it.

Mind – www.mind.org.uk/Depression
Provides information and support on a variety of mental health issues and has an information helpline 0300 123 3393.

Mood Gym – www.moodgym.anu.edu.au
This is an on-line interactive self-help programme developed in Australia. It is available worldwide, but costs 39 Australian dollars to join for a year.

MoodSwings Network – www.moodswings.org.uk
This Manchester based service provides a range of services for people affected by a mood disorder such as depression, including their family and friends. Telephone: 0161 832 37 36

NHS Choices – www.nhs.uk/conditions/depression
Provides information on depression and how to get help.

Overcoming – www.overcoming.co.uk
This website has information on self-help guides you can buy for a range of different conditions. They are not free resources. You can buy the books direct or you may able to get some of the books second hand on auction sites.

Papyrus – www.papyrus-uk.org
Provides information and support for young people at risk of suicide. They have a helpline called HOPELINE UK for people under the age of 35 at 0800 068 4141.

Rethink mental illness – www.rethink.org
Provide advice and information to anyone affected by mental illness and have over a hundred support groups.

SANE – www.sane.org.uk
Provides information and support to people affected by mental illness. They have a mental health helpline called SANELINE at 0300 304 7000.

The Samaritans – www.samaritans.org
Provide a 24-hour service offering confidential emotional support to anyone who is in crisis. Helpline 116 123

The Mix – www.themix.org.uk
Supports under 25s on a wide range of issues including depression.

YoungMinds – youngminds.org.uk
Provides information and advice on children's mental health issues and a Parents'Helpline:0808 802 5544.

References in this chapter

[1] University of London, Institute of Education, Centre for Longitudinal Studies. (2018). Millennium Cohort Study: Sixth Survey, 2015. [data collection]. 3rd Edition. UK Data Service. SN: 8156, http://doi.org/10.5255/UKDA-SN-8156-3
[2] YouGov Survey of British Students 2016
[3] NHS Digital: Mental Health and Wellbeing in England, Adult Psychiatric Morbidity Survey 2014

[4] Boden, J. and Fergusson, D. (2011). Alcohol and Depression - Christchurch Health and Development Study. Society for the Study of Addiction.

[5] Lev-Ran S, Roerecke M, Le Foll B, George T.P, McKenzie K and Rehm J The association between cannabis use and depression: a systematic review and meta-analysis of longitudinal studies. Psychological Medicine, Available on CJO 2013 doi:10.1017/S0033291713001438

[6] Habibi M, Ghaderi K, Abedini S, Jamshidnejad N. The effectiveness of solution-focused brief therapy on reducing depression in women. Int J Educ Psychol Res 2016;2:244-9

Chapter 17

Difficult conversations

Some subjects are difficult to raise, and you might decide to hold off talking to your teenager about various topics, maybe leaving it until you discover a problem or concern or until they raise the subject themselves. For many parents, this includes talking about alcohol, drugs and smoking as well as relationships, sex and sexuality.

Many of these issues are likely to arise after the age of 14, but informal chats on these topics should begin long before then. It is best not to give a major lecture, but to have several smaller, casual conversations over time. Look for times when your child will not be distracted and find creative ways to raise the subject. These may be films or television programmes or items of news or events. Your child may also give you a golden opportunity if they raise the subject first. Younger children may be more receptive than older teenagers, who may think that they already know it all and that you are out of touch. Because of this, you'll need to make sure that they do know as much as possible about the various topics, not just their own views and prejudices, and we have covered each topic in more detail in Part 3 to provide useful information.

Your teenager may already have formed a view from the role model that you have set since they were born. This is not just about how you directly deal with the issues, but also about the views and attitudes that you demonstrate. It is extremely difficult to persuade a teenager not to do something that they have seen their parents do.

When to talk

It's very important that you are as closely involved in your children's lives as you can be and are continually talking to them about what is going on. (See Chapter 7, Getting Communication Right). It is helpful to build this into the daily routine, possibly straight after school or at meal times. Children need to believe that they can talk to their parents about anything without the possibility of an immediate negative or critical response. They need to have evidence from past conversations that you will stay calm whatever you are told and try to understand their point of view. Provided this groundwork has been done, discussions about difficult subjects can be started as early as possible, although obviously the conversation should be age appropriate.

How to talk before the issue becomes urgent

It is important that all talking is a discussion and not a lecture. Although it is natural that you will wish to influence your children, the most important thing is to get an understanding of what they already know or think they know about the topic and what conclusions they have drawn. It is also very useful to know what they think their friends and other people at school are doing and sometimes children are far more honest about this, than their own experiences. Listen carefully, interrupt as little as possible and keep your comments short and try to understand your teenager's point of view.

You may need to inform them about the risks and consequences of their actions and correct any factual misunderstandings but do be as objective and factual as possible and don't just give them your own opinions. Avoid using shock tactics, although a particularly bad incident in a film or in the news may be worth discussing.

Exaggerating risks can lead to teenagers switching off altogether as they may not believe the situation could ever apply to them or their friends. When you are talking about risks, try to talk about how to stay safe. Take the opportunity to talk to your child about whether they feel pressured by their peers or others to behave in certain ways and how they can resist this pressure. (See Chapter 29 for more on peer pressure). You may wish to discuss your own experiences and behaviour as a young person, especially if it might illustrate your concerns and provide examples of coping. If so, those examples need to be honest. Talking about how you dealt with situations and what happened to you and your teenage friends may provide a new perspective for your children, although sometimes teenagers have difficulty in relating their experiences to those of their parents.

How to talk after the issue becomes relevant

At some point it is likely that your teenager will get involved in activities that you disapprove of. They may start drinking or taking drugs or they may start experimenting with sex or exploring their own sexual orientation. They may even be involved in some form of criminal activity. Whatever it is, if they start talking to you about it, it is a very major step for them and suggests either that they feel that they have a good relationship with you and can trust you, or that they are feeling desperate. However, shocked you may be, stay calm and be as supportive as possible. You'll need to show that you appreciate being told and that together you'll will try to find the best way of dealing with it.

Setting rules and boundaries

Parents may well wish to set rules and boundaries to protect their children from risky situations and to give consequences for irresponsible or risky behaviours. If so, it is important that the reason for the rules is explained. Explain how their actions impact not only on them, but also on their family and friends, and that you care about them and the rules are to protect them. (See Chapter 8, Setting boundaries and consequences)

Stay involved in their life and available

The most important thing that you can do to protect your teenagers is to stay involved in their lives by keeping communication lines open and by keeping in touch with what your teenagers are doing and who they are doing it with. Encourage healthy activities and healthy friendships. As teenagers get older it will become more difficult to monitor them, but if they have a mobile phone, this should always be charged and available so that either party can reach the other one in a hurry. It is the aim that at some point, you will have to give your teenagers more freedom, and if you are too overprotective or controlling your teenagers may well rebel. However, you are still responsible for ensuring their safety and do still need to monitor them in as low-key fashion as possible. It's worth remembering that your own friends or other parents might also be a more useful source of information than your own children.

Chapter 18

Drugs

It's frightening to imagine that your child, already growing up so quickly, might be using drugs or drinking. However, drug abuse in teenagers is a very real problem.

Adults and drugs
The level of drug taking among adults has fallen over the last ten years but seems to have been roughly stable recently. In the last year about 9% of all adults have taken drugs, with the highest level among under 25s where the figure was 20%. In the last month alone, the figures fall to 4% for all adults and 10% for under 25s. Drug taking among men is roughly double that of women. Among the drug takers, about a third were using class A drugs (mostly Cocaine and Ecstasy). [1]

Cannabis (Class B) is by far the most widely used drug having been used by 7% of all adults and 16% of under 25s in the last year. The second most commonly used drug is powdered Cocaine (Class A) which has been used by 2% of all adults and 5% of under 25s in the last year. The third most commonly used drug is Ecstasy which has been used by a little over 1% of all adults, but over 4% of under 25s in the last year.

Among under 25s 2% have used Amyl Nitrate in the last year and the levels of use of LSD, amphetamines, ketamine and "new psychoactive substances" are all around 1%. This latter group are new drugs that copy the effects of existing drugs. One of the best known is Spice, which is thought to be in significant use among the homeless and the prison population, both of which are not covered in the usual surveys. Nitrous Oxide use is also significant with around 3% of all adults and 9% of under 25s using it in the last year.

Attitudes to some drugs, particularly Cannabis, have generally been softening around the world and in some countries, some drugs have been decriminalised or even made legal. However, in the UK, the laws on drugs have not changed a great deal.

The Law and drugs
You can get a fine or prison sentence if you take, carry, make or sell drugs or psychoactive substances. The penalties depend on the drug and the amount you have, and whether you're also dealing or producing the drug. The following is a simplified explanation of the law.

Class A Drugs which include Cocaine, Heroin, LSD and Ecstasy
Possession: Up to 7 years in prison and/or an unlimited fine
Supply/production: Up to life in prison and/or an unlimited fine

Class B Drugs which include Cannabis, Amphetamines and Ketamine
Possession: Up to 5 years in prison and/or an unlimited fine
Supply/production: Up to 14 years in prison and/or an unlimited fine

Class C Drugs which include Anabolic Steroids
Possession: Up to 2 years in prison and/or an unlimited fine
Supply/production: Up to 14 years in prison and/or an unlimited fine

Amyl Nitrite (poppers) are not covered by Drugs legislation, but under the Medicines Act.
Glues and gases are not illegal, but it is illegal to sell them to anyone if you think they will be sniffed. Nitrous Oxide is not illegal, but it is illegal to supply it for human "consumption".

Teenagers and drugs
Although drug taking among teenagers has been in long term decline, some recent surveys suggest that this may have stopped and indeed that drug use may be increasing again. The picture is confused by some change in the nature of the substances used, including some new psychoactive substances and Nitrous Oxide.

Younger teenagers tend to sniff glues and gases, whilst older teenagers tend to smoke or take tablets. Over a third of 15year olds say that they have never taken drugs, with 30% having taken them in the last year and 18% in the last month. Unlike with adults, the proportions of boys and girls are very similar. Among 15year olds the most commonly used drugs in the last year were Cannabis (19%), Nitrous Oxide (7%), Ecstasy (4%), glues and gases (4%), Cocaine (3%), new psychoactive drugs (3%) and LSD (2%). [2]

Most 15year olds say that they have been offered drugs with about half of those who took drugs getting them from a friend and a third from dealers. Most drugs are obtained outdoors, although some get them from a friend's house. Most drugs are used with friends. About half of all 15year olds think illegal drugs are easy to get. Most teenagers who take drugs for the first time do it to see what they are like, but afterwards if they take drugs it is most likely to be to get high. Almost all teenagers say that their parents would try to stop or discourage them from taking drugs.

The main drugs and substances

The following gives a brief description of the main drugs used by teenagers. Although each one has its own properties and risks if pure, it is worth remembering that since most of these drugs are illegal, they may contain all sorts of other ingredients, which may be very dangerous in themselves.

Cannabis (Marijuana/pot/grass/skunk/ganga)
Cannabis is made from the cannabis plant. It is usually smoked but may be mixed in cakes/biscuits or drunk in a tea. The main active chemical is tetrahydrocannabinol (THC). When cannabis is smoked the THC is rapidly absorbed into the blood system and quickly affects the brain. It changes peoples' senses and mood. It can make people feel relaxed and happy, but it can also cause anxiety and panic. It makes some people feel light headed or sick. It can affect concentration and decision making and in higher doses it can cause delusions. People who mix alcohol and cannabis are particularly likely to have accidents.

There are both physical and mental long-term effects from using cannabis. The main physical effect on younger people are lung problems with an increased probability of infections. Long-term use of cannabis has been linked to several mental illnesses including Schizophrenia and Depression. There are also concerns that using cannabis during the teenage years, when the brain is still developing, can alter the structure of the brain and cause ongoing problems with concentration, learning and decision making.

Cocaine (Coke/crack/snow/blow/freebase)
Cocaine is a powerful stimulant made from the coca plant. Some forms of cocaine can be inhaled, smoked, or injected, but the most common use is to snort it through the nose or rub it on the gums. Cocaine has a major effect on the brain and increases the level of dopamine leading to a high. It can lead to extreme happiness, energy and alertness, but can also lead to irritability and extreme distrust of others. Some people become arrogant, aggressive and can be violent. The highs produced by cocaine do not last very long and can be followed by a comedown which can last for some time. Cocaine raises the body temperature and the heart rate and large doses can cause heart attacks and strokes. Mixing cocaine with alcohol can significantly increase the effects. Cocaine also depresses the appetite. Long-term use of cocaine can lead to addiction associated with mental health problems, malnutrition and movement disorders.

Ecstasy (MDMA/Molly/E)
Ecstasy is a synthetic drug which is usually taken as a tablet or capsule and acts like a stimulant and a psychotic drug. Ecstasy increases the levels of dopamine, noradrenaline and serotonin in the brain. This can lead to a mental high and a feeling of increased energy with an exaggerated sense of awareness of the surroundings. It can also cause an increase in empathy and emotional closeness. However, some people can feel anxious, confused or panicky. The main short-term risks with ecstasy are caused by impure tablets and body problems caused by overheating and dehydration, which can prove fatal. The elevated feelings of love and empathy can also lead to unwise sexual activity. The high from ecstasy lasts several hours and users can overdose if they take further tablets to lengthen this

period. Following use, there is a comedown which can last for several days and involve irritability, depression and anxiety, as well as affecting memory and concentration. The effects of long-term ecstasy use are not well understood and there is some disagreement about whether it can become an addiction. However, it is believed that long-term use can affect memory and mood.

Glues/gases/aerosols

Sniffing these volatile substances usually has a depressant effect that slows down the brain and makes people feel drunk. They can make people dreamy and giggly, but can also cause mood swings and aggressive behaviour. They can severely affect judgement and cause dangerous behaviours. Sniffing these substances can also cause hallucinations, vomiting and blackouts and is very dangerous. This is the leading drug related cause of death among younger teenagers. It can cause heart attacks and may also cause death by choking and by the slowing down of the respiratory system. Although the drunken effects of sniffing these substances only lasts a few minutes, these dangerous reactions can occur both immediately or sometime later.

Nitrous Oxide (Laughing gas)

Breathing nitrous oxide has a depressant effect and slows down the brain and body. It can give feelings of calm and relaxation, but can also cause dizziness, headaches and hallucinations. Like glues, nitrous oxide affects judgement and can encourage risky behaviours. Too much nitrous oxide, especially in a confined space or when breathing from a bag, can cause blackouts due to lack of oxygen. Long term use can cause vitamin B deficiency and result in nerve damage.

LSD (Acid)

LSD is a synthetic drug that is a powerful hallucinogenic – that is, it creates a distorted view of reality. Colours, shapes and sounds can all be severely affected causing experiences which are very unpredictable. These may be pleasant or frightening. Judgement is severely impaired, and users may put themselves in danger. Longer term effects from LSD can include problems with flashbacks to the LSD experience and mental health problems.

Spotting the signs of drug taking in your teenager

As described above, there are a range of different drugs, which may all affect people in different ways. However, these are some of the physical signs that should raise suspicions:

Eyes that are bloodshot or pupils that are unusually large or small
Impaired co-ordination and unexplained injuries
Shaking and incoherent speech
Runny nose, nosebleeds or sores around mouth or nose
Deterioration in personal appearance and hygiene
Changes in appetite or weight
Unusual tiredness and lethargy
Extreme thirst
Sweating and headaches
Unexplained seizures
Burns on fingers or lips
Changes in sleep patterns
Nausea and vomiting

These are things you may notice around the house:

Missing money, alcohol or prescription drugs
Syringes, smoking pipes, balloons, rolling papers, lighters, straws, foil
Aerosols, gas containers, vials
Strange smells or strong smells of incense or perfume
Strange powders, plant seeds or stems
Plants growing (often under the bed)

Where possible parents should keep any prescribed drugs, volatile glues and aerosols locked away, where they cannot be accessed.

There are also likely to be significant changes in behaviour, although these may have other causes:

Deterioration in school performance, behaviour or attendance
Becoming more withdrawn and secretive
Becoming more defiant, angry and aggressive or more anxious and paranoid
Losing motivation and interest in hobbies/sport
Extreme highs and lows of mood
Lying, making excuses and becoming more deceitful
Problems with memory and concentration
Problems with relationships and changes of friends

If you notice any suspicious signs, you need to discuss the situation with your teenager to establish the cause. If drugs are involved, the earlier the problem can be addressed the better as the behaviour can become ingrained or even addictive.

Where to get help

It isn't helpful to blame yourself if your teenager is taking drugs. Issues with drugs are quite a widespread problem and occur for a whole host of reasons. The most important thing is to get it out into the open and the deal with it before it becomes an entrenched behaviour. Parents can talk to their GP or seek help from charities, local support groups or counsellors. (See below)

Useful organisations

Action on addiction – www.actiononaddiction.org.uk
Provides residential rehab and community-based addiction treatments.

Addaction – www.addaction.org.uk
Provides support for individuals, families and communities to manage the effects of drug and alcohol misuse.

ADFAM – www.adfam.org.uk
Information and advice for families of alcohol and drug users.

DrugFAM – www.drugfam.co.uk
Provide information and support to people affected by someone else's addiction. They have a helpline0300 888 3853

FRANK – www.talktofrank.com
Provides information and support on drug related issues and has a helpline 0300 123 6600. It has a database of support services by area.

Narcotics anonymous – www.ukna.org
A fellowship of men and women for whom drugs had become a major problem, who meet regularly to help each other stay clean.

Scottish families affected by drugs – www.sfad.org.uk
Provides support to families affected by drugs and has a directory of services and a helpline 08080 101011.

Turning point – www.turning-point.co.uk
Provide a wide range of support and services including rehab for those with problems, including drug and alcohol issues and their families.

References in this chapter
[1] Home Office: Drug misuse: Findings from the 2017/2018 crime survey for England and Wales
[2] NHS Smoking drinking and drug use among young people England 2016

Chapter 19

Eating problems and disorders

What are eating problems and disorders

Food and eating play a significant role in our lives and it is important that we eat a healthy balanced diet to sustain good mental and physical health. It is quite normal to think about what we are eating and why we are eating it, but our attitudes to food can become a problem, when they seem to dominate much of our time or when they cause significant weight gain or obesity. Obesity is becoming an increasing problem with young people and is the result of a range of factors including lack of exercise and overeating. The lack of exercise is often exacerbated by long hours spent on social media or computer games. The overeating is often just the result of poor dietary choices or large portion sizes, but can also be linked to psychological issues.

There is little detailed up to date research on the rates of eating disorders, but some detailed research in 2007 suggested that about 6% of the adult population show signs of problems with their relationship with food with around three times as many women exhibiting problems than men. Eating disorders often begin in childhood or adolescence and for younger adults these rates were roughly double with around 20% of young women and 6% of young men exhibiting problems and are thought to be rising. [1] In fact, these rates may well have increased since then, as hospital admissions for eating disorders nearly doubled in the last six years. [2] Very few of these people seek professional help and so it is perhaps not surprising

that the rates of diagnosed eating disorders are quite low and probably less than 5% in total.
Some common indications of eating problems are:

Thinking about food and eating a lot of the time.
Thinking about weight or body shape a lot of the time.
Eating in secret.
Feeling anxious about eating.
Feeling that eating is out of control.
Restricting how much is eaten.
Overeating for emotional not nutritional reasons.
Having very strict rules about the types of food that can be eaten.
Getting rid of food that has been eaten such as vomiting or taking laxatives (purging).
Doing extreme exercise (particularly males),but growing among females.

Eating problems become serious if the attitudes and behaviours associated with food significantly affect the ability to carry out everyday responsibilities at home or at work and to enjoy a normal social life. They can affect people of all ages, male and female, including overweight and underweight individuals.

What causes eating problems and disorders

Many eating problems are linked to coping with emotional issues rather than the food itself and some people with eating problems have other mental health disorders such as depression, self-harm or anxiety. There does not seem to be any single reason that causes eating problems. However, many people with eating problems exhibit some of the following personal characteristics:
low self-esteem
negative self-image
unrealistic expectations of self
obsessive, compulsive traits
very competitive
feeling a lack of control over life
struggling with puberty

Eating problems can arise at times of increased stress and transitions such as changing house or school, doing exams, bullying, abuse or family problems. They can also be exacerbated by social media pressures about body shapes and life styles.

Types of eating disorder and signs to look for

There are four main specific eating disorders, which are carefully defined for diagnosis purposes. However, many people with eating problems may not fit neatly into one or any of these categories. Research shows that the age group 15-19 has the highest rates of eating disorder, with anorexia being particularly prevalent. [3]

Anorexia Nervosa
Anorexia Nervosa is usually associated with extreme thinness and a fear of gaining weight. It is the least common disorder of the four main categories but is much more common among teenagers. It is much more common in females, but male rates are believed to be increasing. Although the thinness can be caused by physical illnesses, some typical signs that could indicate Anorexia Nervosa are:

Behaviour
    Pre-occupation with weight, body shape and food
    strict dieting
    missing meals
    hiding food
    distorted perception of body shape
    excessive exercising
    using laxatives or tablets to reduce weight
    social withdrawal
    sometimes binge eating and purging

Physical
    severe weight loss
    tiredness
    dizziness
    constipation

low body temperature and sensitivity to cold
irritability
concentration problems
poor circulation
thinning hair
growth of fine downy hair on face and body
females missing periods, males having low testosterone

Health implications
low blood pressure
slow heart rate
osteoporosis
dehydration
possibility of heart or kidney failure

These health implications are extremely dangerous, which is why early treatment is essential.

Binge Eating Disorder
Binge Eating Disorder is associated with excessive eating patterns as a way of dealing with emotional problems. It is the second most common of the four main categories and is roughly equally common among men and women. Some typical signs of Binge Eating disorder are:

Behaviour
regularly eating much more than the body needs even when not hungry
eating quickly in an uncontrolled manner
eating until uncomfortably full
eating alone or secretly
uncomfortable about attitude to food
feelings of shame or guilt

Physical
significant weight gain
breathlessness
poor skin condition

mobility problems caused by joint and muscle pains

Health implications
digestion problems
problems linked to excess weight such as diabetes and heart disease

Bulimia Nervosa

Bulimia Nervosa is usually associated with frequent binge eating, which may be a reaction to an emotional trigger, followed by compensatory behaviours such as purging, fasting or excessive exercise. It is the third most common of the four main categories. Some typical signs of Bulimia Nervosa are;

Behaviour
regularly binging
purging by vomiting after meals (may disappear to bathroom)
hoarding food
excessive exercise
abusing laxatives or tablets to help purge
concern about body shape

Physical
fluctuating weight
tiredness and sleep problems
constipation
irregular periods for women
poor skin condition

Health implications
dental problems caused by the vomiting
throat and mouth problems caused by the vomiting
dehydration
digestion and bowel problems
depletion of electrolytes which can result in heart failure

Other Specified Feeding or Eating Disorder (OSFED)
This description is applied when an eating disorder is diagnosed, but it does not fit into any of the above categories. It is the most common of the four main categories, although it covers a range of symptoms.

Other eating and body image disorders
There are many other eating and body image disorders including the following:

Emotional Overeating: This involves using food as a comfort and escape during periods of low mood, but may not involve large amounts of food.

Rumination disorder: This involves regurgitating food and then rechewing it or spitting it out.

Orthorexia: An obsession with eating healthy or pure food.

Pica: This involves eating substances that are not foods.

Avoidant/restrictive food intake disorder (ARFID): This involves avoiding some or all foods because the texture, smell or taste seem repulsive.

Body Dysmorphic Disorder: This is a pre-occupation with an imagined or minor physical defect.

Muscle Dysmorphia (Bigorexia): This is an obsession that the body is too small or not muscular enough.

How can I help to prevent eating disorders?

Although there are many causes of eating disorders there are a number of things that parents can do to try to minimise the likelihood of their children suffering from them:

Build self-esteem: Low self-esteem seems to be one of the most important factors in eating disorders. Parents need to explore all opportunities for improving the self-esteem of their teenagers. (See Chapter 10 Building Self-esteem and confidence)

Communication: Poor communication is another factor in eating disorders. Sufferers sometimes complain of not being listened to or having no control over their lives. (see Chapter 7 Getting communication right)

Food: Parents often make mistakes in the way that they treat their children at mealtimes and in their overall attitude to food. They should try not to
:
 frequently use food as a reward for good behaviour or as a consolation
 use food as a punishment
 force children to eat or finish a meal when they are not hungry

They should try to:
 establish a regular meal pattern
 encourage healthy foods
 encourage them to try new foods

Role model: Parents need to set a good example to their children by eating regular meals and not seeming to be obsessed by diets and by body shape. They should try not to use food themselves as a way of coping with emotional difficulties.

Parental expectations: Most parents are concerned about the academic performance of their teenagers, but some have particularly high expectations or have an expectation that their teenagers should pursue a particular career path. This can put undue pressure on their teenager and cause mental health problems.

What else can parents do to help?

Changing the behaviour of teenagers, who do have an eating disorder, is difficult and time-consuming as this is likely to have become an engrained behaviour for dealing with emotional problems. It allows them a mechanism for relieving distress and having some control over their lives. It is usually not helpful to try to demand changes in eating behaviour without addressing the underlying emotional difficulties. Parents should try to encourage their teenagers to talk about their problems, with a view to identifying what can be done to help. This begins with having a conversation with your teenager, and this can be filled with anger, hostility, denial and sadness. Rarely do these conversations go smoothly, so keep these thoughts in mind.

Get informed before you talk about your concerns with your child. Eating disorders are complex conditions that even the experts don't completely understand. Don't assume that you'll be able to learn everything there is to know about the disorders, but don't enter the conversation without doing at least a bit of homework. There are many websites and organisations that will bring you up to speed on the latest information and advice.

Ask, don't accuse. Explain what you have noticed that has raised your concerns and ask if you are right to be worried, check out with them whether they think there might be a problem, or if they have any questions. Its best to take an inquisitive approach, your child may well deny that there is any problem and may be angry and defiant. Even if they admit it, they may say that they have stopped and won't do it again. Even if they don't admit to the eating problem, at least you will have opened up a conversation.

Go slow. This might be one of many conversations you'll have with your teenager, and the aim is to get their trust so that you can both be open about your thoughts and feelings. You are not trying to prove that you are right, or that you know more than your teenager. This is a crucial time for you to display empathy because unless you too have experienced an eating disorder, you can only imagine what your child might be experiencing. It is important that sufferers do not just define themselves in terms of their disorder and that parents don't let the disorder dictate how they relate to them. The disorder is an illness, which needs to be treated as the enemy, not the sufferer. The important thing is that your child will take time to be persuaded of this too, as at present, they may see the illness more as a useful friend. This is only likely to happen by slowly building self-esteem, good communication, a change in attitude to food and finding alternative strategies for dealing with problems.

Don't criticise your child. Although parents will often blame themselves for their teenager's disorder, the causes are likely to be complex and involve many different issues. For this reason, you shouldn't blame your teenager either. Eating disorders, like any other illness, need to be treated with the same care and compassion as any other physical illness. If it were a broken leg, or migraines, you would not blame your child for having the illness, and an eating disorder should be treated with the same degree of comfort and understanding. Most young people with eating disorders have often spent months and sometimes years trying to deal with it themselves. They might have built up considerable frustration, shame and disappointment in themselves trying to do so. Let your teenager know that you will support their recovery in whatever way is needed. Stay calm and give unconditional love to your teenager in the face of a very difficult struggle.

Emphasise behaviour, not appearance. Eating disorders affect minds and not just bodies. Your child is worrying about how they look and might well have a distorted view of their body shape or size. Telling them how thin they are looking might be just what they are hoping to achieve through restriction of their diet. In your conversations, try not to comment about weight, body shape or eating. Try to concentrate on what they are actually doing, for example skipping meals, over exercising, feeling tired and lethargic during lessons at school, and discuss how addressing the eating disorder will change that. Meanwhile, maintain as normal a lifestyle as possible.

Keep paying attention and listen. Show your teenager that their views are important and that they can be in charge of their future. That means that good mental and physical health is within their own control. The fear of not being able to cope might make this message a frightening one, so its crucial that you reassure your teenager that you will be there every step of the way, that you value their opinions and will work alongside them to overcome their disorder and work towards recovery.

Take action. When your child is in the grips of an eating disorder, it can be difficult for them to see a way through it. Your goal is to try to understand the impact of the illness on their day to day life, and to work out what type of help they need. Once your child has started sharing their thoughts and feelings with you, you will have a better idea, but you might still need help yourself to work out the quickest and best routes into support services. You could start with your GP, the school counsellor or school nurse, or refer to one of the organisations listed below. But what is important is that you don't just leave it and hope that it will sort itself out without you doing anything. It rarely happens that way.

Talking to your teenager about their eating disorder might not be easy, but not doing so can be far worse. Though they can be devastating, eating disorders can also be overcome. Dealing with an eating disorder in the family is very stressful for the whole family and you may need to find your own support mechanisms.

How are eating disorders treated?

The GP will normally carry out physical and emotional assessments. These may result in a diagnosis or referral to a specialist mental health service such as CAMHS. Once a diagnosis is obtained, each type of eating disorder is treated differently as outlined below. For other specified feeding or eating disorders, the treatment is based on the closeness of characteristics to the other three main disorders. Medications are not usually used for eating disorders unless there is another associated mental health disorder. Talking therapies are successful in more than half of cases but can take a long time.

Anorexia Nervosa

Self-help: Joining a self-help group can be useful in conjunction with other treatments.

Dietary advice: Sufferers will probably be given advice on healthy eating and vitamin and mineral supplements.

Family therapy: Several sessions will be undertaken with a therapist, either individually or as a family, to explore how the anorexia is affecting the young person and to find ways for the family to support them. The sessions should include nutrition and meal planning and will also seek to find better ways to manage emotional problems, to maintain healthy eating and to avoid relapses.

Psychotherapy: A planned number of sessions will be scheduled with a therapist to understand how the problem started, and to change the ways the sufferer thinks about themselves, their weight and healthy eating.

Hospital admission: This may be an option if the sufferer has lost so much weight that it is a serious threat to their health.

Compulsory treatment: This only happens if the sufferer is so unwell that their life or health is in danger or they cannot make proper decisions for themselves.

Bulimia Nervosa

Self-help: Joining a self-help group can be useful in conjunction with other treatments and there are many books and other self-help resources available.

Dietary advice: Advice is often given to encourage a regular eating pattern without purging.

Oral care: Advice about minimizing the damage done by vomiting should be offered.

Family therapy: Sessions will be undertaken with a therapist, either individually or as a family, to explore how the bulimia is affecting the sufferer and find ways for the family to support them. The sessions should include information about healthy weight control and regular eating and explain the adverse effects of vomiting, abuse of laxatives or excessive exercise.

Psychotherapy: A therapist will offer support to help understand the role the bulimia plays in the sufferer's life and to change the ways the young person deals with emotional problems.

Binge Eating Disorder

Self Help: People who are suffering from Binge Eating Disorder are usually directed mainly towards self-help programmes.

Psychotherapy: Group sessions may be undertaken with a therapist to support the self-help programme or to help planning and monitoring of meals. Sessions may also try to identify triggers that may provoke the binge eating behaviour and explore other ways of dealing with them.

Useful organisations

Anorexia and Bulimia Care (ABC) – www.anorexiabulimiacare.org.uk
Provide support and guidance to anyone affected by eating disorders. They have a helpline 03000 111213

B-eat – www.b-eat.co.uk
Provide support and guidance to anyone affected by eating disorders. They have a helpline 0808 801 067

Childline – www.childline.org.uk
Provides a free and confidential telephone service for children. They have a helpline: 0800 1111.

Eating Disorders Support – www.eatingdisordersupport.co.uk
Provides information about eating disorders.

Family lives – www.familylives.org.uk
Helps parents deal with changes in family life. They also offer a free helpline at 0808 800 2222.

Men Get Eating Disorders Too – www.mengetedstoo.co.uk
Supports men with eating disorders and their families.

Mind – www.mind.org.uk/Anxiety
Provides information and support on a variety of mental health issues and has an information helpline 0300 123 3393.

NHS Choices – www.nhs.uk/conditions/eating-disorders
Provides information on eating disorders and how to get help.

Overcoming – www.overcoming.co.uk
This website has information on self-help guides you can buy for a range of different conditions. They are not free resources. You can buy the books direct or you may able to get some of the books second hand on auction sites.

Overeaters Anonymous GB – www.oagb.org.uk
Provide group sessions for overeaters.

Rethink mental illness – www.rethink.org
Provide advice and information to anyone affected by mental illness and have over a hundred support groups.

SANE – www.sane.org.uk
Provides information and support to people affected by mental illness. They have a mental health helpline called SANELINE at 0300 304 7000.

The Mix – www.themix.org.uk
Supports under 25s on a wide range of issues including anxiety.

YoungMinds – youngminds.org.uk
Provides information and advice on children's mental health issues and a parents helpline:0808 802 5544

References in this chapter

[1] NHS: Adult Psychiatric morbidity in England, 2007, Results of a household survey
[2] NHS: Finished admission episodes with a primary or secondary diagnosis for eating disorder 2010 - 2017
[3] Micali, N, Hagberg, KW, Petersen, I, Treasure, JL. The incidence of eating disorders in the UK in 2000–2009: findings from the General Practice Research Database. BMJ Open 2013; 3: e002646

Chapter 20

Examinations

Sitting examinations is always stressful and sitting national public examinations is particularly stressful as these examinations are viewed as critical pathways to future study and careers.

This stress and anxiety of exams is not something that will be just felt by your teenager but is likely to affect your whole family. As parents, you have a vital role to play in moderating the worst of the effects of the exam stress by making sure that your teenager is not constantly bombarded or overwhelmed by pressure. When you help to anticipate and respond to these pressures before they build up and affect your teenager, you will be providing valuable and necessary support.

This takes a good deal of energy, time and patience and you'll need to be well prepared in advance, if you are to help your children to do the very best they can and achieve their potential. It can only be made possible by adopting a collaborative approach that includes you, your teenager and their school or college. You can't hope to be fully knowledgeable or an expert in every subject that your teenager is studying, and you may not be a teacher. You just need to know how best to spend your time, in order to support and motivate your child.

The advice, contained below, aims to help you identify the key issues that may affect your children. This will make both your own and your child's lives easier. Being prepared is the key strategy to feeling in control, and a wide range of suggestions is outlined below.

During the period of studying for an exam

Ensure good attendance and punctuality
Leave teaching to the experts but ensure that your child attends school every single day, on time, so that they don't miss any vital piece of information that might make it all come together or that might be tested in the examination. If children have unavoidable absence, however long, try to ensure that the school provides details of all the work that is being missed. Good attendance is one of the key factors in achieving good examination results.

Check that classwork and homework is being completed to a good standard and understood
Many teenagers cut corners with classwork and homework in the belief that they can catch it all up later, when they do their revision, but in reality, work that is not completed, or is not understood during the course leads to substantial gaps in knowledge, which are very difficult to rectify. Encourage your teenager to make the best use of study time by taking notes, participating fully and sorting out any subject areas, which they find difficult. If they are embarrassed to do this during lessons, they should talk to their teachers later.

Teenagers will often tell you that they have no homework or that the homework is "just revision". In fact, it is quite unlikely that they will not have homework in every subject as they near public examinations. If the homework is revision, it is important to make the best use of this time and not use it as an excuse to do very little. It is important that your teenager has a structured approach and knows exactly what it is that they are expected to be revising. Evidence suggests that those students who start early and chip away at revision, do not find the exams such an ordeal. [1] This 'little and often' approach strengthens their memory and steers young people away from the anxiety of leaving their revision until the last minute.

Use mock examinations as a rehearsal for the real thing

Mock examinations or practice runs are usually held by schools in December or January to see how students are progressing. It is important that your child and you see this as a proper rehearsal for the actual examinations. Even though students may not have fully finished the course, they need to treat these examinations very seriously and to achieve the absolute best results that they can. Parents should also try to use this time as a way of implementing some of the advice given below. If students revise as well as they can and do their best, they will get an accurate reflection of their current level of achievement in each subject. This will tell them whether they are on course to achieve their expected or hoped for results or not. If your child's results are disappointing, they will need to talk to their teachers and you are also likely to wish to do so. Use the mock results to decide on whether your child needs to adapt their priorities and their revision strategies to improve their performance. Make sure you and your teenager are fully aware of any special classes or help that is available in schools in this crucial run-up period.

Before the main revision period begins

Don't burden teenagers with parental expectations

Whether you intend to or not, there is a risk that you might burden your child with your own hopes and expectations for their future. If they are conscientious students, they have enough to deal with in coping with their own hopes and expectations. If they don't seem to be applying themselves, try to understand what they want to do in the future and encourage them to make efforts to achieve it, even if it is not the future that you have envisaged.

Decide priorities

Discuss and set priorities with your teenager. No one can please everyone all the time or do everything that others expect of them.

Time management is crucial. During the revision period some activities that they normally do, or are expected to do, may need to be dropped. It is also important to prioritise efforts between revision in different subjects. This will depend on how well your child is currently doing in each subject and which pathway they want to follow in the next year.

Create a revision schedule

Help your teenager to create a revision timetable, bearing in mind the priorities agreed above and the actual examination timetable. To be most effective, it is far better if it is created by your teenager, supported, but not imposed, by you. Working continuously for hours on end and seven days a week is not realistic and will cause mental fatigue and stress. Ideally, there should be a break every hour or so, and it helps to build in as much variety as possible. Working late at night should be avoided. Although there is likely to be less time for leisure than normal, it is still necessary to achieve a balance between work and play.

It is useful to put the schedule up on a wall so that everyone knows it, and adapt it as time goes by, depending on the progress being made in each subject.

Know the examination timetable

It is surprising how many teenagers turn up at the wrong time, or on the wrong day, for examinations. If an examination is missed, it may be a whole year before it can be sat again. Make time to go through all examination documentation with your teenager and make sure that you both have an accurate examination timetable. It is useful to put it up on a wall at home and it can be very useful for everyone to have a copy on their phones calendar. Parents should ensure that no family holidays or important events clash with the examinations.

During the revision period

Create a dedicated work space

Create a dedicated and peaceful space for revision to take place. It is better if this is not the bedroom as this should be kept as a place to relax and sleep, and instead becomes a reminder of what work needs to be done, causing stress and insomnia. It can also become a hiding place with many distractions from work. Even if space is short in the main body of the house or flat, look for possibilities where your child can work peacefully and where you can keep an eye out, encourage rest breaks and offer support when appropriate.

Make sure that they have all the equipment and books that they need

Check that your teenager has all the books, pens, pencils and equipment that they need. If a calculator is required, it is important that it is the correct specification for the course and that your teenager has plenty of practice using it before the examination.

Liaise with the school

Find out if any additional revision sessions are being offered by the school and ask teachers for help on any subjects your child is finding difficult or doesn't understand. A good external tutor can be useful, but make sure that any tutors are keeping to your child's curriculum and exam board subject requirements This might be an option if your child is struggling, but do talk to their subject teacher first, as tutors tend to be costly and of limited value if your teenager fails to engage. Some schools and organisations run internal exam 'boot camps' on particular subjects for free so do check what is available first.

Help them to find the best way of learning and memorising

Allow your child to decide what methods work best for their learning. Sometimes working in pairs with a friend testing each other, working in small groups or listening to quiet background music can help them concentrate better, even if it is hard to imagine! Do encourage the use of a variety of revision techniques i.e. mind maps, brief notes, pictures, spider diagrams, recordings and offer help if it is needed. Studies show that learning through the senses helps information to stick. Just reading things through doesn't always work!

Past papers are a great way of practising for examinations to establish strengths and weaknesses, so encourage your teenager to treat these like a mock examination and do them in as close to examination conditions as possible i.e. at a table, timed, silent, with all of the appropriate equipment.

Nurture their body and mind

Make sure your teenager eats properly and drinks plenty of water. The brain works better when the body is properly fed and watered, and dehydration can cause headaches and loss of ability to focus! Avoid high sugar and high carbohydrate snacks, although these raise energy levels in the first instance they quickly get absorbed by the body, they are often followed by an energy slump and a desire to sleep!

Encourage good sleep patterns

Good sleep is a very important way to combat stress. This is the time when our brains process all the information taken in during the day and organises or makes sense of it. Don't let your teenager work too late and encourage a winding down period of an hour or so before bedtime doing something to help themselves relax.

Use of electronic gadgets during this period should be discouraged and access to them should be stopped altogether overnight. Studies have found that the light from our devices is "short-wavelength-enriched," meaning it has a higher concentration of blue light than natural light—and blue light affects levels of the sleep-inducing hormone melatonin more than any other wavelength. Blue wavelengths suppress delta brainwaves, which induce sleep, and boost alpha wavelengths, which create alertness, so use dim red lights for night lights. Red light has the least power to shift circadian rhythm and suppress melatonin. Although difficult to impose, make a general rule in your household to avoid looking at bright screens beginning one to two hours before bed.

Try to discourage your teenager from using their bed as a workstation. It is better for sleep if the bed is thought of as much as possible as the place set aside for just sleeping.

Encourage some leisure and relaxation activities

Some teenagers sleep a lot and can often be seen relaxed to the point of stop! This can change during the exam period and you might need to encourage your teenager to find ways to relax. The stress hormones affect not only our mood, but also how we feel physically. Exercise is a great way to "burn off" some of this stress. Sport, running, swimming and dancing are all good exercise, but even more moderate exercise like walking, preferably in a relaxing environment, is very helpful.

If your child doesn't like physical activity, try to find another activity that they find relaxing such as listening to or making music, something creative in arts and crafts, hair or nails treatment, watching a film. As the aim is to get the very best out of your child. don't be afraid to use particular leisure activities as a reward or as an incentive to encourage your teenager to work conscientiously.

For some teenagers, "relaxing" may mean playing a computer game or using social media. This is fine in moderation, but other teenagers using social media can create a feeling of mass anxiety when sharing exam concerns, creating a huge amount of stress for one another. If your teenager is getting very anxious, breathing or physical exercises can help. (See Chapter 13 Anxiety and panic)

Plan for all examination outcomes

Discuss together what different outcomes in the examinations would mean for the future. It's very stressful to only think about results as a success or failure. In practice, there may be a whole range of results, so it's useful to have some contingencies in place to deal with them.

Be prepared for meltdowns

Be prepared for your teenager to have meltdowns throughout the examination period. You may hear comments that come from panic like, "Nothing is going in", "I can't remember anything- I'm going to fail" "I'll never pass" "I hate this subject". Talk about the subject and ask questions. Get your teenager talking and explaining the subject. Hopefully, they'll soon realise that they know much more than they realise. Always try to focus on what they do know and not constantly looking at what they don't!

During the examination period

Reassure them that they will be loved whatever happens

Probably the most important message is for you to let your teenager know that you love them before the exams start and will love them afterwards just as much, whatever happens. This kind of reassurance will act as a stabiliser for your teenager and lets them know in no uncertain terms what really matters in life.

Create something to look forward to after the examinations

Giving your teenager something to look forward to can be a huge motivator. The promise of a reward as soon as the exams finish and before the results are announced- just to recognise their effort and commitment to the process will give them something to hold on to and work towards.

Put up with the chaos

Try to relax the helping-round-the-house rules at exam time and put up with the chaos of books and notes littered around the house or dinner table. If your teenager is revising around you, it gives you the opportunity for talking about subjects that are difficult to understand and provides a chance for you to be available to help them with revision or simply to encourage them.

Monitor your teenager's emotional wellbeing

Talk regularly together about how they are feeling, but don't nag them. Do explain that anxiety about examinations is typical and that anxiety, when well-managed, can actually make us perform better. If they are having problems, discuss ways of dealing with them. Look out for signs of stress, particularly if your teenager has struggled with stress or anxiety in the past, but even if they have not. These may include changes in their normal behaviour such as:

Lots of headaches or stomach pains
Changes in sleep patterns
Changes in mood or low spirits
Changes in appetite
Problems concentrating or focusing on issues

If they do seem to be showing changes in their behaviour that are probably caused by stress, be prepared to seek help. Remind them that although examinations are important, they are only one part of our lives and are not worth risking our mental health for. (See Chapter 13 about anxiety)

Be patient

No matter how sensitive and encouraging you try to be, with emotions running high and frayed nerves, don't be surprised if whatever you say is the wrong thing and appears to irritate and annoy your teenager. Accept it, stay calm and put up with the moods and slamming of doors. It will hopefully all be over after the examination. Acting out in this way is often a sign of their failure to cope with the increased stress of the moment, and sometimes your fear that they will not do well. Talk about it when the situation is calm and agree boundaries.

On examination days

Before the examination

Your support on examination days is vital. Your teenager needs to get up on time, dress in school uniform if required, have a sensible breakfast and get to the exam centre in good time before the exam is due to start, making sure they have all the things they need. It is very useful to work together and create a brief checklist of whatever they need to take: clear see-through water bottle and pencil case, black pens and sharpened pencils, an eraser and a ruler, calculator and protractor - the list is not exhaustive! Remind them to put their mobile phone or smart watch or any other electronic device into their lockers before the exam or remind them to switch them off and hand them in. The penalties can be severe for breach of exam rules!

After the examination

When they come home, ask how the examination went. If the exam went well, relax and celebrate, talk about what they were especially pleased about. If it didn't go well, remind them that it is now over and done with and if it was the last paper of the course, they won't have to worry about it again. If they have a second or third paper in that subject, they still have an opportunity and time to recover the situation. Post mortems are rarely helpful, the message is that it is over and done with, move on and concentrate on the future. Marking off the exams on a list as they are completed, is a tangible sign that the end is in sight!

Results day

Results day is likely to be a very emotional day whether things go well or not. If the results are good, be prepared to celebrate, as it is a sign of your teenager's hard work, application and achievement. If the results are less than expected, you will need to demonstrate a positive approach and show your teenager that all is not lost. No matter how disappointed, anxious and worried you are, your modelling of coping is being observed by your teenager and your approach should give the message that 'when one door closes, another opens'. Hopefully, you will have discussed the various outcomes in advance and will have given serious consideration to the best route forward. You might even have agreed on a contingency plan.

Appeals against results are possible, but these are not often successful and can take some time. In the meantime, it is best to proceed on the assumption that the results will not change. Try to discuss options with the school as soon as possible and preferably on the day, if your teenager is in a fit state to think rationally. If an application to a college or university is involved, contact them as soon as possible to find out whether the results are acceptable. If not look for other similar courses with lower entrance requirements or think about another type of course.

Teenagers will face many disappointments in their lives and how they negotiate the early ones is important. They need to think positively, develop a plan, dust themselves off and move forward!

Coursework and revision

There are many sites on the internet that can help in producing coursework and in revising for the examinations, there are also apps. For coursework, it is important that the information is only used as a guide and not copied. Some of the sites like BBC Bitesize are free, but many require a subscription to access the full service.

Useful websites

Exam boards
Assessment and Qualifications Alliance (AQA) - **www.aqa.org.uk**
Council for the Curriculum, Examinations & Assessment (CCEA) - **www.ccea.org.uk**
Oxford, Cambridge and RSA Examinations (OCR) - **www.ocr.org.uk**
Pearson (Edexcel, BTEC) - **https://qualifications.pearson.com**
Scottish Qualifications Authority (SQA) - **www.sqa.org.uk**
Welsh Joint Education Committee (WJEC) - **www.wjec.co.uk**

Careers Advice

Careers Service Northern Ireland –
www.nidirect.gov.uk/campaigns/careers
Careers Wales – **www.careerswales.com**
My World Of Work (Scotland) – **www.myworldofwork.co.uk**
National Careers Service (England) –
https://nationalcareersservice.direct.gov.uk
Careersbox (Videos about careers) - **www.Careersbox.co.uk**
Icould Charity - **www.icould.com**
Apprenticeships - **www.apprenticeships.org.uk**
Future Morph (STEM careers) –
www.stem.org.uk/resources/collection/3338/future-morph

References in this chapter

[1] Kornell, Nate & Bjork, Robert. (2008). Learning Concepts and Categories Is Spacing the "Enemy of Induction"?. Psychological science. 19. 585-92. 10.1111/j.1467-9280.2008.02127

Chapter 21

Friendships, relationships and sex

The importance of friendship

Friendship groups are very important to teenagers. They give them a sense of belonging and security during a difficult period of change and hopefully a safe environment in which to build on their experiences and develop their personality. Teenagers will often change their close friendship groups over time as their interests change and as their maturity develops. This is quite normal but may cause some upset as friends "drop" each other or move on to new best friends.

Teenagers need to develop their social skills and it is important that their role models show them warm, supportive relationships both within and outside the family. Some teenagers find making friends very difficult and they may need help. Try to encourage them to be part of as many group situations as possible such as sports teams, clubs, church or school activities. Try to find their talents and strengths and encourage them.

As they progress through their teenage years, many teenagers spend more and more time with their friends and less and less time with family. This is typical, and a very important part of growing up, so try not to feel "left out" or side-lined.

You might worry about your teenager's choice of friends. Especially if you consider them to be a "bad influence" and someone who might lead your teenager into irresponsible or illegal behaviour.

This is an understandable concern and you can try to address this in three ways:

Model responsible and ethical behaviour yourself (See Chapter 6 The parent's roles and responsibilities)

Talk about the risks and consequences of irresponsible behaviour

Prepare your teenager to resist peer pressure (See Chapter 29 Peer Pressure)

It is perhaps just as important to explain to your teenager how to deal with those relationships which may seriously undermine their self-esteem and confidence and how to create and maintain "good" friendships, that will enhance their happiness by boosting and supporting them.

In general, there are two sorts of relationships that can be particularly harmful. The first is bullying or abuse, which can come from any person with whom your child is in contact. It may be a relative, a neighbour or more likely someone at school or at a club. The second is from "toxic" friendships. These are "friends" or partners, who undermine and demean us for their own purposes. When considering friendships, your teenager should be encouraged to ask "Do they care about my happiness?". Being good friends is a two-way process and people can only truly be good friends if they both care about the other person's happiness. We will consider what makes good friendships in more depth later in this chapter.

In life we meet vast numbers of people and most of them will not really care about our happiness or our child's happiness and we will not really care about theirs or their childrens' happiness. This is usual. No-one can be good friends with everybody, as proper friendship is an intense relationship. Of course, we should treat everybody politely and with respect and expect the same from them, but most of us live independent lives and our relationships with most people are quite detached. Our message to our teenager is that we should never write anybody off, as sometimes good friendships develop over time from the most unexpected places or from relationships which begin as quite distant. However, they will need to look out for anybody who appears to want them to be unhappy. These are enemies and your teenager should avoid or ignore these people. Sometimes, because of lack of experience, and a desire to fit in, teenagers find it difficult to really work out another person's motives, especially if they are determined to invade your teenager's space. It takes practice to recognise the ways in which they are trying to inflict hurt, so enemies can easily become bullies, with our child on the receiving end. (See Chapter 15 for more on Bullying)

What to expect and give as a "good" friend

One of the main secrets of happiness is to have at least one and hopefully several good friends. Good friends not only care about each other's happiness, but they have a deep liking for one another based on shared values, interests or personality traits. They generally have a good understanding of each other and are accepting of the other person even with their faults. They trust each other sufficiently to reveal personal information that may make them vulnerable, but respect each other's right to privacy. They complement each other and try to boost each other's self-esteem and confidence. They are prepared to be critical, but only in a constructive way with advice or information that they think will help the other person. Good friends should feel that they are on the same team and watching each other's backs. They support each other both in private and in public with other people.

We often have many people whom we describe as friends because we have known them a long time or they are part of the same group as us, but many of these do not really meet the description of good friends. It is also important to remember that sometimes our old good friends stop fulfilling this role because something has changed in their or our lives. Sometimes this is just because of the way that we feel. Our instincts may make us suspicious about them or find it difficult to make an emotional connection. If that is the case, we can decide to keep them at an emotional distance or to try to get to know them a bit better to make a final decision. We may also have "friends" with whom the relationship is one sided, where we seem to do all the giving and get very little in return. These are friends we probably can do without. Finally, we may have "friends", who hurt us in various ways. They may mock us or demean us either personally or in public. They may find fault with us at every opportunity without ever giving us constructive advice. They may deliberately exclude us from certain activities. They may betray our confidences or gossip about us behind our back. These are all forms of "toxic" behaviour which if left to continue will lower our self-esteem, confidence and happiness. Teenagers may need advice on dealing with these situations.

If they are not people that the teenager must have contact with, then they should be avoided altogether. If they cannot be avoided, teenagers should be encouraged to assertively challenge the behaviour and say how hurtful it is. Sometimes the person involved simply may not realise what they are doing and may be prepared to amend their behaviour. In any case, the teenager should minimise their contact and make sure that the person concerned does not have access to their most personal information.

Some friendships will be more intense, and this is the age when our teenager might be more physically attracted to their peers. This is a difficult time for teenagers, navigating the world of sex and love, but also a hugely challenging time for parents too. Accepting your child will go on to have a sexual relationship requires a massive adjustment, especially if the evidence of emotional and practical maturity is not always evident at home.

Teenagers and the development of sexuality

In early adolescence, young people begin to physically mature as puberty starts and they will become increasingly interested in sexual topics. Puberty is an exciting time that challenges both us and our children to deal with the physical, mental, and emotional changes that happen between the ages of about 10 and 14.

Girls will begin breast development, have vaginal secretions and will most likely have their first menstrual period. In the first few years of menstruating, periods are often irregular, and might cause abdominal cramping, and their budding breasts can be tender. Some teenage girls can become embarrassed as their new shape starts to attract male attention. This is also a highly charged time as your daughter adjusts to the hormonal changes, and they might also be affected by pre-menstrual tension and fluctuating emotions. You can reassure your daughter by talking about your own experiences at the same age and can broaden the discussion to talk about the positive and pleasurable aspects of maturing. Part of the conversation can be about the sexual feelings that often come around this age, and how these feelings can be managed.

Boys will usually experience their first wet dreams during puberty, and need to be reassured that these are normal, they are also likely to experience more and more erections. These might be associated with sexual arousal or may just occur spontaneously causing embarrassment and confusion. as are the thoughts that accompany them. Conversations with our teenagers about the difference between fantasy and reality can flow naturally from this discussion, and we can provide anticipatory guidance about what might happen in real life when they begin dating.

As they get a little older, they are likely to begin to look for romantic relationships and to experiment with flirting and with physical contact, such as hugging, stroking and kissing. In recent years we have started referring to this as 'skin hunger'- the need to be touched, held, or caressed. This pleasurable aspect of sexuality is critical to normal and healthy development. Young people need to hear from us, the caring adults in their lives, about the pleasure as well as the responsibility of sexuality. Over half of 15 year olds report having been in love and more than two thirds say that they have been in a relationship.[1] Many of them will sooner or later go on to have sex.

Although it is very difficult to obtain accurate information on the level of teenagers having sex, research suggests that the average age for teenagers to have their first sexual encounter is 16 with about 20-30 per cent having sex before then. [2]

Where teenagers learn about sex

Research suggests that teenagers hear most about sex at school usually from their friends, with their parents playing only a small role in information giving, and that when parents do talk about sex, it is mostly between mothers and daughters.[3] The media is playing an ever more important role with pornography also becoming much more prevalent, particularly among teenage boys. Teenagers say that the images portrayed in the media put them under pressure to conform to body images and behave in ways that put them under stress. The girls are worried by the sexualised images used, particularly in the music industry, and many girls and some boys are worried by the pornography that is available. (See Chapter 27 for more on pornography).

There is a feeling that although pornography makes people more open minded about sex, it encourages casual sex with multiple partners and with a variety of sexual activities that not everyone is happy to perform or be expected by others to perform. It downplays the importance of relationships and emotional connection and may involve abuse or disrespect of individuals.

Teenagers, in general, feel that although schools fulfil their role in providing biological information, they still need more information about the emotional and relationship side of sex. This is where parents have an important role, and although it is unlikely that most teenagers will ask their parents about the physical aspects of sex, they may ask about pregnancy, contraception and sexually transmitted diseases. Teenagers will also be keen to sound you out on your views and attitudes, and you have an important function both in role modelling loving relationships, and in discussing what teenagers should expect from their own intimate relationships. It is also very important that teenagers believe that they can talk freely to their parents without instant criticism or judgement.

Discussing sex and intimate relationships with teenagers

When teenagers reach this stage of their development, you should be looking for opportunities to discuss relationships. You don't want to wait for them to become sexually active, so start those conversations as soon as you notice them becoming interested in sex, or as soon as puberty begins. Films, television and news stories can all provide opportunities to raise some issues about how people behave, what is right or wrong, and what are the possible consequences of poor decision making. You can discuss what makes a good friend and this discussion could extend into what makes a good partner. Remind your teenager how to resist peer pressure. Good relationships are initially based on mutual attraction but will only survive if there is a shared closeness and bonding and a commitment on both sides. Good partners should be listening, supportive and should boost your teenager's self-esteem. Teenagers might need help in recognising what makes a great partner.

In a relationship a great partner would:

Respect their wishes and how they feel.
Accept them refusing to do things or changing their mind
Make them feel comfortable about their looks and personality
Make them feel safe
Be prepared to compromise and resolve arguments by talking
Be prepared to admit mistakes
Be prepared to give as well as to take

They wouldn't:

Ask your teenager to do anything with them or others that makes your teen feel uncomfortable
Pressurise or force them to do anything against their will or that is illegal
Hit or hurt them deliberately
Threaten to or share their personal secrets with others either verbally or online
Bully or abuse them to get their own way

Be jealous or possessive
Try to control what they wear or how they behave
Be angry with them much of the time

Teenagers should be warned that even the best relationships have their ups and downs and that they all need work to maintain them. Often, when your young person is having a bad time with a friend or partner, they might choose to talk to you. Beware!

Putting your teenager's potential partner down, rarely works, and forbidding them to continue seeing someone is a red rag. Imagine what you would have said if your parents refused permission for you to see one of your friends! But you can have a conversation, or several, where you explore together what sort of personal characteristics they think a partner should have. These might include things like being honest, trustworthy, caring, reliable, funny. All good relationships are based on good communication and being able to talk things through.

Today, social media plays an increasingly important role in many relationships. It is important for teenagers not to use social media in ways that make their partner uncomfortable by not respecting their privacy or asking them to do something that they should not (including sexting). It is also important to recognise that while difficult conversations, or even breaking up, may seem easier by social media, face to face conversations are less easily misunderstood and more empathetic. Encourage your teenager to be honourable, to end one relationship before starting another, and to always show respect when they choose to leave a relationship by speaking directly with their partner. Although it's difficult when break up's end badly, advise them not to speak negatively about their ex to their friends.

You will also need to make your teenagers aware of the law regarding teenage sex.

Teenagers, sex and UK Law

It is useful to outline the law in the UK, although there are some differences between the different countries. The age of consent is 16, and teenagers of 16 or over are legally allowed to engage in whatever form of sex they wish, with whomever they wish providing both parties consent. We will discuss what consent means in depth a little later. Teenagers of 13 to 15 are technically committing a crime if they have sex, but the guidance suggests that they will not be prosecuted if they are of a similar age and both consenting. Anyone having sex with a child under 13 will be prosecuted. If people are prosecuted they are likely to be charged with rape (men only), sexual or indecent assault. If found guilty they could face a prison sentence and be placed on the Violent and Sex Offenders Register.

It is also worth noting that it is an offence to take, share, distribute or show indecent images of anybody under 18, even if it was done with consent. Indecent images may include naked pictures, topless pictures of girls, pictures of genitalia, pictures of sex acts or even sexual pictures in underwear. These are offences under the Protection of Children Act and can result in a prison sentence. However, since January 2016, the police have said that they will treat sexting by children primarily as a safeguarding issue and may decide to take no further action if they think that this is in the public interest.

Gillick Competency

Teenagers under 16 can be given contraceptives and obtain confidential advice by health professionals to protect their health and wellbeing either with or without their parent's consent, provided they are believed to have enough intelligence, competence and understanding to fully appreciate what is involved in their treatment. It is the responsibility of the health professional providing the advice to assess and ensure that the teenager is what is know as Gillick Competent.

Consenting to sex

A person consenting to sex does not actually have to say that they are agreeing to sex, but must behave in a way that is consistent with agreeing. To consent, they must have freedom and capacity. Freedom means that they are not being unreasonably coerced or pressurised in any way. Capacity means that they are fully aware of what they are doing. If they are under the influence of alcohol or drugs, they may not be able to give consent, nor can they give it if they are not fully conscious. Similarly, the person who believes that they have given consent, must be capable of a reasonable belief that they had consent. Again, if that person is under the influence of alcohol or drugs they may not be capable of exercising reasonable judgement.

Explain to your teenager that the general rule should be not to have sex with someone while either person has been drinking or taking drugs, and that it is far better for both parties to say exactly what they want or don't want with the proviso that they can both change their minds at any time.

Whether or not you believe that your teenager is sexually active, you need to give them information about the physical risks of sex relating to pregnancy and sexually transmitted infections. You aren't expected to be an expert here but do find out where your nearest Contraceptive or Sexual Health Clinic is and advise your teenager to obtain contraceptive advice from health professionals, whilst also encouraging them to use safe sex methods.

Healthcare services for teenagers provided by contraception clinics

Contraception clinics offer of the range of services and can provide:
Confidential advice about contraception
The combined oral contraceptive pill
The progesterone-only pill
Progesterone contraceptive injections
Insertion or removal of the contraceptive implant
Limited supplies of free condoms
Free emergency contraception

Confidential advice about Sexually Transmitted Infections (STIs) and STI testing
Cervical screening
Unplanned pregnancy advice
Free pregnancy tests
Pre-contraception (pre-pregnancy) advice and information on fertility problems
Fitting and checking of caps, diaphragms, IUDs (intrauterine devices, or coils) and IUSs (intrauterine systems, or hormonal coils)

Some contraception clinic may also offer specialist services, including:

Counselling for incest, rape and sexual abuse
Pre-abortion and post-abortion counselling and referral
Well women screening

Teenage pregnancy
The rates of teenage pregnancy in the UK have fallen dramatically over the last forty years and this decline has continued recently. In 2016 there were 18,076 conceptions to women aged under 18 in England and Wales – the lowest number ever recorded. [4] There are a number of reasons for this, including more sex education in schools, teenage girls becoming more focused on education and less young role models in the media becoming pregnant.

Research suggests that fewer younger teenagers are having sex although the rates for older teenagers are high. However, one of the major reasons is likely to be a wider availability of contraceptive advice and contraceptives including some long-lasting options. Society in general, and many parents as well, now recognise that many teenagers will have sex and contraception is the only way to stop unwanted pregnancies and safe sex is needed to prevent sexually transmitted infections.

Sexually transmitted infections (STIs)

Around 80% of 15year olds claim to have used contraception when they had intercourse with about 60% of these using condoms. The rate of condom use appears to be falling with perhaps more reliance on female contraceptive methods. This may be an adequate protection against pregnancy but may leave young people more vulnerable to STIs. Young people are more likely to be diagnosed with an STI than any other age group. In 2017, under 24year-olds accounted for 63% of those with chlamydia, 37% with gonorrhoea, 51% with genital warts, and 40% with genital herpes (English figures). [5] Although under 24year-olds only account for about 12% of new HIV diagnoses, infection can occur many years before a diagnosis is made.

It is important that teenagers know about STIs, whether they are told by you, their parents, schools or someone else. As outlined below STIs. are not always curable, but it is crucial that teenagers know if they have them or not, so that they can receive the appropriate treatment and not pass them on to anyone else.

Chlamydia is the most common STI in the UK and is particularly prevalent among sexually active young people. It is a bacterial infection that can be passed from one person to another by unprotected sex. Although Chlamydia can eventually cause serious health problems, many people do not realise that they have it. Anyone who suspects that they may have it should be tested. Treatment is often straightforward using antibiotics.

Gonorrhoea is another bacterial infection spread by unprotected sex and is the second most common STI in the UK. The symptoms of gonorrhoea are generally more obvious with pain urinating and a yellow/green discharge. However, some people show no real symptoms. A simple test can confirm whether somebody has gonorrhoea and antibiotic treatment is usually successful.

Syphilis is another bacterial infection spread by unprotected sex. It causes small painless sores around the penis, vagina or anus as well as a red rash that can affect the palms of the hand or soles of the feet and white patches in the mouth. It also causes headaches, joint aches and general tiredness. If left untreated Syphilis can cause very serious health problems in the longer term. Syphilis can be detected from a blood sample and can usually be successfully treated with antibiotics.

Trichomoniasis is an STI caused by a tiny parasite. It can cause an unpleasant discharge, soreness and pain urinating. It can be tested by swabbing the affected area and is treated with antibiotics.

Genital warts (HPV) are painless lumps around the penis, anus or vagina. They cause itching and bleeding and can change the direction of flow of your urine. They are caused by Human Papillomavirus (HPV). They can be treated with creams, surgery or freezing but these are not a cure. The HPV virus usually stays in the body and the symptoms may re-emerge. HPV vaccines are now generally available to teenage girls and provide significant protection both against certain forms of cancer and genital warts.

Genital herpes (Herpes Simplex) is a viral infection that causes painful or itchy sores or blisters in the genital area. It is the same virus that causes cold sores on the face. The sores heal but can reappear at any point later in life. There are creams and anti-viral medicines to relieve the symptoms, but again, as with HPV, there is no cure. The virus can be spread even when there are no sores present.

Pubic lice (Pthirus pubis) are tiny parasitic insects that live in pubic hair but can also sometimes live in other coarse body hair including beards and chest hair. They are spread by close contact and sexual intercourse. They cause itching, particularly at night, as well as inflammation and small bite spots. Pubic lice can be treated with creams, lotions or shampoos.

HIV (Human Immunodeficiency Virus) is the virus that causes AIDS (Acquired Immune Deficiency Syndrome). HIV can be spread by sexual contact and sharing needles/syringes used for injections. It can also be passed from mother to baby. Most people who are infected by HIV experience flu like symptoms a few week later. At present, there is no cure for HIV, but there are some very effective drug treatments that can allow most sufferers to lead long and healthy lives and prevent the development of AIDS.

Picking up the pieces

The teenage years are an emotional rollercoaster and intimate relationships only accentuate this. If your teenager has a crush on someone that is unreturned or has been rejected or has a relationship that comes to an end, they can become very depressed or distressed, and their self-esteem can take a big blow. (See Chapter 23 about loss). Parents need to watch out for possible warning signs including withdrawal, quietness, anger and any significant change in behaviour or mood. Don't pester them with questions, but make sure that you are available and that they know that they can talk to you whenever they feel like it, without you being judgmental. If they do talk to you, don't trivialise the situation. Be sympathetic and supportive and explain that most people have problems sooner or later with relationships that don't turn out as they wished. It is very painful and takes time to get over.

Useful organisations

Brook – www.brook.org.uk
Provides sexual health advice, information and services for young people.

Childline – www.childline.org.uk
Provides information and advice on sex and relationships and has a helpline: 0800 1111.

FPA – www.fpa.org.uk
Provides general relationship and sex education information and also produces resources to support parents.

NSPCC – www.nspcc.org.uk
Provides information and advice about healthy sexual behaviour.

Relate – www.relate.org.uk
Provides help and counselling to adults and children to resolve relationship issues.

Terence Higgins trust – www.tht.org.uk
Provides sexual health information and advice and supports HIV sufferers.

The Mix – www.themix.org.uk
Supports under 25s on a wide range of issues including sex and relationships.

References in this chapter
[1] Brooks F, Magnusson J, Klemera E, Chester K, Spencer N, Smeeton N (2015) HSBC England National Report 2014 University of Hertfordshire, Hatfield UK
[2] Hagell A, Coleman J and Brooks F (2015) Key data on adolescence, London Association for Young People's Health
[3] Opinion Research Results June 2014 Online interviews among UK adults aged 18
[4] Office for National Statistics: Conceptions in England and Wales 2016
[5] Public Health England: New STI diagnoses and rates by gender, sexual risk and age group 2017

Chapter 22

Internet

Today's teenagers have grown up with many modern developments in technology and take the use of mobile phones and computers in all aspects of their life for granted. They use the internet for information and to find out what's going on in the world around them, and can access a variety of apps to play, be entertained and socially interact. As a result, they lead lives that look very different to the way we grew up and which you might find rather alien and disturbing. You may worry about the impact of technology on your children's social development, as well as fearing that they are vulnerable, both to exploitation or abuse by others and to their own temptations. In fact, technology probably has as many good points as bad, and whether we like it or not we have all got to learn to live with it. Our teenagers use the internet and apps for a whole variety of purposes, many of which may be beneficial or educational, but this does lead to a whole range of possible concerns. Take a precautionary approach to your teenager's internet use and address problems if they arise, for example:

Appropriate access issues
Access to inappropriate sexual content and pornography
Access to inappropriate violent content
Access to web sites that may incite harmful or criminal behaviour

Controlling temptation issues
Temptation to shop
Temptation to gamble
Temptation to game

Safety issues

Vulnerability to bullying and abuse
Vulnerability to grooming
Vulnerability to radicalisation
Vulnerability to financial or other forms of exploitation
Vulnerability to persuasion to behave dangerously or irresponsibly, including self-harm and eating disorders.

Behavioural issues

Posting illegal or embarrassing content such as sexting
Posting or texting in a bullying, insulting or disrespectful way
Sharing inappropriate content

Of course, it is easy to think of these issues as new problems that parents need to deal with, but in many ways, they are the same old problems, but in a new context. Parents have always needed to warn their children about these issues whether it used to be related to what television they should watch, what strangers they should talk to or where and when they should go to places. The difference is that because the technology is so new and confusing parents feel they do not fully understand or have control over what is going on.

How young people are using the internet

In a recent survey by Ofcom, [1] young people aged 12-15, were asked how they used various media including what equipment they used and how long they did it for. On average this age group spends 21 hours per week online, made up of around two and a half hours per day in the week and four hours a day at the weekend. This is more time than they watch television and does not include offline screen activity. In fact, Youtube is more popular than any television channel. This group also spends 12 hours a week gaming, with boys being heavier gamers at 15 hours. This may be a mixture of online and offline activity. The most popular device is the mobile phone, which is used for 18 hours a week, with girls being heavier users at 21 hours. Over three quarters of this age group now own a smart phone, and most of the rest have a mobile phone of some sort. Among 15 year-olds smart phones are virtually universal. Most of the age group also own a tablet and those who don't usually have access to one at home. Over half also have access to games consoles, which are more popular among boys. The favourite device for accessing the internet is the mobile phone followed by tablets.

What young people are doing on the internet

Over three quarters of this age group have a social media profile. Facebook is used by about three quarters of the age group, but it has been losing popularity. It is followed by Snapchat, Instagram and WhatsApp, which has been gaining ground. In fact, Snapchat has nearly caught up with Facebook as the main platform used. Around half of them have watched other people's live streamed videos and one in ten young people has streamed their own content. Over a third have made a video at some point and most have edited a photo or image. Around two thirds are playing online games, with one in five, often boys, sometimes playing with someone that they don't know and often chatting with them. Although these young people are interested in the news their main focus is on news relating to music (particularly girls), sports (particularly boys) and celebrity lives.

Internet safety

Almost all the age group have been given advice on internet safety mainly by parents or teachers. Around half have blocked messages on social media, around one third changed social media settings and blocked junk mail and a quarter have blocked pop-ups. Nevertheless, nearly half have seen hateful content online in the last year and this figure is increasing. Nearly a quarter have been contacted by someone that they didn't know who wanted to be their friend. Around one in ten had seen something scary or troubling and a similar number had seen sexual content that made them uncomfortable. Many have also been bullied online or are aware of bullying of other people. Some of these young people try to access content that is restricted or possibly unsuitable without detection, by deleting search histories, choosing privacy modes on browsers and resetting filters. Most of this age group think that people are mean to each other online and would like rules to stop people saying hurtful things.

Parents' attitudes and concerns

About half of the parents of 12-15year-olds are concerned about the time that their children spend on the internet and its content, and most of these admit that they find it hard to control the screen time. Generally, parents trust their children to use the internet safely and most believe that the benefits outweigh the risks. Only one in five do not think that they know enough to manage online risks. Parents' main concerns are about privacy and giving out too much personal information, although there is also concern about cyberbullying. There are also worries about sites that might encourage self-harm and about actions that might damage their child's reputation. There is growing concern about radicalisation. A third of the parents are concerned about the content of the games that are played. Many of these also worry about who they are playing with and the pressure to make in-game purchases.

The survey also asked parents about how they try to influence what their children do online. These figures were published for parents of all children aged 5-15 who say that roughly a third of them use network filters, with a similar number using filter software and PIN passwords. Just under a quarter say that they use device settings, a similar number to those who restrict the mode on YouTube or use safe search on search engines. These measures tend to be used more with younger children than older children. Less than a quarter of parents whose children have smartphones have changed or restricted the settings. Most parents say that they talk to their children about internet safety and have rules about internet use. These rules usually apply to who they can contact and what information to share.as well as how long they can spend online and when. They may also cover what they can spend money on. Again, these rules tend to be used more with younger children.

Blocking and filtering mechanisms

Although most parents feel confident about their children using the internet safely, there are a number of reasons to believe that there may be a degree of complacency. Firstly, older children at least now tend to have devices like smartphones that can be used almost anywhere and anytime without supervision. As we stated earlier, nearly a quarter of older children have been contacted by someone that they didn't know who wanted to be their friend. Many gamers are chatting to people that they don't know, and many children are seeing content that upsets or shocks them. Parents may, therefore, wish to consider blocking/filtering internet content or even closely monitoring internet use. They may also wish to restrict the opportunities to chat and to download or purchase. They need to consider not only computers, tablets and phones, but also gaming consoles and smart televisions. The main methods for filtering/blocking are:

Web browser settings – these tend to concentrate on blocking malware and phishing rather than specific content. They can also provide search histories.

Home internet settings – these can restrict adult sites and potential viruses.

Social media settings – these can restrict who sees posts and can be used to block people.

Device settings – most devices now have settings that can restrict various searches or activities. They can also be used to prevent app downloads or purchases.

Parental control software – these can be purchased or sometimes downloaded for free. They restrict content that can be viewed and can restrict access to the internet. In some cases, these can act as spyware and can view everything that is being carried out on a specified device.

Passwords and PINS to restrict access – these can be used to allow access to websites that have not been approved.

YouTube settings – these can be set to restrict access to some unsuitable content.

Netflix settings – these allow certain accounts to be for children only

247

There are clearly a great many ways in which internet access can be restricted and fuller details are available from suppliers and from internet safety websites. However, it should be recognised that none of these measures is completely effective. The European Safer Internet Programme, which monitors internet safety and rates many of the common pieces of software, indicates that they generally allow quite a lot of unwanted content. Although they are generally more efficient at filtering specifically adult content, they are much worse at stopping violent or racist material or content encouraging drugs, gambling or self-harm. It should also be noted that this analysis assumed co-operation from the child. Nowadays many computer literate children are quite capable of finding ways around blocking and filtering mechanisms. In fact, the internet is a ready source of ways to do this and so parents should be careful about having too much confidence in their technical restrictions, particularly with older children.

Should I control my teenager's internet access?

Parental controls are useful tools to protect children online, but they need to be used in conjunction with open communication to ensure co-operation. You might choose to discuss some of the following points with your teenager:

Why it is important not to share personal information.

Why certain content, apps or games are inappropriate.

With whom they should chat or play games.

Why they should avoid chatting to strangers and never meeting them.

Why clicking on unknown files or pop-ups is risky.

How to behave appropriately when using the internet.

When to stop using the internet and how to report disturbing content.

How to respond to cyberbullying.

How to keep passwords secure.

What devices they are allowed to access.

Why they must be careful about posting videos or photos.

The rules for purchasing goods, apps or game add-ons.

Using appropriate device and social media settings

Do try to be aware of how your children are using the internet and this is far easier if devices are used in communal areas and not in bathrooms or bedrooms. You may also need to consider the amount of time that is being spent on the internet and whether this is healthy or not. People who spend very long periods on the internet can become like substance abuse addicts, where the behaviour interferes with many other aspects of life and where they find it very difficult to control or withdraw from this behaviour. However, dealing with this behaviour depends a great deal on what the internet is being used for. We have therefore covered this and other specific issues in much more detail in our chapters on dealing with social media, gaming, gambling and pornography.

References in this chapter

[1] Ofcom: Children and parents: Media use and attitudes report (November 2017)
[2] Safety Internet Programme: Benchmarking of parental control tools for the protection of children (November 2017)

Chapter 23

Loss

Types of loss

Although loss is most often associated with bereavement (death), it can take a great many forms. It is the end of or a significant change in our normal pattern of behaviour often associated with grief. Some examples of loss which, can have a significant effect on us, are:

death of a relative or friend
miscarriage or stillbirth
death of a pet
relationship breakup, divorce and separation
increased or sudden disability
exclusion from friendship group
close friend or sibling moving away
moving home
moving school
failure to achieve ambition such as poor exam results/failed interview
dismissal, redundancy or retirement
confinement in prison or other institution
change in financial circumstances or repossession of or eviction from home

These losses may be easier to deal with if they are predictable and expected, but sometimes they can occur suddenly, without warning, with no time for preparation.

In the following sections, we will talk about death and grief.

Although death is often the cause of our most profound sense of loss, a similar grief process can be experienced with any form of loss. For a sudden event, it will happen afterwards, although sometimes it will be delayed, which can cause some confusion. For an expected or anticipated loss, these processes will also occur in the intervening period as we are coming to terms with the possibility of a forthcoming bereavement.

Attitudes to death

Attitudes to death, and the ceremonies and traditions that are associated with it, vary across different cultures and religions. However, in the UK, death is a topic that is rarely discussed within families or with young people.

With the exception of older people, and people with strong religious beliefs, many adults prefer not to think about or discuss it, even though it is inevitable both for ourselves and all of those around us. Because most people fear death, they often don't make preparation for their own deaths by writing wills or making prior arrangements. When people die, they are usually removed from the home until their funeral, and in many cases, younger children may not be involved. As a result, many children have little experience of death, until a close relative or pet dies. Although we often think we are protecting our children from death, in some ways we are failing to prepare them for it. It is a good idea to raise the topic of death at a convenient and appropriate time to gauge their understanding. A film or television programme can often provide an opportunity for this even if the characters are cartoons or animals.

What is the grieving process?

When we lose something or someone important to us, we go through a grieving process. All deaths and losses are different, and everybody will grieve in their own way. Although support from other people is helpful, grieving is a personal process and no-one else can grieve for you. Nevertheless, grieving is recognised as a process that will go through several stages. These stages are not fixed either in their sequence or their duration and people may move between them at any time.

Denial, shock and disbelief: At this stage, we refuse to accept what has happened. Even if the death was expected, this may still be our emotional response to the actual event. We might think "this can't be true" or "this can't be happening to me". We may enact rituals to carry on as though nothing has happened, like laying a place at the table or expecting a person who has died to be there when we arrive or dwelling on conversations or experiences that we shared. We may even imagine someone even actually being here.

Sadness and searching: At this stage, we feel deeply sad and depressed. We may have difficulties concentrating and dealing with normal everyday life. We may become withdrawn and even lonely.

Anger and resentment: At this stage, anger takes over. People think "why me" or "life is so unfair". If they have been religious, they may be angry at God or even change their views about religion. We can become irritable, agitated and on a short fuse. We can also become angry with ourselves and this can be quite damaging to our mental health.

Bargaining: At this stage, we try to bargain with ourselves or with God to offer something up to reverse or stop our loss and put things back the way they were. We may also feel a sense of guilt, which we might try to put right with those around us.

Acceptance: This is the final stage, when we begin able to accept what has happened and start to move on in our life. We can regain our energy and sense of purpose and start to plan for the future. We retain our memories of the person or thing that we have lost, but we can now move forward alongside and with those memories. Reaching this stage may take a long time, but it usually does happen!

Telling young people that someone has died

If a person or pet, that your child has been close to or loved, has died, telling them may not be easy, especially if you are deeply upset as well. It may be helpful to have another adult present. Generally, children should be told as quickly as possible in case they hear it from someone else, and they are likely to need information and explanations. If you feel too upset or unable to do it, find another trusted adult, whom they know, to do it in your presence. Find a quiet place where you will not be disturbed. For a younger child, sit with them so that you can give them appropriate physical contact and with an older child, sit nearby. Honesty is usually the best policy, so give them enough accurate information as is age appropriate and answer any questions that they may have. The news is likely to come as a shock to them, so it is best to give them some warning both from your mood and seriousness and by how you start. It can be helpful to begin by putting the death into context, particularly if it is not totally unexpected. Some suggestions might be:

> *"I'm afraid I have got some sad news to tell you ..."*
> *"You know Granny hasn't been well for a long time....."*

Keep the message simple and try not to use indirect phrases to disguise the reality and finality of the death. For younger children, it may be necessary to explain that when you die your body stops working and that you stay dead for ever, and won't ever come back. If a question is too deep to be answered easily or would require details that you don't think are appropriate, turn the question back and ask what they think as this will give you a better understanding of what they already know and why they asked the question.

Young people can respond in a variety of ways to bad news. They can go silent, they can cry, or they might be angry, these are all normal reactions. They may want physical comforting, or they may want to be alone. Whatever happens, they may well come back to you later with more questions. It will also be necessary to explain to them about the funeral and whatever other family rituals are associated with death including the possibility of viewing the body.

253

Although some people try to exclude young children from these events to protect them, it is usually thought better to try to include older children and give them a role of some sort.

Supporting someone who is grieving
If your teenager is grieving, they will need your companionship to give them support and to encourage them to continue with everyday life, but they also need time alone to process and deal with their own thoughts. Try to be sensitive to when each approach is appropriate. They may also need you to be patient and tolerant as they may well go through periods of irritability and anger. Teenagers and young people grieve in the same way as adults, but they may not have the same understanding of the finality of death or of the nature of illnesses that may lead to it. When a friend or acquaintance of your teenager dies, it is often hard for them to fathom how frail human life can be and cope with the suddenness of death. Young people can identify closely with the death of a peer and relate it closely to their own situation, generating fear of their own future and realising how unpredictable life can be. It is useful to ask them *"How can I support you best?"* or *"It's OK to cry"*, but do try not to say: *"Cheer up"* or *"It will get better in time"* or *"You hardly knew them"*.

Your teenager may well be experiencing grieving emotions for the first time and because they are struggling to cope with them become very withdrawn. The grief may also present in physical ways such as headaches, stomach aches and changes in sleeping or eating habits. In these situations, make sure that they are properly informed about what has happened or is going to happen and that it not their fault in any way. You will need to tell them that their emotions and reactions are perfectly normal. It is likely that you feel the same way and you should not try to hide your own grief from them. They also need to be reassured about what will happen in the future.

Don't try to make them talk about the situation if they don't want to. If they don't want to talk to you, you may able to suggest another trusted adult they could turn to if they prefer. If they are having trouble expressing and releasing their emotions it can be helpful to explore ways of doing this through mediums such as art, music, writing or sport. It can also be helpful to establish memories of the lost person or thing by creating a picture album or some other form of memorial to reinforce their memory and this can sometimes be a shared activity with other family members. If there is a grave, regular visits may provide a good way to reinforce the memories.

Try to encourage them to carry on life in as normal a way as possible. Ensure that they eat and sleep regularly, and get regular exercise, and encourage them to socialise as much as possible. Monitor their mood and their self-esteem in the ensuing months. Sometimes young people can react to loss by losing a sense of direction and security and blaming themselves for every little thing that goes wrong. They may turn to alcohol or drugs to try to deal with their unhappiness. They can also become entrenched in a depressive state and if this is the case, they will need professional help. (See Chapter 16 on Depression).

Finally, don't forget your own needs. You are probably grieving as well, and you may need your own support.

Useful books

For parents and adults

A child's grief: supporting a child when someone in their family has died. *Di Stubbs*
As big as it gets: supporting a child when a parent is seriously ill. *Julie A. Stokes*
Grief in children: a handbook for adults. *Atle Dyregrov*
Healing children's grief: surviving a parent's death from cancer. *Grace H Christ*
Helping teens cope with death. The Dougy Center
Never too young to know: death in children's lives. *Phyllis Silverman*

For children – activities to help express emotions

Overcoming Loss. *Julia Sorensen*
Help Me Say Goodbye: Activities for Helping Kids Cope When a Special Person. Dies *Janis Silverman*
Muddles puddles and sunshine. *Diana Crossley & Kate Shepherd*
When someone has a very serious illness: children can learn to cope with loss and change. *Marge Heegaard*
When someone very special dies: children can learn to cope with grief. *Marge Heegaard*

For younger children

Always remember. *Cece Meng*
Badger's parting gifts. *Susan Varley*
Gentle Willow: A Story for Children about Dying. Joyce *C. Mills*
Michael Rosen's Sad Book. *Michael Rosen and Quentin Blake*
Nana upstairs, nana downstairs. *Tomie dePaola*
Something small: a story about remembering. *Rebecca Honig*
The heart and the bottle. *Oliver Jeffers*
The scar. *Charlotte Moundlic*
What Does Dead Mean?: A Book for Young Children to Help Explain Death and Dying. *Caroline Jay and Jenni Thomas*
When dinosaurs die. *Laurie Krasny Brown & Marc Brown*

For older children and teenagers

A monster calls. *Patrick Ness*
A taste of blackberries. *Doris Smith*
Goodnight Mister Tom. *Michelle Magorian*
Mick Harte Was Here. *Barbara Park*
Missing May. Cynthia *Rylant Summer*
My sister lives on the mantelpiece. *Annabel Pitcher*
Remembering Mog. *Colby Rodowsky*
The Truth About Forever. *Sarah Dessen*
Tiger Eyes. *Judy Blume*
Vicky Angel. *Jacqueline Wilson*

Useful organisations

Child bereavement   UK- www.childbereavementuk.org
Offer support services for families when a child dies or is bereaved.
It also has a helpline 0800 02 888 40

Children of Jannah - www.childrenofjannah.com
Offers support services to muslim parents when a child dies.

Compassionate friends - www.tcf.org.uk
Supports bereaved families and individuals who are coping with the
death of a child of any age. They have a helpline 0345 123 2304.

Cruse Bereavement Care - www.cruse.org.uk
Provides support, advice and information to bereaved children and
adults. They have a helpline 0808 808 1677. They also have a
website for young people called Hope Again.

Grief encounter - www.griefencounter.org.uk
Supports bereaved children and their families. They have a helpline
020 8371 8455 and run support groups.

Jewish bereavement counselling service - www.jbcs.org.uk
Provides bereavement counselling for the Jewish community.

Rosie crane trust – www.rosiecranetrust.org
Provide support services for bereaved parents and have a helpline
01460 55120.

SOBS UK – www.uksobs.org
Supports families affected by suicide. They have a helpline 0300 111
5065.

Winstons wish – www.winstonswish.org
Supports children and young people who have suffered a family
bereavement. They have a helpline 08088 020 021.

Chapter 24

Lying

There is no doubt, that the first time we catch our teenager out in a lie it is a shock! Our once honest and reliable young person is treating us as if we are stupid. He's lying, we know he's lying, and he knows that we know he's lying, and yet he lies anyway. No wonder we are confused, annoyed and hurt. Not our child, we say, he's just not like that!

We generally view lying as an unacceptable and dishonest form of communication, but psychologists believe that lying is a fundamental part of human communication and is an indication of higher order thinking. Most adolescents will have lied by the age of 12. Of course, people lie for all sorts of reasons, often with very good motives, and young children both copy their parents and indeed are sometimes encouraged to lie by them.

"Tell Grandma you....:

> *....... loved her apple cake"*
> *....... loved her present"*
> *....... wanted to see her but had to go to a birthday party"*
> *....... really enjoyed going to see Auntie"*

These are standard so called "white lies", which are designed to make other people feel better rather than being entirely honest. Most relationships with friends and partners are based on a degree of lying, in order to make them run smoothly, but of course, some lying is just plain nasty and is designed to hurt other people whom we dislike or possibly want to get even with. Other lying is purely for personal gain which may be financial or for other reasons. So, in everyday life we probably all accept that we will be lied to on a regular basis, but we find it particularly difficult to deal with our teenagers lying to us as we see it as a lack of respect, a betrayal of trust and a challenge to our authority and control.

In fact, research does tell us that teenagers are the most frequent liars with about three quarters admitting to lying each day.[1][2] Teenagers also appear to be rather good at lying and seem to treat lying or telling the truth as equally valid spontaneous responses. This may be because they spend much of their time on social networks, where lying is very easy as the other party has no or rather limited visual and other cues to decide if they are being lied to. Teenagers are also not always very good at spotting these cues anyway.

So why do teenagers lie? Or should we ask, why do some children lie more than others? Well, teenagers lie for much the same reasons as the rest of us both for "good" and bad reasons.

The level of lying is often reflected in the amount of troubled behaviour they have demonstrated to date. Avoidance of sanctions or a lecture or fear of punishment appears to be the main reason for lying and lying is more frequent when parents are seen as more controlling.[3] However, it is interesting to note, that most young people say that they want their parents to trust them. This creates difficulties for you as parents, because on the one hand it's important that you trust them. In fact, it's one of the markers of a good parent-child relationship. Feeling trusted inspires them to behave in ways that will maintain your trust, and the more they are trusted, the more they strive to live up to that trust, and the more trustworthy they become. In contrast, if you don't think that your child will ever lie to you, because you trust them, you can miss the opportunity to set rules and act proactively to keep your teenager out of trouble.

So, whilst trying to build an identity for themselves among their friends and classmates, and generally battling against the authority imposed by both you as their parents, and their school, teenagers lie, both by telling falsehoods and by deliberately not giving the whole story.

Of those lies, some will be obvious and others perhaps a bit more worrying:

To avoid a justified punishment/consequence for something they have done
To impress others or attention seek
To get something that they want
To keep activities such as alcohol, drugs, gambling, sex etc secret from disapproving parents
To "protect" other people from punishment or other consequences
To boast about getting away with the deception to other people
To hurt other people

Many of these are the sorts of teenage lies that have always been with us and no doubt will continue to be, but it is well worth talking to your teenager generally about the pros and cons of lying because lying can be considered an important life skill which can be used for good or bad motives. "Bad" lying hurts other people especially our family and friends. The fear of being found out can make our life very complicated, and one lie can easily lead to another. Living a lie is damaging to our self-esteem and can make us hide away in order not to be discovered. It is much easier to live a life where we are true to ourselves and the image we project is the real one.

The less obvious lies occur because:

They don't respect the rules/punishments/consequences imposed
They don't think it matters what they say as they are not listened to anyway
They don't want to disappoint their parents
They don't want to worry their parents
They want to be independent and sort it out themselves
They want privacy and a part of their life that parents don't know about
They are being coerced into lying by another person

So how should parents deal with lying?

Improve levels of communication

Many of these lies are perpetuated because of poor levels of communication, which we have already talked about in Chapter 7. It is essential that teenagers believe that they will be listened to and treated fairly and with understanding and that the reasons for boundaries and consequences are explained properly and clearly. Teenagers also need to understand that parents expect to worry about them. In fact, they are likely to get far more worried if they find out little snippets from other people that concern them, than if their teenagers are honest with them. Admit to your teenager that you will sometimes get it wrong and be suspicious of their motives and actions. Explain that this is a result of your anxiety for them to have as smooth a transition into adulthood as possible. Most distrust arises from fear, keeping the communication channels open can avoid angry accusations and recriminations.

One of the reasons teenagers lie to us is because they think we won't listen, or that there is no room to negotiate or make exceptions to rules so that lying to us is their only option. Prove that you are approachable, and where possible, relax the rule enough to allow a little more freedom whilst still maintaining standards and safety. Praise your teenager when they come to you with their concerns or if they are ever in trouble or feeling out of control in a situation, and when they are being open about what is happening in their life. Be prepared to hear things that might make your hair curl!

Have realistic expectations

In some ways, the most worrying reason that teenagers lie is not to disappoint their parents. We know that a great many teenagers are having trouble coping with life and that many are self-harming or have early signs of mental ill health and it is essential that they can talk to you if they have problems. It is vital that teenagers do not believe that their parents expect them to be great at everything and it is equally important that parents do not have unrealistic expectations of their children. One of the greatest lessons that teenagers can learn is how to deal with failures and disappointments, as these are part of everyday life. Both parents and teenagers should expect these setbacks and be prepared to find ways to deal with them when they occur. Being able to recover and move on from adolescent mistakes without feeling a complete failure and without it being brought up on every occasion will encourage your teenager to be open and honest with you.

Avoid interrogations

Intense interrogations of teenagers are usually counter-productive. They rarely get to the truth and just undermine your relationship even more. So, can we spot when our teenagers are lying to us? Well, this can be very difficult as teenagers are often very proficient at lying and have few qualms about doing it. The best way is to know as much as possible about what is going on in their lives, but this needs to be done subtly and not to be too intrusive or interfering.

Nevertheless, these are some of the physical signs that can indicate that we are being lied to:

Avoiding eye contact
Repeatedly touching their face
Stiff or no arm and leg movement
Facial expressions/body language not matching the statements
Facial expressions/body language not synchronised with the statements
Sentences that are garbled
Speech that is unusually quiet or high pitched
Not using 'I or my' pronouns

Discuss the downside of lying

Although lying can sometimes be well motivated, it usually creates far more problems than it solves. Lying to friends and family is a betrayal of trust that can lead to rejection and shame. Maintaining lies is very stressful as liars need to remember what they have said before and one lie can easily lead to another to try to cover it up. Liars live in fear of being found out and may increasingly isolate themselves. Liars also hurt their self-esteem and confidence as they are leading a false life, not content to demonstrate the real them. They may also experience feelings of guilt. Teenagers need to be aware that by lying in order to gain more freedom, they can lose parental trust, and as your trust erodes, so does their freedom.

Although it might not feel that way to you, most teenagers still value your opinion and want you to approve of them, and they don't want to let you down. If you can handle their lies in a calm way, without taking it personally or overreacting, and show them that you are approachable and flexible, you will both get through this difficult period of adolescence.

References in this chapter

[1] Serota, K. B., Levine, T. R., & Boster, F. J. (2010). The prevalence of lying in America: Three studies of self-reported lies. Human Communication Research, 36, 2-
[2] Debey, E, De Schryver, M, Logan, GD, Suchotzki, K & Verschuere, B 2015, 'From junior to senior Pinocchio: A cross-sectional lifespan investigation of deception' *Acta Psychologica*, vol. 160, pp. 58-68. DOI: 10.1016/j.actpsy.2015.06.007
[3] Jensen, L.A., Arnett, J.J., Feldman, S.S. et al. Journal of Youth and Adolescence (2004) 33: 101. https://doi.org/10.1023/B:JOYO.0000013422.48100.5a

Chapter 25

Online gaming

The development of gaming

Since its modest beginnings in the 1950s, video gaming has expanded out of all recognition and is now the largest sector in the entertainment industry. There are now games for consoles such as Xbox, Playstations and Nintendos, as well as games for laptops, tablets and phones. As a result, games can be played at home or on the move.

There are now games to appeal to adults, teenagers and young children of both sexes and all ages. The quality of the games has now improved to such an extent that it can be difficult to distinguish between the virtual world and the real world. At the same time, the range of genres has expanded considerably and now includes action, adventure, survival, role play, simulation, strategy and sports. Some of these, like the sports and shooter games, seem to appeal much more to men, while others involving role play and fantasy appeal more to women. Games can now involve just one person or involve hundreds or even more in online co-operation or competition. They can last for minutes, hours or even sometimes for many days. Consoles and games can be expensive and although there are many free games to download for computer, tablet and phone, many of the "free" games have paid for extras, add-ons or skins, which we will discuss later in this chapter.

Who are the gamers and how do they play?

In the US there are slightly more male gamers, but a survey in the UK suggested that there were slightly more female gamers in the UK driven by 25-44year old women using puzzle and trivia games. [1] [2]

The same survey showed that 69% of the population were gaming with the heaviest gamers being young people with 99% of 8-17year olds and 89% of 18-24year olds having played a video game in the last six months.

According to a detailed survey of media use in the UK, [3] around two thirds of 12-15year olds play online games, with 61% sometimes playing on their own, 42% sometimes playing with someone in the same room, 39% playing against someone they know elsewhere and 22% against someone they don't know elsewhere.

Over half of 12-15year olds who play online use the chat function within games with 19% chatting to the people that they don't know. The average 12-15year old spends about 12 hours a week gaming, consisting of around an hour and a half on school days and over two hours a day at the weekend. The most used gaming device, a games console linked to the television, is used by over half of 12-15year olds, followed by phone (42%), tablet (29%), computer (21%) and hand-held console (18%).

An international comparison of gamers suggests that UK gamers are amongst the heaviest gamers in the world and are more likely to buy hard copies of games, possibly because they experience download problems. [4]

Should you worry about your teenager's gaming?

Gaming can have both beneficial and harmful effects on young people. Although there has been a considerable amount of research over the last twenty years on the effects of gaming, this research is sometimes disputed and may also become out of date as the nature of gaming develops and changes. It is often difficult to separate the effects of the time spent gaming from the actual content of the games, which can clearly vary enormously from game to game and person to person. Nevertheless, it is now recognised that in some cases excessive or inappropriate gaming can have serious effects on young people. You will need to need to assess the impact that gaming is having on your own children and react accordingly.

What does the research tell us? Let us look at some of the beneficial effects first.

Beneficial effects of gaming

Gaming as a learning medium. Games are now widely used with younger children as a learning aid in schools. They can be used not only as a means of acquiring specific skills or knowledge, but also as a way of influencing behaviours such as bullying and developing social skills. Gaming is also being developed to help in behavioural therapies.

Gaming as an exercise medium. Some games encourage physical exercise, which can improve both physical and mental health.

Gaming as a form of relaxation. For some people playing casual short games provides a ready means of distraction and can help them to relax and deal with stress.

A means for teenagers to develop their own identities. Teenagers are going through an important transition stage and need to try to develop their own personalities, independent of their parents. Gaming can give them the opportunity to have a part of their lives that is theirs alone and where they have a good deal of control that they may not have elsewhere. It can improve their sense of status and improve self-esteem. They may also adopt or experiment with a persona that is different from the way they usually behave.

To develop relationships with others. Gaming can provide the opportunity to share experiences with other people and to become part of a wider community of gamers. If your teenager has difficulty making friends, this can provide a useful alternative to combat loneliness and isolation. Some games also provide a valuable requirement to co-operate with other players.

To develop creativity. Gaming can provide a wide range of opportunities for developing creativity in a wide range of settings including art, music design and construction.

To develop problem solving skills. Many games involve players overcoming challenges to achieve set goals and this requires understanding and obeying instructions, serious thinking around the problem and in some cases developing overall strategies to maximise their performance.

To improve physical and mental agility. Many games require players to improve their concentration, reaction times, visuospatial processing and hand-eye coordination.

Damaging effects of gaming

Games involving violence. Playing games that have a significant level of violence has been linked to aggressive behaviour, a desensitisation to violence and a reduction in empathy and sociable behaviour.[5]

The impact of excessive gaming. Whatever the content of the video games, spending too much time playing reduces the amount of time that can be spent on other activities and on social interaction with other family members. School work can suffer, and other hobbies and sports can be neglected. This can affect eating and sleeping habits and be detrimental to both physical fitness and mental health. It can also have a negative impact on family relationships. It is now recognised that excessive gaming can become an addiction, and this will be discussed in much more detail later. We already know that teenagers may be particularly susceptible to developing addictive behaviours.

Lack of real-world social development. The gaming world can be very attractive to those who find it difficult to make friends by providing an alternative virtual community. However, too much reliance on this form of interaction denies the opportunity to spend time trying to develop and improve social skills in the real world.

Brain development. As we discussed in Chapter 3 teenage brains are plastic and develop structurally to meet the demands placed upon them. Excessive gaming is likely to result in brain structures specialised to meet the needs of the games whether they be reaction times, spatial awareness, problem solving etc. Depending on the game, this specialisation may be valuable in everyday life or it may be completely unhelpful.

Risks of grooming. During gaming, many young gamers are chatting to people that they have never met. This presents the risk that they may be groomed by older players wishing to take advantage of them.

Encouraging gambling. In the last few years, there has been a huge increase in "skins" for games. These are virtual items that can be won or purchased to enhance characters. These skins can now be bought and sold between players for real or virtual currency. They can be gambled for loot/mystery boxes to try and win a more valuable skin. There are also sites where skins can actually be used as stakes to gamble on esports, play casino type games or try to win a jackpot. A recent survey found that 10% of 13-18year olds have skin gambled [6]. The UK Gambling Commission has warned parents to be vigilant and monitor how their children are spending their money. (See Chapter 26 Online and other gambling)

Spotting potential problems or addiction

Gaming manufacturers compete to produce games that are the most appealing, and successful games are clearly those that encourage players to spend as much time as possible playing them. It is therefore not surprising that gaming can become addictive like other types of behaviour. Although clearly playing games for many hours a day can cause problems, it is not in itself an indication of addiction.

Addiction is more about the attitude to gaming and is likely to be demonstrated by:

A pre-occupation with gaming spending a lot of time thinking about gaming when they are not playing.
Withdrawal problems causing irritability, anxiousness or anger when not playing.
Need to keep playing for longer or find more exciting games to maintain response levels.
Not being able to cut down gaming even if they recognise the damaging effect on sleep, work or relationships.
Lying or covering up how much they are gaming

Whether or not the level of gaming should be considered an addiction some signs of excessive gaming are:

Physical signs
Problems with the thumb, hand, wrist or arm such as tendinitis, bursitis or carpal tunnel syndrome
Loss of weight due to missing meals
Gain in weight due to lack of exercise or snacking
Tiredness due to disruption or lack of sleep
Eye strain and possibly migraines
Neglect of personal hygiene
Mood signs
Becoming more aggressive to other family members
Having mood swings
Behavioural signs
Poor academic performance
Spending long periods in bedroom
Gaming late at night
Avoiding mealtimes and chores
Withdrawal from hobbies, sports and friends
Problems managing money due to gaming related spending

Who is most at risk?

Many researchers have tried to analyse the behaviour and attitudes of young gamers to investigate their susceptibility to addiction. A study in 2009 estimated that around 8.5% of gamers aged 8-18 exhibited these characteristics, with males much more at risk.[7] The most at risk players played over twenty hours a week. More recent research has indicated that addictive players display more signs of anxiety, depression, aggression and lower wellbeing. [8] Many of them appear to use gaming as a way of escaping from mental health problems including stress. [9]

Which games are most addictive?

In the past gaming was largely male dominated and first-person shooter games were often the most obsessive games. However, in recent years the development of online games has added a whole new dimension. The multi-player role playing online games are now thought to be the most addictive, as they now form part of a constantly evolving situation interacting with other people. Players feel an obligation to the rest of the community to keep on playing and characters often develop into progressively more powerful characters with rewards being available as play continues. Games can last for long periods and have no natural pauses or ending. These games provide an endless challenge in a community in which it is easy to lose oneself.

How can parents try to avoid the potential problems of excessive gaming?

Role modelling. You need to ensure that your own gaming habits are under control. Gaming can provide a useful way of interacting between you and your children or between siblings, but it needs to be fitted into convenient times when there are not more important things to be done.

Be aware of what your teenagers are doing. you should be aware of which games your teenagers are playing and whom they are playing them with. Keep a close eye on whom your teenagers are chatting to and warn them about the risks. Monitor how much your teenager is spending on gaming. Although the cost of purchased games might be known to you, regular spending on skins should be monitored and your child warned about the risks of gambling skins. Be careful and check that your teenager can't gain access to your card details and use these to purchase games or game add-ons.

Be aware of the age rating of the game. Most countries grade games according to the appropriateness for different age groups. In the UK and much of Europe, the PEGI system is used which uses ages 3,7,12,16 and 18. Ensure that not only are the games that are purchased appropriate, but also that games that may be played with older siblings or adults are.

Restrict access to gaming. Consider setting limits on gaming both in terms of time and location. Gaming should be a privilege that is only permitted provided homework and other household duties are carried out. Allowing unsupervised gaming in bedrooms can easily lead to excessive gaming and sleep deprivation. Careful monitoring and control of all screen time is important and do give consideration to screen-free time slots or screen holidays. (See Chapter 22 & 35 for more on the internet and social media.)

Restrict the time spent gaming. Although there is no clear-cut level at which gaming becomes a severe problem, too many hours spent gaming disrupts other aspects of life and clearly presents a greater risk of addiction. Research carried out in 2013 suggested that gamers playing for more than 3 hours a day show significant negative effects. This is broadly consistent with the research mentioned earlier which showed "addicts" game on average for over 20 hours per week. Some people believe that even this level is too high and may certainly not be appropriate for weekdays.

Encourage non-screen activities. Try to encourage your teenager to carry out activities, hobbies and sports outside of the home either with the family or with other teenagers.

Ensure regular meals. It is best not to allow snacking during gaming, but to encourage having a proper meal time.

Ensure enough sleep. Lack of sleep due to excessive or late gaming or social media is a major problem and can have serious effects on academic performance and mental health. (See Chapters 22 and 35 for more on the internet and social media)

If your teenager is addicted to gaming

Gaming addiction like other addictions is difficult to deal with and you will need to be patient and determined. A discussion with your teenager about the nature of the addiction and its impact on their own and family life is a good place to start. Explain how much you love them and are concerned about them. Addressing the gaming addiction is not a form of punishment, but is necessary to improve their future life satisfaction and success.

You may wish to point it out that many adults have also become addicted to gaming and is now considered a major cause of relationship breakdown and divorce. You'll need to explore whether the gaming addiction is an escape mechanism from some form of external stress, that can be addressed separately either by removing it or learning techniques such as relaxation to deal with it. (See Chapter 13 Anxiety). Other family members may need to be made aware of what is going on, as it may well impact on them, and although you may not want to tell others outside the family about the problem, don't try to hide any negative outcomes that may result from not completing schoolwork or any other responsibilities. Teenagers need to realise that success and social interactions in the virtual world, are not nearly as important as what they are doing in the real world.

Those young people addicted to gaming may well already recognise some of these negative effects but may still not wish to stop or may have trouble coping with reducing or giving up the gaming. If possible, try to develop a joint strategy for addressing the problem that will reduce the amount of gaming. It may be helpful to complete a log or diary of how much time is being spent on the gaming and it will almost certainly be necessary to remove gaming access from the bedroom. It can be helpful to make changes in your teenager's daily routine to try to break the habit of gaming at particular times. It is useful to use distraction techniques to encourage the teenager to spend as much time as possible away from screens and preferably out of the house. If this does not work, screen time restrictions will need to be imposed.

For an addicted teenager, this is likely to involve a withdrawal reaction, which may well lead to angry outbursts, irritability and even depression and you should expect this. If all else fails, remove the gaming device or turn off access to the internet and have a gaming holiday.

Help and treatment for gaming addiction

If you have tried to reduce your teenager's dependence on gaming without any success, you may need to seek help from your GP or a specialist clinic. Since gaming addiction has only been recognised in recent years it may not be easy to obtain treatment although the NHS has recently opened its first dedicated clinic., Treatment for video game addiction is likely to be similar to treatment used for other types of behavioural addictions. Counselling and behaviour modification are two of the most important components of treatment. Counselling can help gamers to work towards reducing their gaming and finding healthier alternatives, while other forms of treatment, such as family therapy, may be necessary to help to identify other issues that may be contributing towards the addictive behaviour.

Useful Organisations

Action on Addiction-www.actiononaddiction.org.uk. Offers treatment for addictions of all sorts.

Clik-adix – www.clik-adix.co.uk. Gives advice to people about screen addiction

Stem4-www.stem4.org.uk. Addresses teenage mental health issues including addiction to gaming

References in this chapter

[1] Entertainment Software Association: Essential facts about the computer and video games industry 2018
[2] Internet Advertising Bureau: The gaming revolution study 2014
[3] OFCOM: Children and parents media use and attitudes report (November 2017)
[4] Limelight Networks: The state of online gaming – 2018
[5] Anderson C, Carnagey, N, Flanagan M, Benjamin Jr A, Eubanks J & Valentine J. (2004). Violent Video Games: Specific Effects of Violent Content on Aggressive Thoughts and Behavior. Advances in Experimental Social Psychology. 36. 10.1016/S0065-2601(04)36004-1
[6] Parentzone: Skin gambling: teenage Britain's secret habit (2018)
[7] Gentile D, (2009). Pathological Video-Game Use Among Youth Ages 8 to 18. Psychological science. 20. 594-602. 10.1111/j.1467-9280.2009.02340.x
[8] Stockdale L,& Coyne, S,. (2017). Video Game Addiction in Emerging Adulthood: Cross-Sectional Evidence of Pathology in Video Game Addicts as Compared to Matched Healthy Controls. Journal of Affective Disorders. 225. .1016/j.jad.2017.08.045.
[9] Loton D, Borkoles E, Lubman, D & Polman R, (2015). Video Game Addiction, Engagement and Symptoms of Stress, Depression and Anxiety: The Mediating Role of Coping. International Journal of Mental Health and Addiction. 10.1007/s11469-015-9578-6.
[10] Przybylski A, (2014). Electronic Gaming and Psychosocial Adjustment. Pediatrics. 134. 10.1542/peds.2013-4021.

Chapter 26

Online and other gambling

Gambling among adults

The latest report from the Gambling Commission 2017 (covering adults over 16) shows that gambling has been steadily declining, although this decline is largely explained by a fall in the popularity of the National Lottery. [1] Just under a half of adults have gambled in the last four weeks, but this falls to around a third, if the National Lottery is excluded. Among this third, gambling rates are higher among men and the younger age groups. Not surprisingly the main reason for gambling is the hope of winning, but other reasons include for the fun of it, or to support good causes. Despite declining, lotteries remain the most popular form of gambling, followed by scratch cards and sports betting. Football and horse racing are the most popular sports bets, and these are much more common among men.

Online gambling is one of the few sectors to have been increasing and just under one adult in five gambles online. Online gambling has been taking a larger share in almost all forms of gambling, but is particularly important to in-play betting. The most common online device is a laptop, but phones and tablets are increasing quite rapidly. Although most online gambling takes place at home, younger gamblers are far more likely to gamble while commuting or at work. Among younger gamblers betting on esports (video gaming competitions) either with money or with other items is also on the increase. (See Chapter 25 for more on gaming) Younger gamblers are also more likely to follow betting companies through social media with Facebook being the most popular, followed by Twitter. Among this group social casino and bingo style games with money or non-money prizes are also popular particularly with women, often being downloaded as apps.

Overall attitudes to gambling are generally declining with less people thinking gambling is conducted fairly and most people thinking that gambling is dangerous to family life and that there are too many opportunities for gambling nowadays. The biggest concern about gambling policy is that children and young people should not be exposed to gambling. There is also concern about regulating the number of gambling premises on the high street and regulating overseas gambling operators.

The survey also includes an analysis of respondents' answers to try to identify the likelihood of gambling being or becoming problem gambling that would have negative effects on the gambler and those around them. This suggests that around 4% of the population are at risk of becoming problem gamblers and about 1% already are. These rates are much higher among the younger age groups with about 7% at risk and 2% already a problem.

Gambling among children and teenagers

The latest report from the Gambling Commission 2018 covering children aged 11-16 shows that gambling has stopped its long-term decline due to the decline in the National Lottery. [2] This survey monitors gambling in the last week and showed that 14% of this age group had gambled with their own money in this period, slightly up on last year. Boys are roughly twice as likely to be gambling than girls. Unlike adults, gambling for the excitement is virtually as important as the possibility of winning money. The most popular form of gambling is private bets, followed by the National Lottery scratch cards and fruit machines. Around half of the gamblers spent less than £5 a week on their gambling, but worryingly 15% said that they spent more than £50. Gambling rates were higher among those who took drugs, smoked or drank alcohol.

Although only 1% of the age group had gambled their own money online in the past week, these were the most regular gamblers, and this rose to 5% over a one-year period. However, 6% report gambling online in the last year using parent or guardian's money with the most popular form being National Lottery games. Around a fifth of these gamblers admit to using this money without permission.

13% of young people also play online gambling-style games that do not involve money with bingo and fruit machines being the favourite among girls and casino type games most popular with boys. These games are usually downloaded as apps but are also accessed via social media sites such as Facebook.

A recent development in the online gaming market has been the ability to trade and bet on skins. (See Chapter 25 for more on online gaming). These are extras that can be rewarded or purchased in many of the most popular games, which provide cosmetic alterations to a player's appearance or weaponry. Some online sites allow these skins to be used to gamble for real money prizes or for items that have real monetary worth. The Gambling Commission believes that these unregulated websites should be licensed, as they believe that this is legally gambling, and have successfully prosecuted FutGalaxy. 15% of the age group were aware of skin betting and 3% had done it.

In addition, over half of the age group were aware of loot boxes in games, which provide a similar experience to gambling and over a third had used them. This activity seems to be much more common among boys.

As with the adult survey, an analysis of respondent's answers is undertaken to identify problem gamblers. This analysis suggested that nearly 2% of the young people were problem gamblers with another 2% at risk.

Gambling and UK Law

Apart from spread betting on financial markets, which is regulated by the Financial Services Authority (FSA), gambling in Great Britain is regulated by the Gambling Commission under the Gambling Act 2005, with a similar regime in Northern Ireland. Since an amendment in 2014, this Act regulates the licensing arrangements for both British based and overseas gambling organisations who advertise and trade with UK customers. Advertising for gambling is also regulated and should not be directed at under 18s. This Act not only aims to ensure that gambling is fair and not associated with criminality, but importantly that children and other vulnerable people are protected from harm or exploitation from gambling. As a result, the Act places restrictions on how children can gamble.

For under 18s it is illegal to:

Enter licensed premises such as casinos, betting shops and adult entertainment centres (adult only arcades) unless there is a designated area separate from the adult gaming activities.
Gamble on race courses, bingo halls or online.
Play most gaming machines or be allowed access to them, except those described below.

For 16 and 17 years olds:

It is only legal to play the National Lottery and other lotteries as well as scratch cards and football pools.

All children are allowed to:

Play on simple gaming machines (category D) which include very low stakes machines, coin pushers and grab machines, which are likely to be found in licensed Family Entertainment Centres (non-adult only arcades).
Indulge in private non-commercial betting.
Indulge in equal chance gaming with prizes under a prize gaming permit or by a licensed family entertainment centre (non-adult only arcade).
Indulge in prize gaming at non-licensed family entertainment centres or travelling fairs.

The Gambling Commission report discussed above suggests that at least some of the gambling being undertaken by children and young people is illegal under the Act. It is not always easy to distinguish between adult and children's gambling, when bets are placed, or lottery tickets purchased, when children are accompanied by adults. However, adults should bear in mind that under the Act it is an offence to Invite, cause or permit a child or young person to gamble illegally with a penalty of fines or imprisonment.

Should you worry about your teenager gambling?

For many people, gambling provides some fun and entertainment and does not cause problems. These people gamble in moderation, sticking to financial limits and avoiding high risk activities. They limit the time they spend gambling and may well largely gamble socially either with or against friend or family. For others, gambling can become an obsession which they cannot stop. They gamble for emotional reasons often for the thrill of the gamble and often overspend. They chase after big wins, will keep playing despite losses and are prepared to increase their betting stakes. Here are some signs to watch out for that could alert you to your teenager struggling or getting out of depth with gambling.

Spotting potential signs of gambling addiction

Physical signs
  Tiredness due to disruption or lack of sleep
  Changes in eating patterns
  Concentration problems
Mood signs
  Becoming more aggressive to other family members
  Having mood swings
  Being anxious or depressed
Behavioural signs
  Preoccupied by gambling
  Problems managing money with unexplained debts or cash
  Obsessed by sports results
  Stealing and lying about the gambling
  Poor academic performance
  Spending long periods in bedroom
  Withdrawal from hobbies, sports and friends

Who are most at risk?

Although anyone can develop gambling problems, research has suggested that certain types of people are more susceptible. [3][4][5][6] It should be noted that the higher risk characteristics listed below are very similar to those seen for problem gamers. (See Chapter 25 Online gaming) This makes the possibility of excessive gamers moving on to become problem gamblers a real concern particularly with the growing popularity of skins betting as well as the popularity of online games which simulate or copy games on which gambling is common.

The most at risk individuals are:
boys
Asians
children of single parents
those who start gambling early in life
those who also take drugs, smoke or drink alcohol
those with family members who gamble regularly
those who are impulsive and thrill seeking
those who wish to escape from stress
those who use it to help their mood
those who are bored or lonely
those with mental conditions such as anxiety and depression
those who have more money or access to credit cards

Which forms of gambling are most risky?

Teenagers under 18 cannot gamble themselves in casinos, betting shops or high stakes gaming machines. However, slot machines generally seem to be a high-risk activity as, even if the stakes are low, the games are very short and the experience intense. Although online gambling is not widespread among younger teenagers, similar activities such as free casino style games are popular and skins betting is becoming commonplace. These activities could potentially act as a stepping stone to real online gambling. This is another high-risk form of gambling as it can be carried out privately or out of the home and can be funded by credit or debit cards.

How can you help your teenager to avoid the potential problems of excessive gambling?

Role modelling.
You need to ensure that your own gambling habits are under control and that they demonstrate responsible gambling. Discuss with your teenager the potential dangers of gambling and suggest how to gamble responsibly. Explain that with most forms of gambling people are highly likely to lose money over time and that gambling should only be viewed as a form of entertainment, not as a way of making money. Talk about the dangers of gambling when they are feeling low, depressed or under the influence of drugs or alcohol.

Be aware of what your teenager is doing.
Be involved in your teenager's lives and be aware if your child is gambling and what they are gambling on. Teenagers who are gambling should be encouraged to set aside a fixed amount of money that they can afford to gamble, so discuss what would be a sensible amount bearing in mind their adolescent income and commitments. Monitor spending on gambling and be aware that teenagers may also gain access to your card details and use these to gamble online.

Support the legal age limits
Don't encourage or facilitate underage gambling that is illegal. Under 16s should be limited to family arcades and fairs and under 18s to lotteries and scratch cards. Not only is encouraging illegal underage gambling an offence, but early gamblers are at risk of developing serious gambling problems later.

Restrict access to gambling.
Consider setting limits on gambling both in terms of money, and how and where the gambling is carried out. Allowing

unsupervised gambling in bedrooms can lead to problems as well as sleep deprivation. The monitoring and control of all screen time needs to be looked at as soon as it seems to be causing problems. Consideration should be given to filters or blocking devices if necessary. (See Chapter 22 on the internet.)

Encourage other activities
Parents should encourage social activities with friends or family, especially physical activities out of the home.

If your teenager is addicted to gambling

If you believe that your teenager has a gambling problem, there are several steps that can be taken. Discuss the problem with them and try to come up with an agreed strategy for reducing or stopping the gambling. Tell them how much you care about them and how worried you are. Try not to get angry or issue ultimatums. You can't solve the problem without co-operation. Try to find out why they are gambling and if it is a form of escape from other stresses or problems. If it is, try to address these or find better ways of coping with them such as relaxation techniques. (See Chapter 13 for more on anxiety). Keeping a diary of how and when they gamble can help identify ways of addressing the issues.

 If their problem is with a particular form of gambling or one organisation, they may be able to enter a self-exclusion arrangement whereby they agree with the organisation or organisations involved to cease gambling for a period usually of at least six months. If, as is likely, the problem is causing financial problems, it will be necessary to try to restrict the access to money or credit/debit cards. It can also be useful to use a blocking software to stop access to gambling sites on computers or phones. However, it needs to be recognised that these methods will only work if the gambler themselves are committed to stopping as they will always be able to find alternatives if they really try.

Gamblers also need to change their patterns of behaviour. you can try to change family routines to encourage more social and physical activities. If none of these things appear to be working you should seek help. Problems associated with gambling addictions have been recognised for a long time and there are clinics and counsellors who use well established therapies to change behaviour. These treatments are available both at private clinics and at NHS clinics and charities, and it is usually possible to obtain free treatment.

Useful organisations

BeGambleAware – www.begambleaware.org
Provides help, advice and support in relation to gambling. It gives advice on gambling responsibly and how to spot problems,

Bigdeal – www.bigdeal.org.uk
This is part of Gamcare targeted at young people.

CNWL National Problem Gambling Clinic
Treats problem gamblers in England and Wales who are aged 16 and over who have an engrained gambling problem for which other approaches have failed. It assesses the needs of problem gamblers as well as those of their partners and family members and offers evidence-based treatments as well as interventions to assist with financial, employment, social and relationship difficulties.

Count Me Out – www.countmeout.org.uk
A not for profit social enterprise that aims to help vulnerable children and adults who are addicted to, harmed or exploited by gambling by promoting self-exclusion and social responsibility.

Gam-anon – www.gamanon.org.uk
A group of husbands, wives, relatives or close friends who have been affected by problem gambling, which gives support to those affected.

Gamblers Anonymous – www.gamblersanonymous.org.uk
A group of men and women who have joined together to do something about their own gambling problem and to help other compulsive gamblers do the same. They organise regular meetings throughout the UK and have a chatroom.

Gamcare – www.gamcare.org.uk
Provides information, advice and practical help in addressing the social impact of gambling for gamblers and their friends and relatives. They have a chatline and a helpline 0808 8020 133 and can offer free support and counselling for gamblers and other people who are affected.

Gambling Therapy – www.gamblingtherapy.org
Offers online services for gamblers and their friends and relatives including online groups and forums. They also offer self-help exercises as well as a GTapp to support gamblers trying to stop.

Gordon Moody Association – www.gordonmoody.org.uk
Provides online advice and support to problem gamblers through free residential treatment for severely addicted gamblers, as well as providing outreach support and an internet counselling service

References in this chapter
[1] Gambling Commission: Gambling participation in 2017: behaviour, awareness and attitude (February 2018)
[2] Gambling Commission: Young people and gambling 2018. A research study among 11-16 year old in Great Britain (November 2018)
[3] Calado F., Alexandre J., Griffiths M. D. (2017). Prevalence of adolescent problem gambling: a systematic review of research. J. Gambl. Stud. 33, 397–424. 10.1007/s10899-016-9627
[4] Forrest D & Mchale, I.G. (2011). Gambling and Problem Gambling Among Young Adolescents in Great Britain. Journal of gambling studies / co-sponsored by the National Council on Problem Gambling and Institute for the Study of Gambling and Commercial Gaming. 28. 10.1007/s10899-011-9277-6.
[5] Floros, G. D. (2018). Gambling disorder in adolescents: prevalence, new developments, and treatment challenges. *Adolescent Health, Medicine and Therapeutics*, *9*, 43–51
[6] Richard J, Derevensky J (2017) Identifying the Relationship Between Mental Health Symptoms, Problem Behaviors and Gambling Among Adolescents. Ann Behav Sci. Vol3 No. 2:30. doi:10.21767/2471-7975.100030

Chapter 27

Online pornography

What is pornography?

Pornography can be defined as printed or visual material containing the explicit description or display of sexual organs or activity, intended to stimulate sexual excitement. Of course, this is not a very precise description and it is not surprising that it is difficult to legislate against the various forms of pornography.

UK law on pornography

UK laws that relate to pornography are summarised below. Generally, pornography on the internet is difficult to stop or control as much of it originates overseas or from unknown sources. Viewing pornography is normally not an offence, but downloading, storing or sharing pornography may be. The UK government is currently considering ways to impose age limits on internet pornography sites.

The Obscene Publications Act mainly covers items that are produced in the UK. The guidance for this Act lists categories that are 'suitable for prosecution':
Sexual act with an animal.
Realistic portrayals of rape.
Sadomasochistic material which goes beyond trifling and transient infliction of injury.
Torture with instruments.
Bondage (especially where gags are used with no apparent means of withdrawing consent).
Dismemberment or graphic mutilation.

Activities involving perversion or degradation (such as drinking urine, urination or vomiting on to the body, or excretion or use of excreta).
Fisting.

The possession of extreme pornographic images Act makes it illegal to possess an explicit and realistic pornographic image, other than in a film that has been classified by the British Board of Film Classification (BBFC). The Act covers images that depict:

Acts which threaten a person's life, such as hanging, suffocation or threat with a weapon.
Acts which result in or are likely to result in serious injury to a person's anus, breasts or genitals, which include mutilation or insertion of sharp objects.
Bestiality (sexual act with an animal).
Necrophilia (sexual act with a corpse.

The Protection of Children Act 1978 makes it illegal to take or permit to be taken any indecent image of a child under 18. It is also illegal to distribute (share) such images or to show them. (See Sexting)

Revenge pornography Where an indecent or explicit sexual image is shared without the consent of the subject and with the intention of causing distress several laws may be broken. These include crimes covered by The Malicious Communications Act, The Communications Act and the Protection from Harassment Act.

The Video Recordings Act covers the classification of videos with certain exemption such as educational videos. It is undertaken by the British Board of Film Classification, who also classify films. The classification of videos is legally enforced and selling to under age customers is an offence. The showing of films in cinemas is technically controlled by local councils, who issue licences, which ensure that cinemas apply the age restrictions. It should be noted that films classified as R18 are not considered suitable for general release, but only through licenced sex shops and specially licenced cinemas.

The accessibility of pornography

Pornographic images have been around for thousands of years, pornographic books for hundreds of years and pornographic films for over a hundred years. Nevertheless, before the widespread use of video recordings and the internet, pornography was not easily accessible especially to young people, because pornography was generally restricted to adult only book shops or cinemas and could not be widely shared. Although the internet is a major source of pornography, it is useful to remember that young people still access a wide range of sexually explicit material through magazines and films. In addition, sexual imagery is commonplace both in music videos, advertising and in late night television.

The reason why this section will focus on the internet is because this has become a very easy way to assess pornography both on laptops and on mobile phones. Research [1] suggests that of over one thousand online providers of adult material only one is regulated in the UK. Many of these provide hard core pornography free and with little or no age checking of viewers. In the month that was monitored the five most popular adult websites each had over two million different UK viewers. Although this research only monitored computer use in the home, it still identified a significant rate of underage access to adult sites. Of those who went online in the 12-17 age group, one in five boys and one in nine girls visited adult only sites. Even among young children aged six to eleven, the rate was around three per cent of those going online.

The website that is reported to be the largest pornography site in the UK reports [2] that worldwide it has 81 million visits a day with the UK having the second highest volume of traffic after the USA. In the UK its' viewers view for an average of 10 minutes a visit with three quarters of viewers male. Although only around a quarter of viewers are said to be under 25, age verification is very difficult. The four most searched for items were lesbian, milf (a sexually attractive

287

older woman, typically one who has children), step sister and step mother, with the latter three all suggesting that viewers may be more likely to be younger males. Two thirds of the visits were carried out using phones, with laptops next. and then tablets. It is also worth noting that some access was via games consoles.

Is pornography harmful to young people?

Although there is a general view that pornography can be harmful, this is not universally accepted, and some pieces of research have suggested the opposite. Of course, it is difficult to research pornography because the term covers a very wide range of content varying from the erotic soft porn to hardcore pornography which may feature violence and degradation. The effects will also depend on the character of the viewer and the circumstances under which it is watched. The benefits that are sometimes stated are consistent with some research carried out among some Australian adult users of pornography. [3] These included:

Attitudinal
Becoming more relaxed about sex
Becoming more open-minded and experimental about sex
Becoming more tolerant of other peoples' pleasures in sex

Educational
Becoming more knowledgeable about body functions and sexual techniques

Social
Helping maintain a long-term sexual relationship
Helping them find an identity or a community

It is easy to see how teenagers can be attracted to pornography in the same way, both as a means of finding out about sex and as a way of exploring their own identities and sexuality. (See chapter 32 about Sexuality). For people who do not identify as heterosexual this may be particularly useful.

Other research suggests that pornography can relieve stress, improve libido and improve the perception of the opposite sex, but these results are all disputed and often contradicted by other research. It is useful to bear in mind that these beneficial effects are self-reported and may not be supported by objective analysis.

The general view from the substantial amount of research on pornography is that it can have detrimental effects, at least on some people. There are also specific concerns about young people because they are at a developmental stage, where any intensive behaviours run the risk of both long-term effects on brain structure and of possible addiction.

There are many kinds of pornographies, both professional and amateur, which include a wide-range of genres such as erotica, hardcore, group sex, feminist and a rapidly growing lesbian and gay sector. Nevertheless, most pornographic content on the internet has been and remains heterosexual, made by men for men, with women portrayed as objects of male gratification. As a result, there are considerable concerns about the potential for the images viewed to have a detrimental effect on sexual practices, social relationships and on mental health. The main areas of concern are:

Sexual practices

Casual sex: Sex is often between strangers or people who exhibit no significant level of affection. This is believed to encourage permissiveness and not to encourage healthy stable authentic relationships.

Unsafe sex: The use of condoms is rarely seen in heterosexual pornography and this could encourage unprotected sex. Combined with the possibility of casual sex, this could increase the possible spread of STIs, (See Chapter 21 for more on sex and relationships).

Normalising minority sexual practices: Many sexual practices portrayed in pornography including anal sex and deep oral sex are not commonplace among the population at large. This can encourage people to believe that they should indulge or expect their partners to indulge in practices that they find uncomfortable or physically unpleasant. Many of these practices are now far more common with younger rather than older people, which may be a direct result of pornographic influences.

Consent: In pornography, women often put up token resistance to sex saying no initially, but then co-operating and enjoying the subsequent sex. This "no means yes" portrayal can encourage sexual advances and actions that do not have the proper level of consent. (See Chapter 21 Friendships, relationships and sex)

Social relationships

Gender stereotyping: The males are often depicted as being in control and directing the woman's behaviour to maximise their own pleasure. The women are often obedient and submissive and largely seen as sex objects. This can encourage a view of male/female relationships which are very unequal and even abusive. In addition, coercion involving threats or violence is sometimes depicted which is thought to encourage sexual violence.

Mental health and self-esteem

Body images: At a time when we know that body image is a real concern for many young people (See chapter 10 on Building self-esteem and confidence), male bodies in pornography are usually very muscular and well-endowed, while the women are often slim with disproportionate sized breasts, which are often implants. This can lead young people to feel a sense of physical inadequacy.

Sexual performance: Pornography portrays people indulging in a wide range of sexual practices for long periods of time with no apparent lack of energy or enjoyment. Trying to emulate this can lead to sexual acts which are not fulfilling and can lead to confusion, frustration, disappointment and a sense of failure.

Distress: Pornographic images, particularly if they are not viewed deliberately can cause distress to the viewers. This is especially so for pre-teenage children, but also applies more to girls than boys.

Addiction and excessive viewing: Young people generally are more susceptible to addictive behaviours and it is thought that some of them, like some adults, can become addicted to watching pornography. As with other addictions, this is especially true of those who use pornography as a form of escapism from everyday life or for sexual arousal or masturbation. Excessive use of pornography has been linked to anxiety and depression. It can also cause desensitisation, with a need to watch more and more extreme content. This can cause problems with obtaining sexual arousal in normal life.

How many young people are viewing pornography?

A recent major study was commissioned by the NSPCC and the Children's Commissioner to investigate the impact of online pornography on young people [4]. It studied 11-16year olds and used the following description of pornography:
'By pornography, we mean images and films of people having sex or behaving sexually online. This includes semi-naked and naked images and films of people that you may have viewed or downloaded from the internet, or that someone else shared with you directly, or showed to you on their phone or computer.'

Unlike the survey mentioned earlier this covered access to pornography using any sort of equipment. Within this age group about half reported having seen online pornography with 56% of boys and 40% of girls. Although only 28% of 11/12year olds had seen pornography this rose to 65% of 15/16year olds. Interestingly, the first time that pornography had been encountered was often as an unrequested pop-up or being unexpectedly shown it by someone else.

However, among those who had seen pornography, around a quarter of 11/12 year olds and over a half of 15/16 year olds had actively looked for pornography. The most likely place to first view pornography was at home, followed by at a friend's house.

How does viewing pornography affect them?

In the survey young people were asked how they felt when they first saw pornography and many of the responses were negative including shocked, confused and disgusted. Only 17% had felt turned on. However, when asked about the pornography they are currently watching about half felt turned on and a quarter excited. When asked about the characteristics of most of the pornography that they had seen around a half described unrealistic and arousing. About a third described it as silly or amusing, while a similar number viewed it as exploitative and degrading. Around a quarter described the pornography as repulsive or upsetting.

It is interesting to note that although curiosity was a major reason for viewing pornography, only a few young people described it as informative. Younger children are more likely to find pornography upsetting, while older children are more likely to see it as fun, but also as more exploitative and unrealistic. Boys were more likely to be aroused and excited and to think pornography was realistic, while girls were more likely to be shocked or upset and to see pornography as exploitative. Nearly half of the boys and over a quarter of the girls indicated that pornography had given them ideas about the sex they wanted to try out. There was also a tendency to agree that pornography had led them to believe that men and women should behave in certain ways during sex and even that they should be pressured into this.

What can parents do?

Be aware of what sites your child is accessing

Be vigilant about what sites are being accessed. This is often difficult to do if children are allowed access to the internet in their bedrooms or other private locations. This is becoming increasingly difficult with internet access via phones, tablets and game consoles. Try to monitor which websites, games, apps and social media sites are being accessed and ensure that they are age appropriate.

Reduce access to pornography

It is clear from the research that the first time that children see pornography is often accidental resulting from pop-ups or legitimate searches and can cause upset. Once you become aware of this, try to address it by using blocking/filtering technology to stop inappropriate adult content. (see Chapter 22 on the internet). However, you should be aware that none of these methods are completely successful even when children are co-operating. Encourage your children not to click on pop-ups and to shut down or minimise any images or pages that they find upsetting and to tell you about it. Make it clear to your children that this is not their fault and that they won't be punished or have their internet access suspended. They should also be warned against pop-ups that demand money as a penalty for watching inappropriate content. It is useful to have wider discussions with younger children about whether anything that they are experiencing on-line is upsetting them or causing them to worry or be frightened. This could also apply to something that someone else has shown them.

Discuss healthy relationships

Since many teenagers will eventually see pornography it is important that teenagers are prepared for when they do so and are not punished or shamed, if discovered doing it. It is useful to admit to teenagers that it is perfectly natural to be curious about sex and masturbation, but that pornography is not a good way to learn as it provides a distorted and misleading picture of real life. It is important to counter any messages with discussions about healthy relationships and the role of sex within them. (See Chapter 21 on Friendships, relationships and sex). If you find it difficult to talk to your children about these issues or if children find it difficult, there are several useful websites which can be helpful including Childline, Think U Know and Brook.

Discuss the nature of pornography

Although pornography is often talked about, watching pornography is not the norm for teenagers. Less than half of younger teenagers have watched pornography and those who do, often do so quite infrequently. It is important to explain to young people that pornography is primarily a money-making activity. It is not real but is usually actors being paid to perform for the camera and being paid according to what acts they are prepared to perform. It does not reflect the reality of how most people behave either in terms of how they treat each other or the acts that they perform, and often shows disrespectful, abusive and violent behaviour, which in real life would be unacceptable or even illegal. The actors are selected because of their appearance and willingness to perform and not based on their acting skills. In real life bodies come in all shapes and sizes as do breasts and penises. If age appropriate, it is useful to also discuss safe sex and consent. (see Chapter 21 Friendships, relationships and sex)

If your teenager is regularly viewing pornography

If you discover that your teenager is regularly viewing pornography, you can try to use appropriate technology to block the sites, but this may well not prove successful as they may find ways around the block or seek the pornography elsewhere. Try to discuss why they are viewing the pornography. If it as a form of escapism try to find alternative strategies to achieve this and if it is out of curiosity about sex, try to discuss the issue or direct them to a more appropriate source of information. Discuss how they think different people are portrayed in pornography and whether they think that it reflects real life. It is also useful to discuss whether people are being abused and whether they are consenting to the acts being performed upon them.

If your teenager seems to be viewing pornography so often that it is becoming an obsession and interfering with other aspects of life, you need to discuss the risks involved. Although porn addiction is not a universally accepted condition, it does seem likely that since pornography stimulates dopamine release within the reward system, it could lead to obsessive behaviour like other addictions. Some research does suggest that heavy users of pornography have brain structures similar to other addicts. [5] Research also suggests that this can affect performance in other areas such as school work. [6] There is also an increasing volume of research that suggests that heavy pornography use, often linked to masturbation, can lead to eventual desensitisation. This can result in some people finding it difficult to be aroused by real life situations or eventually by any stimulation. [7] Research also suggests that male heavy pornography users have less satisfaction with their sex lives and relationships. [8]

If the problems persist it may be necessary to seek help from a GP or from a relevant charity. Although not every organisation recognises pornography addiction as a condition, talking therapies aimed at modifying the compulsive behaviours may well be effective.

Useful Organisations
ATSAC - www.atsac.co.uk
Provides information and support for sex addictions including pornography and gives information on courses and therapists.
COSRT - www.cosrt.org.uk
An organisation that provides information and therapists who deal with sexual and relationship problems.
Sex Addicts Anonymous – www.saauk.info
Provides meetings for sex addicts f various sorts to meet and address their addiction.
Sex and porn addiction help - www.sexaddictionhelp.co.uk
Provides free self-help resources.

References in this chapter
[1] ATVOD: For Adults Only? Underage access to online porn A research report by the Authority for Television On Demand ("ATVOD") (March 2014)
[2] Pornhub: 2017 Year in review

[3] Mckee, A. (2007). Positive and Negative Effects of Pornography as Attributed by Consumers. Australian Journal of Communication. 34.
[4] Martellozzo, E., Monaghan, A., Adler, J.R., Davidson, J., Leyva, R. and Horvath, M.A.H. (2016) I wasn't sure it was normal to watch it. London: NSPCC
[5] Kühn S., Gallinat J. Brain structure and functional connectivity associated with pornography consumption: The brain on porn. JAMA Psychiatry. 2014;71:827–834
[6] Beyens, I., Vandenbosch, L., & Eggermont, S. (in press). Early Adolescent Boys' Exposure to Internet Pornography: Relationships to Pubertal Timing, Sensation Seeking, and Academic Performance. The Journal of Early Adolescence. doi:10.1177/0272431614548069
[7] Voon V, Mole TB, Banca P, Porter L, Morris L, et al. (2014) Neural Correlates of Sexual Cue Reactivity in Individuals with and without Compulsive Sexual Behaviours. PLoS ONE 9(7): e102419. doi:10.1371/journal.pone.0102419
[8] Wright, P. J., Tokunaga, R. S., Kraus, A., & Klann, E. (2017). Pornography consumption and satisfaction: A meta-analysis. *Human Communication Research, 43,* 315–343

Chapter 28

Parties, discos and unsupervised holidays

If your teenager asks you if they can have or go to a party or go on an unsupervised holiday, don't be rushed into providing them with an answer. Give yourself time to find out all the details and to weigh up the likely risks involved. Parties are a great opportunity for teenagers to develop their social skills and meet new people but attending an inappropriate event or mixing with inappropriate people can encourage them to misbehave or take unnecessary risks as well as being places where alcohol or drugs may be present.

Attending other people's parties

If your teenager wants to go to someone else's party contact the host parents and make sure that the party will be supervised. Find out whether alcohol will be available, what other rules are in place and who else is invited. It is essential to know the start and finish times and whether there is a sleepover. If you are happy with what you are told, you can agree to your teenager going provided that they accept whatever conditions you wish to impose. These conditions will depend on your teenager's age and how responsible they are but may include:

Taking your teenager to the party at the start time. This avoids pre-loading with alcohol or gathering on the streets before the party and going somewhere else or misbehaving.

Collecting or arranging collection of your teenager at the finish time. This ensures that they do not stay after they are welcome and don't risk coming home late on public transport. It is also sensible to have a plan in place should they wish to leave early for any reason. Make sure that both you and they have fully charged phones and that you are available to receive the call.

Know their travel arrangements. If you are not taking or collecting them, find out how and when they will be travelling and who they will be with. Make sure that they have enough money or travel cards for their journeys.

Decide whether you want them to drink alcohol. If you don't wish them to drink alcohol, but there will be alcohol at the party tell the host adult. If there will be alcohol at the party, your teenager should not need to take any with them or buy it on the way.

Decide whether you want them to sleepover. You may not want them to sleepover, if you are not sure how well they will be supervised.

On the night of the party Ensure that you can contact both your teenager and the adult supervising the party if necessary, and be available to cope with any unforeseen events. If you are not collecting your teenager try to check that they have left at a sensible time and wait for them to come home. Whether you collect them or not, you need to check whether they are drunk. This is also a good time to find out how the party went and whether there were any problems. If there were, this may affect which parties you allow your teenager to attend in the future.

Hosting a teenage party

If your teenager wants to have a party at home, never let them do it without you being present. Although they may be the "host" of the event as far as their friends are concerned, you remain responsible for the safety and organisation of the event. If you don't want to take on this responsibility, don't feel you have to say yes. Suggest alternatives such as a group visit to a restaurant or the cinema or a smaller event at home. If you do agree that the event will take place, you may decide that you need some other adults present to help you out.

Parties provide an ideal opportunity for teenagers to learn some planning and catering skills as well as providing a way to introduce their friends to their parents. However, It is really important to have a detailed discussion with your teenager to agree on exactly how the party will operate to avoid things going wrong. The kind of party you have will very much depend on the age of your teenager and whether they are legally allowed to consume alcohol. Some areas to consider are:

Timing: Agree the start and finishing times and whether anyone will be staying for a sleepover. It is usually a good idea not to make the party too long and to finish at a time convenient for parents to collect their teenager, and so that the neighbours (who should have been informed) are not annoyed by the noise. Sleepovers should be kept to a minimum as they usually result in little sleep both for the teenagers and adults.

Food and drink: Agree what sort of food and drink is going to be served and who is paying for it. If alcohol is to be available, it is better to provide it than to let the guests bring their own. Make sure that there are plenty of non-alcoholic drinks available and try to choose lower alcohol or alcohol-free brands of beer/cider/wine and to avoid spirits. Providing plenty of tasty carbohydrate heavy food is also a good way of slowing up drinking and moderating its effects.

House rules: It is usually a good idea to create some no-go areas in the house to preserve your privacy. You may, for example, decide that you don't want boys and girls hiving off to bedrooms for obvious reasons. It is also sensible to lock up valuables and remove fragile or expensive items from the party area. If you are allowing smoking, you may wish to designate a smoking area. Make your teenager responsible for enforcing these rules in the first instance. Your teenager should also be responsible for tidying up the house afterwards.

Activities: Agree on what activities are going to be available such as disco/dancing, games, videos etc. Make sure that they are appropriate for the age group and consider how much noise and disturbance will be involved for any neighbours.

Invitations: Try not to make the event too big and make sure that there is a complete list of those who are being invited. It is useful to have a formal invitation, which states the times of the party, exactly what the guests are expected to bring or not bring, and whether alcohol is available. You may wish to show these to the guest's parents if necessary. Warn your teenager that there must be no open invitations or invitations that appear on social media that may be shared. Only invited guests will be allowed in.

On the night of the party: You may need several adults to ensure that the party goes well, but don't have your own party and do stay sober yourself. It is best to have only one entrance and for someone to check that only people on the guest list are allowed in and that they are not bringing alcohol or anything else that you don't want. Try to stop random comings and goings or guests roaming around the local area. If you are serving alcohol, keep it all in one place and have an adult monitoring it. If you have some younger guests, make sure that they are not given alcohol. Although you may wish to keep a low profile, circulating with plates of food, provides a perfect excuse for checking how things are going and watching out for any early signs of problems. If anyone is sick or ill either through alcohol, or otherwise, contact their parents and don't leave them alone. (See Recognising and dealing with drunkenness and alcohol poisoning below)

As the party approaches its end, time be prepared to turn the music down and turn lights back on. Check how the guests are getting home and don't let them leave noisily or with alcohol. If all has gone well, congratulate your teenager and their friends that you meet.

Recognising and dealing with drunkenness and alcohol poisoning

If your child comes home drunk or you need to deal with one of their friends who is drunk, try not to talk to them about who is to blame – that can wait until the next day when they are sober. If it is one of their friends, contact the parents as soon as possible. Concentrate on ensuring that the teenager is safe by:

Asking if they have taken any other drug.
Keeping them awake and encouraging them to drink water.
If they vomit or think that they might, try keeping them sitting up to avoid choking.
If they can't sit up, put them on their left side in the recovery position and support them with a pillow to maintain the position.
Never leave them alone

Being drunk can be a life-threatening situation. Alcohol depresses the central nervous system and binge drinking can lead to alcohol poisoning that can lead to a loss of consciousness. Signs of alcohol poisoning include:
A semi-conscious or unconscious state
Asleep and can't be woken
Cold, clammy or bluish skin
Slow breathing at a rate of less than 12 times a minute or stopping breathing for periods of 10 seconds or more

If you see signs of alcoholic poisoning contact the emergency services immediately. Stay with them until help arrives. If they have taken any drugs give them to the ambulance personnel or tell them what you have been told.

Festivals and unsupervised holidays

Many teenagers now wish to go to festivals and other unsupervised holidays, particularly after they have finished their examinations. If you decide to allow this, it is important to plan early, and importantly, before they make their own arrangements with friends.

You want to ensure that they can have fun, while minimising the possible risks involved. Areas for discussion are likely to include:

The exact nature of the event or location Where exactly is your teenager going and what are they likely to be doing there? You may be able to check some of this on the internet or by discussion with other parents or older children.

Who will be there Who are they going with and who else they may be meeting at the event?

Travel and sleeping arrangements How will they get there and back, where will they stay and what will they eat? How will they pay for all of this?

Keeping in touch How can they contact you either daily or in an emergency?

Safety How will they keep themselves and their property safe while they are away?

Chapter 29

Peer pressure

Even as adults, we experience peer pressure and it can have both positive and negative effects upon us. On one hand, it can encourage us to try new things, take a few risks and expand our comfort zones, but negative peer pressure can be a major problem for all of us and often makes us do things that we don't want to do, or not to do those things that we really want to. Because of this, it can affect, not just our happiness, but can also impact on our mental health.

For teenagers, this can cause problems, because they become susceptible to outside influences as they are trying to build relationships and develop their own values and personality independent of you and away from your watchful eye. If you notice changes in your teenager's mood or behaviour, this may be the reason, but in any case, you need to discuss negative peer pressure with your teenager. Since this pressure is likely to come from their friends, it is useful to discuss what a good friend is and how good friends should support each other, accept each other for how they are and not coerce, or insist that your teenager change (See Chapter 21 Friendships, relationships and sex)

You will need to encourage ways to help your teenager resist negative peer pressure. These could include:

Keep communication going
It is important that parents try to maintain as much day to day communication with their teenager as possible, even when their teenager is becoming more distant. It is essential for parents to know as much as possible about what is going on in their teenager's lives and for teenagers to feel confident that they can tell parents about their problems. These talks must not be lectures

or necessarily very long but must be a two-way conversation respecting your teenager's views and trying to understand their situation. You'll need to find appropriate early opportunities to discuss the issues you're most likely to worry about, including alcohol, smoking, drugs and sex, but again this needs to be done in a calm and balanced manner. During these discussions try to find out what your teenager knows, understands and already has experience of. You're likely to want your teenager to adopt your own attitudes to these issues, but these can't be imposed. They need to be explained and justified with an honest and accurate discussion of the consequences of making the "wrong" choices.

Know your teenager's friends
Try to meet your teenager's friends and judge how good an influence they are likely to be. It is difficult to persuade a teenager to drop a friend of whom you disapprove, but it is often possible to encourage friendships which seem to be supportive and positive.

Encourage a variety of social networks
The more friends in different situations your teenager has the better. If their only friends are at school, they will have little backup if things are going wrong. Encourage sporting activities, joining clubs and time spent with neighbours or relatives of whom you approve. This will also develop their social skills and build their confidence.

Build their self-confidence
Give your teenager the opportunity to make as many decisions in their life as possible and praise them whenever they make wise and appropriate choices. Teenagers who have faith in their own ability to choose, are less likely to follow a poor example. Encourage them to recognise their strengths and talents.

Build their own values
Parents need to establish their expectations of acceptable behaviour, but it is important not just to impose these, but to explain them. Teenagers need to learn what is right and what is

wrong, but also what is sensible and safe and what is reckless. They need to build their own instincts for decision making, so that they can be confident that if something feels wrong or uncomfortable, they shouldn't do it.

Encourage their individuality
Each of us is different and we all deserve to be respected no matter how nature has made us or how we choose to be, so try not to inhibit your teenager's choices of clothes, music, hobbies and activities provided they are safe and not anti-social. Teenagers should learn that we all have the right to make individual choices and to decide whether we wish to fit into a specific group or not. Other people are entitled to try to influence us but not to coerce us. At the same time, we are responsible for our own decisions and actions and if we make the wrong decisions, we can't blame others.

Plan ways to deal with unwanted peer pressure
You will never be able to protect your teenager from experiencing all unwanted peer pressure and teenagers need to be allowed enough time and space to develop their own strategies, but you can help your teenager think and draw their own conclusions by talking through the various options. This may just be by offering general advice or in response to a particular situation.

Avoid the situation
If a certain situation is known to be presenting problems or is expected to, encourage your teenager to avoid them altogether or be prepared to walk away. It may be helpful to provide them with an excuse so that they can blame you for avoiding the situation. It can also be useful to have a coded message that your teenager can use to phone you to let you know that they need to be "rescued" if they are feeling vulnerable or are in an unsafe situation.

Practise possible situations
It can be very useful for teenagers to practise how to resist peer pressure in certain situations. Parents can help them to play out scenarios and encourage their teenagers to be assertive and to find

appropriate phrases to use to either reject the pressure directly or to challenge the actions by pointing out the consequences. It is useful to ask questions such as: "What if your friends say this, what will you say?"

Teach them to be able to say no!

This is one of the most important assertiveness skills for all of us, if we are to be in control of our lives. With younger children, parents expect absolute obedience, but if parents are to teach teenagers to make their own decisions, they must encourage them to say no, when it is appropriate, even to them! Saying no to anyone who is pressurising us is difficult and so we need to learn a number of different strategies to use. Teenagers must understand that everyone has the right to say no to anything which makes their life more difficult, which makes them feel uncomfortable, or which is against their personal values.

Teenagers should be prepared to say no politely, but clearly and directly, so that the listener knows that they mean it. Saying "No thanks, I don't want to do that" should be enough and their friends should respond by respecting their wishes, but some people prefer to say no and then give an explanation as to why they can't do it. If they do give a reason, they should generally try to use an honest reason that can't be challenged as they need to be prepared to resist persistent pressure from someone trying to undermine these reasons. If the pressure does persist and someone won't take no for an answer, teenagers need to be prepared to just keep repeating why they don't wish to do it and not back down. If this doesn't work, they may need to put a stop to the conversation by saying *"Can you stop pestering me please, I'm not going to do it"* or even to just walk away.

Supporting your child to recognise peer pressure, when it helps and hinders them, and how they can develop their own individuality, is an important role for parents.

Chapter 30

Self-harm

What is self-harm?

Self-harm is a term used when someone injures or harms themselves on purpose rather than by accident. In the most severe cases, the self-harm results in a hospital admission or even death.

In the majority of cases, however, the motive is not suicide, but trying to cope with distressing situations, and strong emotions. Whatever the motivation, self-harming is always a sign that something is seriously wrong and must be taken seriously.

How do people self-harm?

People self-harm in a wide variety of ways including:

Cutting
Self-poisoning
Over-eating or under-eating
Self-biting or excessive nail biting
Picking or scratching skin
Self-burning or scalding
Inserting objects into their body
Hitting themselves against walls
Overdosing
Exercising excessively
Pulling their hair

Between 2007/8 and 2016/17, hospital admissions for under 18 year olds rose by 40%, with a particularly marked increase for girls, [1] and over three quarters of these admissions are the result of self-poisoning.

Cutting is the second biggest cause of admissions and the fastest growing. A detailed analysis of self-harm health records from 2001 to 2014, showed a dramatic increase of 70% for girls aged 10-13.[2] Among most people who self-harm as a coping mechanism, and do not have suicidal thoughts, cutting seems to be the most common method. While the numbers of young people with suicidal thoughts may be relatively low, the number of teenagers who self-harm is thought to be substantial and to have been growing. One study among 15 year olds in 2015 found that around one in nine boys and one in three girls reported that they had self-harmed. [3]

Why do young people harm themselves?

Young people self-harm for a variety of reasons. Some are suicidal, some are punishing themselves for some perceived failure, but the most common reason seems to be as a way of coping with emotional distress and to help manage and control their feelings and create a sense of calm. Creating 'real' pain can be easier to deal with at the time than addressing the underlying cause or emotional pain. The effect is usually only temporary though, as the feelings and emotions are still there after self-harming, and there is a risk that young people can turn to self-harm automatically when they are distressed out of habit. As a result, the incidences of self-harming can become more frequent or the impact more severe over time. This is clearly very serious and, in some circumstances, can be life threatening.

Teenagers who say why they self-harm cite the following reasons:

Some young people use it as a way of generating immediate relief from intense or difficult emotions that build up inside them and cause them distress.
Some say that they have been feeling very worried about a problem and don't know where to turn for help. They feel hemmed in and vulnerable. They can feel more in control when they self-harm.
Guilt or feeling ashamed may also become unbearable. Self-harm is a way of punishing themselves.

Some young people are unable to discharge feelings of resentment or pressure that get bottled up inside. Self-injury helps to relieve the tension that they feel.

Some are facing personal circumstances, such as loss, abuse or other types of trauma that they wish to escape or disassociate from emotionally. This can lead to a feeling of numbness that creates a calming sensation. Young people say that they can then feel detached from the world and their bodies, and that self-injury awakens them, and they can feel more connected and alive.

Who is most likely to self-harm?

There's no such thing as a typical person who self-harms. It can affect anyone of any age, background or race, regardless of whether they are an extrovert or an introvert. It can be one short episode lasting hours or days, or it can continue for months or years. For some, it's part of coping with a specific problem and they stop once the problem is resolved. Others self-harm for years whenever certain kinds of pressures and problems arise.

A survey carried out in 2014, showed that one in three 18-21year-olds say they've self-harmed, but some individuals seem to be more likely to self-harm [4] [5] [6]

These include:

Girls and young women, although there has been a significant increase in the number of boys using self-harming as a coping mechanism.

Teenagers and younger adults aged between 15 and 25 years old.

People with mental health disorders including depression and eating disorders, loneliness or isolation

People who are affected by loss e.g. death of relative or close friend, parental divorce or separation.

Those with negative thought patterns, and low self-esteem, poor body image or poor life satisfaction or who feel that they are not accepted or belonging.

Teenagers and young people who have difficulty forming or maintaining relationships, or who experience communication problems with parents, teachers and classmates.

Gay, bisexual, transgender men and women or those young people confused about sexuality or sexual orientation.

Asian women.

People who are or have experienced bullying or abuse – sexual, physical and emotional.

Those facing sudden changes in behaviour and academic performance or a dislike of school.

Perfectionists and young people under pressure from family, school and peer groups to conform or to perform well (for example in getting good exam results).

People who are dependent on alcohol, drugs, smoking and other risk-taking behaviour to manage emotions. Drinking a lot of alcohol can significantly increase the risk of self-harm in young people who are already feeling stressed or depressed, or who demonstrate an impulsive personality.

People who live in residential care or secure institutions, prisoners and those with learning difficulties or disabilities.

Young people of lower economic status, or who are homeless or in severe debt.

The psychological reasons behind this behaviour can be complex and young people often need to have counselling or medical help to work through their problems and to find healthier coping mechanisms, so they can choose to move away from self-harm.

Spotting signs of self-harm

Although many people believe that self-harm is attention seeking, it's often carried out in a very secretive way and therefore is can be easy to miss. Although there are often physical signs, young people who self-harm can go to great lengths to hide these. The physical signs might also be evidence of abuse or bullying. Some signs to watch out for are unexplained cuts, burns or bruises to arms legs or abdomen, but many people who self-harm will make this difficult by:

not changing in front of others
avoiding swimming and PE
keeping covered up which may involve wearing inappropriate clothes, e.g. long- sleeved shirts in the summer, or a refusal to wear shorts or a bikini.
avoiding inoculations or visits to the G.P.
hiding blood-stained clothes or washing separately

People who self-harm may spend long periods alone in their bedroom or the bathroom. They may hide razors, knives or other sharp objects and may use elastic bands to numb areas.

They may well also exhibit changes in their behaviour including:

changes to sleeping or eating patterns
changes in school performance
becoming more withdrawn
becoming very moody, aggressive or down
losing interest in normal hobbies and activities

How can I help my child?

As a parent, it's very hard to cope with a child/young person with self-harming behaviour or who attempts suicide. It's natural to feel anger that your teenager is indulging in such dangerous and irrational behaviour and to feel frightened or guilty that you must have let them down in some way. It may also be difficult to take it seriously or know what to do for the best. These feelings are understandable, but most important is the need to recognise that your teenager is in distress, find out what is causing it and try to find ways to address it.

Your initial reaction and your first conversation will have a big impact on your child and whether they feel safe discussing it with you. Try to keep calm and caring and don't show disgust or anger, even if you feel cross or frightened. This will show your teenager that you can manage your own distress and that they can come to you for help and support, confident that you are able to help them manage theirs.

Remember that your child is the same young person as before and self-harming behaviour is just a small part of who they are, so do treat them as usual.

It is important to remember that most young people who self-harm do not intend to commit suicide. At the time, many people just want their problems to disappear, or to be blocked out. Be aware that although self-harm is non–suicidal behaviour, the emotional distress that leads to self-harm can also lead to thoughts of suicide. If you think your child is at risk, seek urgent medical assistance.

Find out as much as you can about the issues surrounding self-harm and share the information with your child and other close family members if they are affected or are finding it difficult to cope with their sibling's self-harming behaviour. This will provide an openness and a shared understanding of the issues. Your child might beg you not to tell anyone, and whilst it is helpful to consider carefully who needs to know about what is happening with your child, and to respect their privacy and their need for confidentiality, it is vitally important that this does not stop you from seeking help. The earlier your teenager addresses the self-harm, the less entrenched the behaviour will become.

Notice when your teenager seems upset, withdrawn or irritable. Encourage your child to talk about their worries and take them seriously. Let them know that you are there for them and show them you care by listening, offer sympathy and understanding, and help them to solve any underlying problems.
Offering to go with them to the doctor or counsellor can be helpful and a visible sign of your support but accept their decision if they choose to go alone.

If your teenager does start talking to you about their self-harming it is important to find out what situations, people or emotions trigger the self-harm. How were they feeling before they self-harmed, and how did they feel after the event. A diary can be useful in documenting this and teenagers may be prepared to write a diary or a letter, even if they won't talk directly to you about it. A diary can also provide a useful way of recording whether any alternatives to self-harming helped the situation.

Here is a summary of how to respond to self-harming disclosure or discovery

listen carefully and calmly without being critical or judgmental
try to understand how they are feeling
focus on the cause of the distress, not on the injuries
assure them that you want to help them address their distress
assure them that self-harming is quite common and can be helped
offer to find them professional help
try to keep things generally as normal as possible

Try to avoid:

trying to take control of the situation
trying to be their therapist
expecting or trying to force them to stop immediately
telling other people without the teenager's permission
constantly inspecting injuries

Accept that you are not to blame for your child's self-harming behaviour but take time to review your relationship especially as it may be perceived by your child and make improvements where possible.

Buy blister packs of medicine in small amounts. This helps prevent impulsive overdoses. Getting pills out of a blister pack takes longer than swallowing them straight from a bottle. It may be long enough to make someone stop and think about what they are doing. Keep medicines locked away.

Don't suggest that your child just stops hurting themselves. If it were easy to do, they might have stopped already! Remember that this is a coping mechanism for dealing with distress, so withdrawing it suddenly can lead to even more dangerous outcomes, and they will need to have healthier alternatives in place first before they stop.

Self-harming needs to be treated almost like an addiction, where people find ways of reducing it over time using alternative techniques and by resolving underlying issues. This may take a long time. Many teenagers will find it difficult to talk to their parents, when they are discovered due to shame and sometimes their own confusion over why they do it.

Young people are very resourceful! If you remove tools and implements used for self-harm they will simply replace them with something else. Talk together about what could be less harmful methods for managing feelings.

Distraction strategies
Some teenagers who find it very difficult to stop self-harming behaviour in the short term will need help from you to think of less harmful ways of managing their distress to achieve similar effects. When there is a delay in accessing services to address your teenagers' self-harming behaviour, or if you want to support your teenager more immediately, here are some useful distraction strategies that can help to alleviate stress and painful feelings and replace the self-harming behaviour. Some will work much better than others, and it's also helpful to discuss with your teenager what solutions they have already found that helps them to cope in other less harmful ways.

Distractions (anger management)
   hit a pillow or punchbag
   tear up sheets of paper
   squeeze ice cubes
   breathing exercises
   scream or swear to yourself

Distractions (soothing)
   stroke a pet
   listen to calming music
   have a bath with fragrances/bubbles
   try some yoga or meditation

Distractions (sadness)
  wrap in blanket
  hug a soft toy

Distractions (indoor)
  create something: drawing, writing, collage, music or sculpture
  listen to loud music
  write a diary or letter about your feelings
  do some exercises or dance
  sing to karaoke
  write lists of five blessings or good things in life
  watch a favourite video that lifts your spirits
  paint nails
  colour or restyle hair

Distractions (outdoor)
  go for a walk, looking at things, listening to sounds and touching
  objects
  go to the park on the swings
  go for a run

Replacement activities (sensual)
  hold an ice cube
  take hot or cold baths/showers
  chew a hot spice
  drink very cold water
  snap an elastic band on the wrist
  smell a strong smell such as a vapour rub
  use an embrocation to make the skin tingle

Replacement activities (visual)
  draw on skin with red pen, lipstick, nail polish or paint
  put plasters on the skin
  apply a fake (temporary) tattoo
  apply ice or warm water that has been made with red food colour

Dealing with wounds

Self-harm is often kept secret, but as already discussed, there may be clues. In some situations, you will only become aware of injuries when your child, or one of their friends, come to you in panic, especially if cuts or burns are extreme. You can help practically by checking to see if injuries (cuts or burns for example) need hospital treatment and if not, by providing them with clean dressings to cover their wounds.

If their self-inflicted injuries are sufficiently serious, you will need to take your teenager to a hospital for treatment. If teenagers are continuing to self-harm by cutting it can be a good idea to provide a first aid kit with antiseptic wipes and dressings. Although this may seem like colluding with the problem, it can prevent infections and scarring until the underlying problems are addressed.

If you are worried that your teenager is suicidal
We have already said, that most young people who self-harm do not intend to end their life. Sadly though, some young people who self-harm can signal a warning that they are considering suicide.

Although many people who commit suicide have had no previous dealings with mental health services, suicide is rarely an instantaneous decision and there are usually warning signs in advance. Suicide rates among boys are over twice as high as those for girls, although the rates for girls have been increasing recently. (See Chapter 2 Worrying times) The most important signs of suicidal thoughts are spoken, although this may be to friends rather than parents. Any talk of not being able to go on or wishing to end it should be taken very seriously and parents should be ready to seek professional help.

Other signs to watch out for are:

being depressed
becoming withdrawn
showing significant changes in behaviour or attitudes
preoccupation with death
lack of appetite
lack of energy
showing lack of self-worth
a sense of helplessness
self-harming
risk taking and impulsive behaviours
drug or alcohol abuse

Of course, many of these can also be associated with other mental health issues as well. The risk of suicide is often aggravated by other events such as:

recent death of a close friend or relative, especially by suicide
family history of suicide
divorce and family breakup
failure in school examinations
breakdown of close friendship or relationship
abuse or bullying

If you are worried that your teenager may have suicidal thoughts, try to talk to them about it. Listen carefully and take any risks seriously. If your teenager is in despair, they need to be told that they can be helped and that there is hope that they can change the situation. If you are at all worried, seek professional help. Try to ensure that their home is as safe as possible by locking away medicines and alcohol and keeping any household products that are poisons in a safe place. Teenagers with suicidal thoughts should not be allowed to drive and should not be left alone if possible.

How is self-harm treated?

This will obviously depend on the severity of injuries and whether your teenager needs hospital treatment, but generally, if professional help is sought it will normally be from the GP or from a therapist or counsellor. Some schools can provide this service or will have contacts with agencies that can. GPs may refer the teenager on to another service such as Child and Adolescent Mental Health Service (CAMHS), a self-help group or to a therapist. Unless there are other mental health issues, treatment is normally by talking and does not require medication, although it may involve treatment of injuries or scars.

All young people who attend hospital following harming themselves should also have a specialist mental health assessment before leaving. It is often difficult to work out what prompted your teenager to self-harm and mental health professionals have the expertise to make sense of these complicated situations. As parents or carers, it is usual for you to be involved in the assessment and any treatment. This makes it easier to understand the background to what has happened, and to work out together whether more help is needed.
Assessments in Emergency Departments (also known as A&E), which include a short 'talking therapy' session have been shown to help young people come back for ongoing help and support. A lot of young people continue to self-harm if they do not receive the help they need.

Usually, treatment for self-harm and attempted suicide, other than any immediate physical treatment, will involve individual or family 'talking therapy' for an agreed number of sessions. Your child will need help with how to cope with the very difficult feelings that cause self-harm. The talking therapies usually have two main objectives. The first is to try to discover the underlying causes of the distress and to find ways of addressing these. This will vary considerably from person to person and may involve issues such as helping with relationship issues, helping to raise self-esteem, helping solve problems and managing expectations. They may also deal with coping with emotional states such as anger and anxiety. The second, which applies to everyone, is to make clear plans on how to help and how to keep your teenager safe. Families often need help in working out how to make sure that the dangerous behaviour doesn't happen again, and how to give the support that is needed. This is something your local CAMHS could have on offer.

Dealing with self-harming teenagers is extremely serious and you may simply feel too upset, angry or overwhelmed to effectively help your child/young person. If so, you should seek advice from your GP or from local support groups or charities. Try not to take on the role of therapist yourself but do find out as much as possible about self-harming. If there are a lot of problems or arguments at home, get help if they are upsetting you or your family.

If your teenager agrees to see a professional, you may well be involved in suggested strategies or techniques, but often they refuse to seek professional help, and they are uncooperative. In this situation, you could consider involving your teenager's school, or a close or trusted friend. However, if there are warning signs that they may be suicidal, you must seek professional help no matter what your teenager says. If depression or another serious mental health problem is part of the problem, it will need treatment. Some young people who self-harm may have suffered particularly damaging and traumatic experiences in their past and may need specialist help over a longer period.

How can schools help to reduce the incidents of self-harm?

As part of the Life Skills programme, the school will discuss the dangers of self-harming with pupils. Key factors of the topic are often introduced using outside speakers with follow up discussions. Tutors should ensure that pupils know what support is available both within and outside the school.
Pupils can be encouraged to self-refer to the school counsellor or to specialist groups in the area and to talk to their parents.
One of the main problems with self-harming is that the pupil can make themselves very ill by their actions and long periods of absence from school can then follow.

For this reason, schools that take a proactive role in such situations, may encourage pupils to take time away from school temporarily, if:
their condition is not improving
they refuse to acknowledge they have a problem
they refuse to co-operate with the management of their condition
their behaviour is having a detrimental impact on other pupils in the school, in the judgement of medical, teaching, academic or pastoral staff.

Useful organisations

Childline – www.childline.org.uk
Provides a free and confidential telephone service for children. Helpline: 0800 1111.

Family lives – www.familylives.org.uk
Helps parents deal with changes in family life. They also offer a free helpline at 0808 800 2222.

Harmless - www.harmless.org.uk
Harmless is an organisation that provides a range of services about self-harm including support, information, training and consultancy to people who self-harm and their families.

Heads above the waves – www.hatw.co.uk
Raises awareness of depression and self-harming in young people and gives advice for dealing with it.

Lifesigns – www.lifesigns.org.uk
Helps understanding of self-harm and provides information and support to people who self-harm and their families.

Mind – www.mind.org.uk/Self-harm
Provides information and support on a variety of mental health issues and has an information helpline 0300 123 3393.

National Self-Harm Network – www.nshn.co.uk
Offers support and advice to people who self-harm and their families. They have an on-line forum.

NHS Choices – www.nhs.uk/conditions/self-harm
Provides information on self-harm and how to get help.

Overcoming – www.overcoming.co.uk
This website has information on self-help guides you can buy for a range of different conditions. They are not free resources. You can buy the books direct or you may able to get some of the books second hand on auction sites.

Self Harm Organisation – www.selfharmorganisation.org.uk
Supports those struggling with self-harm and gives advice to families.

Self Harm UK – www.selfharm.co.uk
Supports young people affected by self-harm.

Self Injury Support – www.selfinjurysupport.org.uk
Supports girls and women who self-harm or are supporting someone who self-harms. They have a helpline at 0808 800 8088.

The Samaritans – www.samaritans.org
Provide a 24-hour service offering confidential emotional support to anyone who is in crisis. Helpline 116 123

The Mix – www.themix.org.uk
Supports under 25s on a wide range of issues including self-harm.

YoungMinds – youngminds.org.uk
Provides information and advice on children's mental health issues and a Parents' Helpline:0808 802 5544.

References in this chapter

[1] Hospital Episode Statistics, Admitted Patient Care - England: External causes
[2] Morgan, C., Webb, R.T., Carr, M.J., Kontopantelis, E., Green, J., Chew-Graham, C.A., Kapur, N., & Ashcroft, D.M. (2017). "Incidence, clinical management, and mortality risk following self harm among children and adolescents: cohort study in primary care." BDJ (2017).
[3] Brooks, F., Magnusson, J., Klemera, E., Spencer, N. and Morgan, A. (2011). HBSC England National Report: Health Behaviour in School-aged Children: World Health Organization Collaborative Cross National Study. Hatfield: University of Hertfordshire, CRIPACC
[4] Public Health England: Intentional self-harm in adolescence: An analysis of data from the Health Behaviour in School-aged Children (HBSC) survey for England, 2014
[5] Mars, B; Heron, J; Crane, C; Hawton, K; Kidger, J; Lewis, G; Macleod, J; Gunnell, D; (2014) Differences in risk factors for self-harm with and without suicidal intent: Findings from the ALSPAC cohort. JOURNAL OF AFFECTIVE DISORDERS , 168 pp. 407-414. 10.1016/j.jad.2014.07.009
[6] Hawton, K, Saunders, K & O'Connor, R. (2012). Self-harm and suicide in adolescents. Lancet. 379. 2373-82. 10.1016/S0140-6736(12)60322-5

Chapter 31

Sexual harassment

The level of online sexual harassment

Sexual harassment can occur at any time and in any place, but increasingly it is being carried out wholly or partly on the internet and social media. Although most teenagers have received advice about internet safety, presumably often including the topic of sexting, a recent survey [1] suggests that the sending and receiving of sexual images and messages is still quite common. Among secondary pupils about one in eight pupils has been sent a naked or semi-naked picture from a young person, with a similar number receiving a sexual message from a young person. One in twenty has received these pictures or messages from an adult. At the same time around one in twenty-five admits sending images of this sort or messages to another young person, and around one in fifty to an adult. These rates may be even higher in the older age groups.

Two recent reports from the Internet Watch Foundation suggest that a significant amount of child abuse imagery on the internet is now self-generated, often in children's bedrooms or in a bathroom. [2, 3] Nearly half of these images show secondary school age children often aged 11-13 with most of it showing girls. For some young people, this may just seem like a bit of fun, or a way of getting followers or likes, and although many young people believe that they can delete these postings, they can be copied and redistributed by others. In fact, these sexual images and messages can cause a range of very serious issues.

Firstly, as explained elsewhere they may well be committing an offence by posting an indecent image. (see Chapter 27 Online pornography). Secondly, they may be leaving themselves open to sexual grooming, blackmail or other forms of coercion or exploitation, either from another young person or from an adult.

A recent European study of 13-17year olds in three countries including the UK found that online sexual harassment between young people is commonplace. This included the following four categories:

Sharing of intimate images or videos without consent.
Receiving unwanted sexual requests, comments or content.
Being bullied by sexual content that humiliates, upsets or discriminates against them.
Receiving sexual threats, being coerced to participate in sexual behaviour online or being blackmailed with sexual content.

Around a quarter of the respondents reported having had rumours about their sexual behaviour shared online, while a similar number reported receiving unwanted sexual messages or images or had had sexual comments made about a photo of themselves that had been posted. Over one in twenty had had a nude or nearly nude picture of themselves shared online without permission, while nearly one in ten had received sexual threats. Many of the age group reported seeing other young people taking sexual images of other people or editing photos of other people to make them sexual and sharing them online, sometimes using fake profiles. They had also seen homophobic and transphobic comments used, as well as derogatory terms about girls such as slut or sket. These various forms of harassment were generally felt to have a greater negative impact on girls' reputations than boys.

The victims of online harassment were most likely to try to block the site or to speak to a friend or tell the perpetrators to stop. Less than half would tell parents and only about a quarter tell the police. Teenagers are generally reluctant to get their families or teachers involved and are also worried about getting themselves and the perpetrators into trouble. They also worry that if they tell parents or teachers, it could make matters worse. As a result, families and schools are often unaware of the problems until they escalate.

Although the above research only asked limited questions about whether the teenager had sexually harassed someone else, a study in America, which followed a group of young people over a six-year period[5], found that one in four males and one in six females admitted to sexual harassment with the average age of the start of harassment 15. Many of these young people later went on to more serious offences including sexual assault and in some cases rape. Some factors which appeared to be linked to the perpetration of sexual harassment were aggressive and delinquent behaviour, being the victim of harassment and watching violent pornography. (see Chapter 27 Online pornography). Peer pressure and attitudes also plays an important role, while one of the major factors preventing harassment is a sense of empathy.

Another survey[6] which asked young people who admitted sexual harassment, why they did it, found the four main reasons in rank order to be:

It's just part of school life
I thought it was funny
I was being stupid
I wanted to get back at someone

Clearly, all these reasons show little concern for the victim.

The impact of sexual harassment

Sexual harassment is a problem throughout wider adult society, but it often begins in the teenage years and it is quite widespread in schools and colleges. It may also be experienced by teenagers in the workplace.

Harassment can take many forms including:

Verbal – using derogatory sexual remarks or jokes
Non-verbal – using sexual images or gestures
Indirect – spreading sexual rumours or images online or elsewhere
Physical – being touched, bumped into or held in an inappropriate sexual way or being physically bullied or coerced into sexual behaviour

Research[7] over the last twenty years has suggested that sexual harassment is even more damaging to the physical and mental health of adolescents than bullying. Both bullying and sexual harassment have negative effects with girls, with sexual minorities being particularly vulnerable, but sexual harassment appears to have a more damaging effect on self-esteem and general mental and physical health. It has been linked to a range of mental health issues including depression, anxiety, self-harm and suicidal tendencies as well as low self-esteem and body image. Sexual harassment also has an adverse effect on academic performance and sometimes school attendance.

Of course, the growth of the internet and social media has changed the nature of sexual harassment in recent years and so it is useful to take a closer look at the impact of this type of harassment. Some recent research [8] has looked at the impact of non-physical harassment. This showed that this is just as damaging to mental health with similar negative effects on depression, self-esteem and body image. Female victims of harassment seem to be particularly linked to depression, while sexual and ethnic minorities are more affected by self-esteem and body image issues.

Sexual harassment is a major factor linked to mental health issues among young people, which can have repercussions on their whole life satisfaction and happiness, so what can you do if your teenager is affected?

How do I raise this subject with my teenager?

The current 'Me Too' movement and various associated news stories can give you a good opportunity to raise this issue. These discussions are needed both to stop teenagers being perpetrators or victims. It is valuable to talk about what is or what is not acceptable behaviour. Although much harassment is deliberately unpleasant, there is also harassment where teenagers don't realise the impact of what they are doing. What can appear to be a bit of fun or a normal part of teenage sexual development, can be very harmful to the recipient. Also, a one-off comment or sexual advance may be part of typical relationships, but continually behaving in this way becomes harassment. Sexual harassment and bullying is defined as any behaviour that causes the victims to feel intimidated, humiliated or degraded and can include:

Making sexual jokes, comments, innuendos or gestures to or about someone.
Sexualised name calling and insults.
Spreading rumours concerning sex, sexuality or sexual orientation (in person, by text, or online).
Writing sexual messages about people on bathroom walls or in other public places.
Unwelcome looks or comments about appearance, attractiveness or sexiness.
Pressurising someone into sexually related behaviour using emotional blackmail.
Showing someone inappropriate sexual pictures or videos.
Asking someone to send you naked pictures of herself or himself ("nudes").
Posting sexual comments, pictures, or videos on social networks like Facebook, or sending explicit text messages.
Making sexual comments or offers while pretending to be someone else online.
Touching, grabbing or pinching someone in a deliberately sexual way.
Pulling at someone's clothing and brushing up against them in a purposefully sexual way.

Asking someone to go out repeatedly, even after the person has said no.
Flashing or mooning at someone.
Calling someone gay or lesbian in a negative way.
Taking inappropriate and unsolicited intimate photographs, including upskirting.

Encourage your own teenager not to behave in this way, but to also challenge it when they see it being carried out by or to their friends.

Minimise the opportunities for online sexual harassment

It is important to advise your teenager not to deliberately or inadvertently post images online that might later be used to embarrass or intimidate them. Even images of themselves sunbathing or swimming, that they might believe are fairly harmless can result in unwanted comments or can be edited to cause offence, and so it is important to set privacy settings on social media to restrict access. They need to realise that images that are posted can be copied by other people even if they later decide to delete them.

It is important that teenagers are not communicating online with strangers without your supervision. This can occur during gaming), on chat forums and social media or during live streaming. This can provide adults with a way of grooming them either to encourage them to meet or to persuade them to film themselves in inappropriate ways. Sometimes these adults will pretend to be teenagers themselves and will start by using dares or games to encourage inappropriate behaviour. If an embarrassing image is sent, this can be used as a threat to either coerce them into even more damaging behaviour or sometimes for blackmail.

Warn your teenager about the dangers of sexting. Not only is this often illegal, but the images can later be used against them (see Chapter 15 about bullying). Social media now forms an important part of teenage relationships and this includes sending images. The research discussed earlier [4] found that about one in seven teenagers had sent a nude or nearly nude image of themselves to a boyfriend or girlfriend. Obviously, this runs the risk of this image being shared with other people and this may be particularly likely if the relationship breaks down. 'Revenge porn' is now a well-known phenomenon and was made illegal in 2015/6 in the UK.

Responding to sexual harassment

Encourage your teenager to talk to you or another responsible adult if they are the victims of sexual harassment either online or in everyday life. You need to acknowledge that teenagers may find it very difficult to talk about this and so you may need to discuss who else the teenager might confide in, such as a teacher or school counsellor. They should also be made aware of helplines, if they would rather talk to someone who does not know them. The key message is that as with any form of bullying, they must tell someone.

Many forms of sexual harassment are illegal under harassment, equality and other legislation and it may be appropriate to involve the police, but this should be discussed with the teenager first. Most social media platforms have mechanisms for reporting sexual harassment and potentially removing it, although of course, the damage may already have been done. If social media platforms are asked to remove content, take a screenshot of it first so that it can be shown to police, schools or other relevant organisations. It should be noted that schools have a legal duty to safeguard pupils and this includes protecting them from degrading treatment and eliminating unlawful discrimination, harassment or victimisation. This includes activities that may not occur in the school itself. Schools should be promoting healthy and respectful relationships and be prepared to intervene to counter unacceptable or illegal behaviours such as derogatory sexual remarks, sexual touching or grabbing, lifting skirts and taking photographs without consent.

Useful organisations

Childline – www.childline.org.uk
Provides a free and confidential telephone service for children.
Helpline: 0800 1111.

Family lives – www.familylives.org.uk
Helps parents deal with changes in family life. They also offer a free
helpline at 0808 800 2222.

Revenge porn helpline – This is a helpline run by charity and is
mainly for adult victims. The helpline is at 0345 6000 459.

The Mix – www.themix.org.uk
Supports under 25s on a wide range of issues including sexual
harassment and abuse.

The Samaritans – www.samaritans.org
Provide a 24-hour service offering confidential emotional support to
anyone who is in crisis. Helpline 116 123

YoungMinds – youngminds.org.uk
Provides information and advice on children's mental health issues
and a Parents'Helpline:0808 802 5544

References in this chapter
[1] NSPCC and LGfL Digisafe: Children sending and receiving sexual
messages (2018)
[2] Internet Watch Foundation: Annual Report 2017
[3] Internet Watch Foundation: Trends in Online Child Sexual
Exploitation:
Examining the Distribution of Captures of Live-streamed
Child Sexual Abuse (May 2018)
[4] Project DeShame: Young People's experience of sexual harassment
(December 2017)
[5] Ybarra, Michele & E. Thompson, Richard. (2017). Predicting the
Emergence of Sexual Violence in Adolescence. Prevention Science.
19. 1-13. 10.1007/s11121-017-0810-45

[6] AAUW: Crossing the line – Sexual harassment at school (2011)

[7] Gruber JE, Fineran S (2008) Comparing the impact of bullying and sexual harassment victimization on the mental and physical health of adolescents. Sex Roles 59:1–13

[8] Bendixen, M., Daveronis, J., & Kennair, L.E. (2017). The effects of non-physical peer sexual harassment on high school students' psychological well-being in Norway: consistent and stable findings across studies. *International Journal of Public Health, 63*, 3-11

Chapter 32

Sexual orientation and sexual identity

The teenage years are the years when teenagers explore who they are and develop their independence. This is particularly true of their sexuality. As they reach and go through puberty their bodies mature and change and they are likely to experience a whole new range of feelings, both physical and emotional, related to their sexuality. This can be both exciting and confusing as they come to terms with their new bodies and become aware of their gender identity, their sexual orientation and develop their values around sexual behaviour. This chapter explains some of the terms identified with sexual orientation and sexual identity.

Gender identity relates how comfortable someone feels with their biological sex, where the inner sense of being male, female, or both -- doesn't always match their biology. In other words, it describes a person's perception of having a particular gender, which may or may not correspond with their birth sex. Conflict can arise when the biological sex or society's expectations of that sex doesn't fit with the way they feel or view themselves. People who feel closer to the other sex or do not have any sex at all, are often described as transgender.

A **Transsexual** person feels emotionally and psychologically that they belong to the opposite sex and have usually sought or been in the process of undergoing medical or psychological treatment to acquire the physical characteristics of the opposite sex.

Pansexuality means that an individual is physically, emotionally and/or romantically attracted to a person, regardless of the other person's gender identity and/or sexuality.

Sexual orientation is about what kind of people we find sexually attractive. Everybody is different, but the most common orientations are:

Heterosexual/Straight – Attracted to the opposite sex
Homosexual/Lesbian/Gay – Attracted mostly or solely to the same sex
Bisexual – Attracted to both sexes
Asexual – Not really attracted to anyone

Sexual behaviour is not always the same as sexual orientation, as people sometimes have sexual relationships with others who are not their main orientation.

Although feelings about gender identity and sexual orientation are most likely to develop over the teenage years, they are not fixed and may change at any stage of life. The number of people who fall into these different categories is not accurately known as it is very difficult to get honest survey data due to problems of discrimination. However, official population statistics suggest that 95% of the population is heterosexual. Whilst among young adults under 25 in the UK, the heterosexual percentage falls to 91% with nearly one in twenty identifying as gay/lesbian/bisexual, but this may still be an underestimate. [1] Whatever the figures, it is known that teenagers who are transgender or gay/lesbian are far more likely to have mental health issues. These result from a feeling of not fitting in, feelings of rejection as well as bullying and discrimination.

What should I do as a parent?

The message loud and clear to your teenager must be that everybody is different and unique, and that you love your child unconditionally. Letting them know that they can talk to you about anything affecting them, without fear of punishment or criticism. Become knowledgeable, and review your own thinking about sexual orientation, keeping as open-minded as possible. Look for opportunities to discuss these issues with your teenager using news items, television shows or films as prompts. Remember. that whatever your teenager feels about their gender identity and their sexual orientation, you can't change them by expressing your own personal disapproval and it would be wrong to try to do so.

Many younger children may want to behave in ways that are not normally associated with their biological sex and this does not mean that they are transgender, but if this becomes an ongoing pattern that lasts for months or years, they may well be. Children, who struggle with their gender identity or identify as transgender, may well find the body changes that occur during puberty very difficult. If this affects your teenager, you will need to be as supportive as possible as transgender teenagers can feel very isolated. Together, you will need to discuss the situation with your child's school and agree on how your teenager wishes to be addressed and treated. If these issues are causing deep unhappiness for your child, professional help should be sought.

Whether teenagers are heterosexual or not, the teenage years are likely to be a rollercoaster of emotions as they try to build relationships both of a sexual and non-sexual nature and experience the elation and disappointments that go with it. However, gay and lesbian teenagers generally have an even tougher time and may need extra support. They are particularly likely to be bullied or to become bullies. Gay teenagers may also need to pay particular attention to safe sex, as they generally have a higher risk of infections.

If your teenager tells you that they are gay/lesbian, or think that they might be, the same approach as we discussed in the earlier paragraph applies. Try not to be shocked or judgemental. Just telling you is probably a major act of courage and a recognition that your opinion is important. Gay teenagers not only fear rejection from those around them, but may also feel isolated by a lack of role models or friends who feel the same way. Some may already be being bullied, because they are viewed as different, even if they are not known to be gay. It is very important that you accept the situation and offer to help your teenager in whatever way you can that will meet their needs.

Research suggests that sexual minorities suffer from worse mental health than heterosexuals with a greater incidence of depression, anxiety and suicide attempts. [2] Gay teenagers who are rejected by their parents are thought to have added problems. It will help them if you reassure your teenager that they are not alone and that everyone has the right to whatever sexual orientation they wish without bullying or discrimination. Your teenagers may wish to "come out" and tell other people or may already have done so. This needs to be their choice. If they do choose to "come out" try to support them as much as possible and defend them against bullying or homophobic comments or perceptions.

Whatever orientation your teenager may have, they need to develop healthy physical and emotional relationships as discussed in Chapter 21.

Useful organisations

Albert Kennedy Trust – www.akt.org.uk
Provides safe home, mentoring, training, advocacy and support to LGBTQ young people, who are homeless or living in a hostile environment.

Beaumont Society - www.beaumontsociety.org.uk
Provides support, help and advice to the transgender community.

Childline – www.childline.org.uk
Provides a free and confidential telephone service for children. Helpline: 0800 1111.

Fflag - www.fflag.org.uk
Supports parents and their LGBTQ sons and daughters.

Galop - www.galop.org.uk
Supports LGBTQ people who are the victims of hate crime, sexual violence or abuse and who may have problems with the police.

GIDS – gids.nhs.uk
Provides a specialist clinical service for young people with gender identity problems.

Gires - www.gires.org.uk
Supports and empowers trans people and those with non-conforming gender.

Gendered Intelligence - www.genderedintelligence.co.uk
Supports trans children and young adults.

Imaan - imaanlondon.wordpress.com
Supports LGBTQI Muslims. Founded in London in 1999, that campaigns to ensure that no LGBTQI Muslim person in Britain feels excluded from their family, their faith or their communities.

LGBT Foundation – lgbt.foundation
Gives advice, support and information to the LGBTQ community.

Mermaids UK – www.mermaidsuk.org.uk
Supports transgender children, young people and their parents.

Pink Therapy – www.pinktherapy.com
Provides information about specialist therapists for the LGBTQ community.

Stonewall www.stonewall.org.uk
Provide information, advice and support to the LGBTQ community.

Switchboard LGBT – switchboard.lgbt
Provides a helpline for the LGBTQ community at 03003300630.

Terence Higgins trust www.tht.org.uk
The leading HIV and sexual health charity, which provides STI testing and sexual health information and advice.

The Mix – www.themix.org.uk
Supports under 25s on a wide range of issues including sexuality.

The Samaritans – www.samaritans.org
Provide a 24-hour service offering confidential emotional support to anyone who is in crisis. Helpline 116 123.

References in this chapter

[1] Office for National Statistics: Annual Population Survey 2017
[2] Plöderl M & Tremblay P (2015) Mental health of sexual minorities. A systematic review, International Review of Psychiatry, 27:5, 367-385,

Chapter 33

Sibling rivalry

"Equal, but different"

Sibling rivalry is not just about how brothers and sisters treat each other. It's about how parents and other people treat them. We tend to think of sibling rivalry as kids fighting over who should have what or who should be entitled to what, but it is often made worse by how other people treat different siblings. Of course, parents need to treat children differently according to their age and stage of development, but most parents, although they won't admit it, often have favourites. This might be the happy child, the compliant child, the only daughter or even the child who has had the most health problems and needs the most support - there are many reasons for it. At one level, it is a recognition of the most important point – we are all different. We probably all make comparisons between our kids, but it should never be used as a weapon to throw in our children's faces. Parents should avoid using comparisons with other siblings when talking to their children. Remarks such as:

"Why can't you behave like your sister?"
"Why can't you just come home and do your homework like your brother?"
"Why can't you be good at that like your brother?"
"Why haven't you got lovely hair like your sister?"

These kinds of statements are not helpful and breed resentment and division between siblings. Even positive comparisons such as *"You're much better at that than your sister"* should be avoided as they are unnecessary and can also have a detrimental effect on children's self-esteem and motivation. Of course, it's not just

338

parents. Many relatives also overtly favour one child over another. It also happens in schools. If your older brothers or sisters were super-academics or paragons of virtue, it can be a hard act to follow. Equally if they have a reputation as disruptive or difficult you can feel that you are automatically being tarred with the same brush. Parents need to remember all children deserve to be respected as individuals. They are not reflections of their siblings, nor are they automatically responsible for or sharing in their siblings' good or bad points. Parents should avoid throwing comparisons at them and treat them as individuals with all their good and not so good characteristics.

Of course, even if parents are not aggravating the situation, they are very likely to have to deal with sibling rivalry which exists in most households, and as many households are now getting more complex, with step-siblings and step-mothers and fathers, the rivalries can become even more entrenched. Although sibling rivalry can be very annoying for parents and a cause of constant bickering, it needs to be recognised as an important part of growing up. All children will gradually learn to tolerate, accept and relate to the people around them and much of the time this will be other family members. Children can choose their friends, but they cannot choose the brothers and sisters with whom they share their household. Teenagers often face increased sibling rivalry as they are developing independence and trying to establish their own importance and place in the family pecking order and in the wider world. There are many factors that contribute to sibling rivalry including:

Competition for love and attention from parents
Jealousy of sibling's looks, talents, friends, privileges.
Arguments over privacy and personal space.
Arguments over sharing, or borrowing things.
Differences in age, sex and temperament.
Perceptions of unfair treatment or inequality.
Having to spend too much time together.
Boredom.
Outside pressures.

If you are trying to reduce the causes of unnecessary sibling rivalry or deal with the issue, you will always have a difficult challenge, knowing when or how to intervene, so here are some useful strategies.

Model positive family relationships
You should aim to get the message across early, through discussion and example, that the relationships between all family members must be kind, respectful and considerate. When disagreements arise, they need to be resolved in a calm and controlled fashion.

Set ground rules
Establish family ground rules that prohibit hitting and other forms of abusive or insulting behaviour with appropriate consequences.

Value each child's uniqueness
Don't compare your children, they are as different as apples and pears! Make sure to spend individual time with each of them to show them that they are loved and valued in their own right.

Don't show favouritism
In general, children must be treated fairly and given the same opportunities and advantages as one another, but these are different for each child and it is often not practical to treat them exactly the same. Differences in age, sex and other characteristics often require diverse levels of freedom and responsibilities, but if you explain the reasons why one child has or does something, and not another, most young people will understand and accept that on this occasion it is not their turn.

Pay attention to good and co-operative behaviour
We often leave our children to get on with it when things are going well and all is quiet and only intervene when things go wrong. Look for opportunities to give your teenager attention and praise for co-operative and supportive behaviours. Otherwise, the message you give is that it is only bad behaviour which gets your

attention and, if they don't wish to be ignored, that is how they will behave.

Create individual spaces
Teenagers need their own space where they can escape from their siblings and their parents. This will often be their bedrooms, but if this is not possible try to make somewhere else available, if only on a temporary basis.

Try not to intervene at all
If children are to learn the skills involved with dealing with other people such as compromising, negotiating, empathising and conflict resolution, they need to be left alone to sort their problems out as much as possible unless there is a risk that they will physically abuse one another, or if the insults are becoming personal, degrading or aggressive. Sometimes, your intervention can just make the underlying problem worse. If your natural inclination is to always intervene early, try to sit back and see how things develop. If they sort it out themselves give them some praise.

Don't act as referee
Unless the culprit is entirely obvious, do not try to referee your children's squabbles. Trying to establish who started it or who is in the right or wrong is usually very difficult and not very helpful. Both children should be held responsible and should experience any consequences. This will encourage them to find their own solutions in future. Getting in the middle encourages both young people to escalate the situation by telling tales.

Establish ownership rules
It is important that children are clear who owns what in the household and understand that they should not use or borrow other people's things without permission. Where common resources are shared such as computers or television, rules may be needed to establish who has priority or to create a rota.

Address ongoing causes of friction
If there seem to be certain issues that are constantly causing conflicts, discuss these with your children individually and in private. It may be useful to call a family conference to try to resolve issues by compromise and agreement.

Teach relationship skills
Parents can play an important role in teaching their children relationship skills. This begins with showing respect, but it is also important to know when to withdraw from or ignore provocation and when to assertively maintain your position. It is also necessary to learn how to see the other person's point of view and be prepared to make concessions.

Useful organisations

Relate (Family counselling) – www.relate.org.uk
Provides family and individual counselling services

The Spark – www.thespark.org.uk Provides family and individual counselling services in Scotland.

Chapter 34

Smoking

If you don't smoke and your partner doesn't smoke. it will probably come as a big surprise when you find or hear about your teenager smoking. How should you handle the situation so that he doesn't continue with this deadly habit? We know that smoking kills more people than car accidents, suicides, murder and AIDS combined. Every year, thousands of teenagers smoke their first cigarette. In fact, close to 90% of adult smokers smoked their first cigarette before the age of 18.

Adults and smoking
In the late 1940s, following the end of the war, smoking in the UK reached its peak with around two thirds of the population smoking. This reduced a little over the next few years partly because of price increases, but the major decline began following reports of the health effects of smoking.

These reports began in the fifties but became much more public in the sixties. As a result, most people began to recognise the dangers of smoking and the rates of smoking have been on a steady decline ever since. In recent years the dangers of passive/secondary smoking, particularly to children have also been widely recognised. It is now estimated that about 15% of adults smoke, with slightly higher rates among men and the under 35s.[1]

Smoking rates are higher among those with less qualifications and lower earners and are particularly high (29%) for the unemployed. In recent years, electronic cigarettes have also become available. Around 5% of adults "vape", although most of these also smoke or have recently switched from cigarettes. At present electronic cigarettes are widely viewed as less harmful than ordinary cigarettes.

Although there are beginning to be research articles questioning their safety, the general view of professionals seems to be that they appear to be less harmful than cigarettes and may be a useful way of stopping smoking.

Smoking and health

Smoking is one of the main causes of premature death in the UK. It is widely recognised as being a cause of 90% of lung cancers, but, in fact, is linked to a great many illnesses. These include:

Cancers of the lungs, mouth, throat, bladder, liver, kidneys and stomach.
Higher risk of circulation diseases such as coronary heart disease, strokes and heart attacks.
Higher risks of lung diseases such as bronchitis, emphysema and chronic obstructive pulmonary disease.
Smoking can also affect fertility and aggravates many other conditions such as asthma and chest infections.
Smoking during pregnancy has been linked to miscarriages and stillbirth as well as premature and low weight births.

Why adults smoke

Most adult smokers started smoking in their teenage years. This may have been for a whole range of reasons that we will discuss later. However, the basic reason that most adults smoke is because of the effects of nicotine on the brain. Nicotine is rapidly absorbed during smoking and almost immediately gives a "kick" as adrenaline is released. This raises blood pressure and increases the respiration and heart rate. There is also an increase in levels of dopamine, which is associated with a feeling of euphoria. However, these effects are very short lived, which encourages the user to keep smoking. Regular smoking changes the way in which the body and brain respond to smoking and the user can become dependent on the nicotine. If they stop smoking, they experience withdrawal symptoms, such as irritability and mood problems, difficulties concentrating, as well as changes in sleep and eating patterns.

Around two thirds of adult smokers say that they want to quit, usually for health reasons, but also because of the cost, but many people struggle to do so.

Smoking and the law (UK Law)
As the effects of smoking and passive smoking have become established the laws on smoking have become much stricter. the main laws now are:

Enclosed spaces: Smoking is no longer permitted in enclosed public spaces. This generally includes places of work, shops and pubs. It also includes public transport, cars used for work purposes and any car carrying a passenger under 18.

Buying tobacco products and e-cigarettes: It is an offence to sell these products to anyone under 18 or for an adult to buy them for anyone under 18.

Shop displays: Most shops must cover up cigarette displays.

Teenagers and smoking
The rates of smoking among teenagers has been falling in a similar way to that for adults along with the number of cigarettes smoked. The attitude to smoking is also changing with fewer young people thinking that it is okay to try or use cigarettes. In the last 10 years the number of 11-15year olds, who have ever smoked has roughly halved to 19%. [2] However, among 15year olds about a third have ever smoked and about 15% are currently smoking. This is almost the same as the average adult rate. Most regular smokers have friends or family members who smoke and parental attitudes to smoking are an important factor. Although most teenagers report that their parents would try to stop them smoking, the rates of parental opposition are lower among regular smokers. Their main source of cigarettes are friends or family members, but some are still managing to buy them from shops.

Use of e-cigarettes among teenagers has been increasing with about 11% of 15year olds currently using them. As with adults, the users are usually cigarette smokers or recent non-smokers. Teenagers who don't smoke cigarettes, like their adult counterparts, rarely use e-cigarettes.

When asked why teenagers are smoking, teenagers give the following reasons in order of importance:
To look cool
Because they are addicted
Peer pressure
To break the rules
Others in the household smoke
To cope with stress
To feel good/relax
To stay slim

Spotting the signs of smoking

The following are signs to look out for if you suspect that your teenager is smoking:

Clothes or hair smelling of smoke: If your teenager smokes their clothes and hair are likely to smell, although this may also be true if they spend time with smokers. They may try to hide this with perfume or deodorant.
Bad breath: Smokers often have bad breath, although many try to hide it by chewing gum or mints.
Yellow staining of teeth or fingers: Smoking causes yellow staining of the teeth, although some will try to treat this with teeth whitening products. Smoking can also cause yellow staining of fingers and fingernails.
Coughing: Coughing, sore throats and hoarseness can all be signs of smoking, although there may be other causes. The cough is usually worse early in the morning and may be associated with phlegm.

Breathing problems: Smoking can cause wheezing and shortage of breath after exercise, although there are many other causes. Smokers are more likely to suffer from chest infections and colds.
Moodiness and short temper: These are not unusual characteristics in a teenager, but if these problems suddenly disappear with a visit outside or to their bedroom, they may well be smoking (or using some other substance).
Smoking equipment: Check to see if they have matches or a lighter.
Smoking damage and litter: Holes or burn marks in clothes or furnishings are often caused by cigarettes. There may also be cigarette ends in outside bins or near the house.
Lack of money: If your teenager is getting the odd cigarette from friends, they may well be free, but if they are smoking regularly the habit becomes quite expensive.

Where to get help

If teenagers want to quit smoking, parents can help them to achieve this. It often needs careful and consistent planning and it is not always easy or successful at the first time of trying. If they find it difficult and need more help it is useful to visit a GP who may prescribe nicotine replacement patches, gums, inhalers or tablets or may refer to the local Stop Smoking Service. Make a date for them to cut down significantly or preferably quit altogether. Try to avoid times which may be stressful due to other events. If they wish to quit completely suggest that they throw out all cigarettes and lighters. If they have been regular smokers, they may well have withdrawal symptoms, such as irritability, cravings, or general aches and pains.

Some people also find that e-cigarettes can be useful in quitting smoking, but it is better if this is only a short-term solution. Teenagers can remain dependent on the nicotine and the long-term effects of e-cigarettes are not really known.

Giving up cigarettes can be a difficult process and teenagers will need support and encouragement. Try not to criticise them if they stop and then start again but try to encourage them to keep going with their efforts to quit. Parents may need to investigate what triggers are causing the smoking and try to find other ways to deal with these. Creating distractions or exercising can often help.

Useful organisations

ASH – www.ash.org.uk
Provides information on smoking and health and campaigns to reduce smoking.

QUIT – www.quit.org.uk
Provides information on how to give up smoking.

Smokefree – www.nhs.uk/smokefree
Provides information and support to help people give up smoking.

References in this chapter

[1] NHS Digital : Statistics on smoking England 2018
[2] NHS Smoking drinking and drug use among young people England 2016

Chapter 35

Social media

Is social media harmful?

Social media is often the greatest use of technology by teenagers, particularly girls. Teenagers and young adults are the heaviest users of social media with its use approaching 100% in these age groups and with the majority having their own profile. It is therefore likely that any detrimental effects of social media are likely to impact on them the hardest. However, before we look at the problems caused by social media, we need to recognise that it can have benefits for many people. These include:

Enhancing friendships and other relationships.
Minimising isolation and loneliness.
Providing emotional support, advice and information both from friends and other sources.
Promoting a sense of community and belonging.

For teenagers, social media can allow them to develop their own identity and friendships as well as giving them an area where they have some privacy and can escape from everyday stresses. The use of social media by teenagers has also been associated with a reduction in some risky behaviours as they spend much less time on the streets, where they may be more susceptible to criminal activities, alcohol and drugs.

Some of the disadvantages of social media apply to us all:

Depiction of other peoples' lives that appear to be better than ours.
Images of bodies and fitness that appear to be much better than ours.
These can easily lead us into what some describe as a 'compare and despair' mentality, where we feel that we must be totally inadequate as we don't measure up to these 'perfect' lives. This is especially likely for teenagers, who are at a very self-conscious stage of development and pay a lot of attention to the apparent world of their idols in the entertainment industries. Teenage girls and increasingly teenage boys, are very influenced by the issue of body image and this can lead to problems of self-esteem as well as issues with eating, exercising and overtraining. (See chapter 19 dealing with eating problems and disorders)

Fear of missing out. (FOMO)

Any of us who use social media, or the internet in general now suffer from this problem. Wherever, we are, we feel that we must stay in contact with the online world in case we miss out on the latest information or gossip. Teenagers, as the heaviest social media users feel this keenly. Many of them literally dare not turn off their phones in case they miss out on something that is going on in their community. As we will see later this has turned the phone into a form of addiction.

Personal abuse and bullying

This is a huge problem among teenagers with nearly three quarters of them claiming to have been victims of cyberbullying and over a third experiencing it on a frequent basis.[1] Although some bullying and social competition has always been prevalent among this age group, social media has intensified these issues and allowed them to be a 24 hour a day issue. Social media can also provide a way of excluding and isolating individuals from a group. (See Chapter 15 Bullying).

Another widespread problem is sexual harassment both from peers and from strangers. Teenagers sometimes facilitate this by providing images of themselves, either voluntarily or because of coercion. However, sometimes images are falsified or edited by others to cause embarrassment, this is a form of bullying. Whether the images are real or not, they can be used to threaten or to extort money. (See Chapter 31 for more on sexual harassment)

Radicalisation and other similar unwanted influences

Social media is now widely used by many organisations and individuals trying to influence our thinking and behaviour. This runs the risk of vulnerable young people being susceptible to various forms of radicalisation and to be receptive to the extreme views of small minorities.

Lack of meaningful, intimate relationships

Although, as we mentioned earlier, social media can alleviate loneliness and isolation, virtual relationships can come to dominate heavy users' lives. The less they go out into the world the less time they have for meeting and interacting with others in a face to face relationship. They can become very introverted and miss out on the most valuable and lasting human relationships, as well as not developing the subtle techniques required in direct communication.

Lack of sleep and 'downtime'

The pressures of social media are constant and 24 hours a day. It is not just the fear of missing out, but research suggests that many teenagers get an emotional kick from the 'likes' that they get on social media and become dependent on them in a similar way that they might do with gambling [2]. In addition, the huge amount of time and energy that they spend on their phones means that they rarely fully relax and miss out on opportunities for outdoor exercise and other pursuits. Heavy social media users are poor sleepers, and this has a knock-on effect on their wellbeing. Nearly half of teenagers admit to looking at their phone after they have gone to bed and some of them are checking their phones throughout the night.[3] In fact, there is constant social traffic going on between teenagers 24 hours a day.

Although social media has both positive and negative effects on the individual, there is now a considerable body of research [4] [5] linking heavy social media usage with a lack of satisfaction with life and higher levels of anxiety and depression. In addition, teenagers themselves report that social media adversely affects their mental health [6].

Lack of sleep and downtime is also experienced by teenagers who spend many hours playing computer games. These tend to be boys and with some, this has now become a recognised form of addiction and is included in the recently updated International Classification of Diseases (ICD-11). (See Chapter 25 dealing with gaming) Some researchers have linked excessive usage to relationship problems, worse academic achievement and less participation in face to face communities. They have also found that those who could be more vulnerable to a social media addiction include those dependent on alcohol and the highly extroverted. [7]

Experiments where people have turned off social media for a while have reported that those people felt less stressed, more satisfied and more sociable.[8] So what strategies should parents adopt?

How do I manage my teenager's social media use?

Be aware of age restrictions on social media

Most social media sites in the UK are for children aged 13 and above. This currently includes Facebook, Snapchat, Twitter, Instagram, Musical.ly, Linkedin, Pinterest, Twitch, Tinder and Skype. It is also the YouTube age for having your own account. WhatsApp have recently announced that they are moving to 16. It should be noted that some sites have different rules for teenagers than adults and some have different age limits in different countries.

Instigate screen free times for the family

As adults and parents, we need to not only set rules, but also set an example to our young people, as we are also often permanently tied to our phones. In a recent survey, teenagers admitted that their use of social media had a detrimental effect on family life, but they felt that their parents also contributed to this.[9] Consider creating some family screen-free times during school days and the weekend. Communal occasions like meal times may be a good place to start, but everybody needs to be on board. Car journeys should also be considered. Phones are a distraction for drivers, but also these journeys can provide good opportunities to talk to our teenagers.

Instigate screen curfews or screen free times for your teenager

Given the sleep related problems discussed above, a screen curfew is a good idea. It is easier to instigate this with younger children and carry it on through the teenage years with appropriate changes in the time. However, even for older teenagers and indeed ourselves, move towards not having phones or screens in the bedroom, or if we must have them, to turn off certain functions, such as notifications, and place them out of sight and out of reach. Exposure to the "blue light" associated with most devices has been shown to cause sleeplessness and anxiety and suppress the secretion of melatonin, which aids sleep. Curfews and screen free times are best established by negotiation and agreement, but there are settings and apps for phones, which can be used to impose them. Perhaps surprisingly, in a recent survey, nearly two thirds of teenagers said that they wouldn't mind if social media had never been invented, and even more young people had undergone a digital detox and were prepared to do so again. [10]

Address our dependency on social media

Discuss with your teenager why we are so dependent upon our phones. In general, the more time we spend sitting and not doing much, the more likely we are to get drawn into the temptations of social media. Developing indoor hobbies or outdoor activities for the family will help to counter this. If our teenagers are immersing themselves in the virtual world because they cannot cope in the real world, we need to find ways to boost their social skills and confidence.

Use screen time punishments appropriately

Lastly a word on punishment and consequences for bad behaviour. Many parents now see the withdrawal of phones or screen time as one of the main penalties for transgressions by their children. They know that our young people find this particularly difficult and quite rightly they see screen time as a privilege that can be withdrawn. However, do be careful about the message you are giving to your children. It is difficult to give out the message that the family needs to reduce its screen time to improve their mental wellbeing and family life, if this is also used as a punishment. Of course, it is an appropriate sanction if your teenager has been using the phone in the middle of the night, sending unpleasant messages or has been on social media, when they should have been doing homework or jobs around the house.

Improve their understanding of their children's technology

Become aware as far as possible of the sites and apps that your children are regularly visiting as social media, entertainment and information. Look for information online or if possible try them out and see what they do so that you can identify potential problems. For some of them, your children or older siblings, or relatives may be able to demonstrate them for you. They may even be activities that you can share in a positive fashion with your children.

Teach and model respectful behaviour online

If you discuss with your children in advance how they should behave online, you may avoid later problems. They need to understand that some behaviours are illegal, while others are just plain nasty and hurtful or silly. In general, your teenager should behave towards others online in the same way as they would face to face, or in the way that they would like to have others behave towards them.

Discuss appropriate content

Discuss with your children which content, websites and apps are appropriate for their age and which are not. Try to instil a level of scepticism about all online material, so that children are prepared to question its authenticity and motivation, just as they might a newspaper or advertisement or any other media. There are some people currently posting a great deal of 'fake news' online, and we are all susceptible to being drawn in to believing it. This includes the real age and character of any strangers that they meet online. Your children need to understand the difference between virtual relationships, which may be based on false impressions and real face to face ones. They should never arrange to meet these online "friends" except in a supervised environment.

Discuss what should not be posted

Clearly teenagers should not post in a way that is harmful to others and need to be careful that posts do not harm themselves. Posting embarrassing information or images about themselves which they will later regret should be avoided. Posting any indecent image of anyone under 18, including themselves, is illegal. (See sexting) Personal information such as their full name, addresses, school etc should generally not be revealed.

Discuss self-control and impulsive behaviour

Resisting temptation is difficult for all of us, but children need to be made aware of the consequences of overspending on shopping or spending too much time or money on gaming or gambling. This includes using your credit cards either with or without your permission. Controlling their impulses is an important life skill and is no different to not eating the whole bag of sweets. They also need to learn how to deal with temptations that come from other people. If they are not to be led astray, they need to have a sensible set of values and be prepared to live by them. The ability to be able to say no to others is another essential life skill, that may need to be taught as discussed in Chapter 29 Peer pressure.

Monitor your teenager's online activity

The issue of how much freedom to allow teenagers online and how much to monitor their activity is a difficult issue which needs to be responsive to teenagers age and behaviour. At one level it is an invasion of privacy, like reading their diary and it can also be over intrusive, restricting their ability to develop their own independence. When the activity took place on a family computer, it was easier to keep an eye on what was going on, but now most activity occurs on phones which are available to your teenager for most of the day and therefore is harder to track. Nevertheless, you do have a lot of options which are available using the device settings or apps (see Chapter 22 dealing with the internet):

Know your children's passwords (and keep yours secret)
Restrict times or content using parental controls on equipment
Befriend your child on social media to see postings
Monitor their location
Monitor their chat room content and texts
Monitor websites visited
Monitor all screen activity
Keep up to date about new social platforms, it's not just Facebook that is in use these days. Consider Snapchat, Instagram, Musical.ly, Tumblr, HouseParty, Live.me, YouNow, Whisper, Omegle, MeetMe, Yubo, Amino- to name but a few!

As far as possible the amount of monitoring should be discussed and explained to your teenager. Spying, that is monitoring without them knowing, should only be used as a last resort. You'll also need to be aware that the more the monitoring is imposed without agreement, the more likely teenagers are to try to find a way around it. They may change phone settings or use airport mode to interfere with the monitoring. They may create accounts that you don't know about, use other peoples' devices or identities or even have a secret phone that you don't know about. As with all forms of parental supervision you'll need to be prepared to adapt to the level of maturity and responsibility shown by your child.

References in this chapter

[1] Ditch The Label (2013), the Annual Cyberbullying Survey
[2] Turel, O.; He, Q.; Xue, G.; Xiao, L.; Bechara, A. Examination of neural systems sub- serving facebook "addiction". *Psychol. Rep.***2014**, *115*, 675–695
[3] HMC Digital Awareness UK Survey (2016), Teenage use of mobile devices during the night
[4] Sampasa-Kanyinga Hugues and Lewis Rosamund F.. Frequent Use of Social Networking Sites Is Associated with Poor Psychological Functioning Among Children and Adolescents Cyberpsychology, Behavior, and Social Networking. July 2015, 18(7): 380- 385. doi:10.1089/cyber.2015.0055.
[5] Thomee S, ICT use and mental health in young adults, Institute of Medicine, University of Gothenburg 2012
[6] Royal Society for public health, (2017) Status of mind: Social media and young people's mental health and wellbeing,
[7] Kuss DJ, Griffiths MD, Karila L, Billieux J. Internet addiction: a systematic review of epidemiological research for the last decade. *Curr Pharm Des.* 2014;20(25):4026–4052
[8] The Happiness Research Institute Denmark (2015) The Facebook Experiment
[9] HMC Digital Awareness UK Survey (2017) Parent/Pupil Digital Behaviour Poll
[10] HMC Digital Awareness UK Survey (2017) Tech control of your future on social media

Chapter 36

Stealing

When our child steals from us or someone else, it's hard to come to terms with what has happened! Today, we believe that most children are privileged, and generally get all that they need or want, and we worry that this is the start of a slippery slope into delinquency. but there are many reasons why young people steal, and many ways that they do it.

Stealing by teenagers can take many forms and teenagers often believe that there is a big difference between stealing from someone in your own household, usually from parents, and stealing from other people at school or elsewhere. The difference is considered both in terms of likely consequences and in the effect on relationships.

Parents are also role models, and even if you have taught your child the difference between right and wrong, or about property rights and the consideration of others, they will still look to see how you act in day to day life. So, if you have taken equipment or stock from your workplace, or brag about a mistake at the tills in your favour, your lessons about honesty will be much more difficult to take on.

Stealing outside the home may also involve other people either encouraging or joining in with the stealing. The main reasons for stealing are:

Thrill seeking such as shoplifting.
Trying to fit in with peer pressure by having what others have.
To get money to pay for something they shouldn't have/do such as drugs, cigarettes, alcohol, gambling, food (in the case of eating disorders).

To get money for something that they are too embarrassed to ask for such as condoms, sanitary products, medicines.
Attention seeking.
Feeling of entitlement that it is deserved.
Jealousy of someone else's possession, often a sibling considered to be more favoured.
"Borrowing" without permission.
Deliberately hurting someone else.
Impulse – couldn't resist the temptation.
To get money that they can use to spend on others to improve their image.
To get money because they are being bullied/intimidated.

Clearly the response to stealing needs to reflect the wide range of reasons indicated above. However, before anybody is accused of stealing it is essential that there is adequate proof of who the culprit is and that the item has actually been stolen. We all mislay things or forget what we have spent from time to time, so be very careful that the theft has indeed taken place. If you have several possible culprits it may be very hard to track down the person responsible, especially if this is the first time. Give people the chance to own up or rectify the situation, which may have been accidental. "Has anyone seen my wallet?" "I didn't leave some money on the side did I, has anyone seen it?" Whether you can prove it or not, if money seems to be going missing in the household you need to start locking things away and not leaving temptation in anybody's way.

You also need to establish clear cut rules in your house. If you allow people to borrow from you or other household members without proper permission, do not be surprised if things disappear possibly never to be seen again. Similarly, if you let your children regularly take money from your purse or wallet, or use your credit card to buy things online, it is easy for things to get out of hand.

If you do establish that your teenager has deliberately stolen from you or someone else, you need to take immediate action to confront them. You will probably be extremely angry, so give yourself time to cool down and try to stay calm. Remember that although you may feel it, this is not a direct reflection of your parenting or your moral standards. Rather it is your teenager having problems and dealing with them in a totally inappropriate fashion. The ideal situation is for them to admit it and so it can be useful to give them a little time to think after you have told them that you know that they have stolen. Clearly it is very important to understand why they have stolen something, and your response will be partly dependent on that, but a number of issues are critical.

If you find out that your child or teenager has stolen these are the recommended steps to take:

Tell them that stealing is wrong.
Help them pay for or return the stolen article.
Make sure that they don't benefit from the theft is any way.
Avoid lecturing, predicting future bad behaviour or saying that you now consider your child to be a thief or untrustworthy, or a bad person.
Make clear that this behaviour is totally unacceptable both within the family morality and that of the community and society as a whole.

Explain the implications of their actions

You need to explain how disappointed you are with them and how they have let themselves down. Stealing is wrong and illegal and whoever they have stolen from is right to feel hurt and that trust has been broken. Hopefully you can make them appreciate what they have done is wrong and how they need to make amends. An apology is certainly a useful beginning, if it is sincere. Clearly, they have made a mistake, but people will trust them again provided the situation is not repeated. You need to explain that if they get a reputation for stealing, their friends and other people will not trust them or want to be with them. Generally, it is not helpful to tell other people about the stealing unless it is repeated, or you feel that there is a real risk of the other people also becoming victims.

Return or replace the stolen goods

Whatever they have stolen needs to be given back. If it has been spent or gone in some other way, an equivalent of similar value needs to be found from the culprit. Stealing should never be allowed to pay or feel successful.

Impose consequences

You need to impose consequences upon their behaviour. These are likely to be consistent with the boundary setting and discipline that we discussed in Chapter 8. However, they will also need to be appropriate not just to the scale of the theft, but also to the reasons for it. If money is being spent online or on phone apps/games a restriction on access to these needs to be imposed. If money is being spent outside of the home a curfew might be needed.

It may also be useful to look at how your teenager might be able to afford the things that they want either by better money management or by earning money from a job or by some other legitimate activity.

Labelling

Labels stick! A teenager who believes himself to be a 'thief' may well have the behaviour further entrenched, believing that there is no hope for them. Stealing is a choice, not something that we are all born with as a character defect, and just as people can make bad choices, they can also determine to make different ones on another occasion.

Encourage your teenager to know that whilst you have acknowledged that they made a bad choice in stealing, you fully expect that this was a mistake or aberration and that you do not anticipate a recurrence in the future.

Try to move on

If the stealing is a one off, forget about it and try not to mention it again as it will only bring back bad memories for all concerned. If something else is stolen later, don't assume it is the same person doing the stealing, but investigate as you would normally do in any new situation. If there are other siblings in the house or other visitors, it may not be the same person.

If the stealing continues and nothing that you are doing is working, you will need to get external agencies involved. The police may well need to be involved, even if the stealing is only going on within the family. Some form of counselling may be helpful and may uncover causes that you are not aware of. Getting to the underlying reasons for stealing and making appropriate interventions so that the trusting relationships are restored is important to helping your child change to a healthier path of development.

Stealing and eating disorders

Stealing appears to be strongly associated with bulimic symptoms in people with eating disorders, and the presence of stealing may serve as a marker of eating disorder severity. This is further addressed in Chapter 19 Dealing with eating disorders.

Final Thoughts

Being the parent of a teenager can be really challenging and it is getting harder. The world is rapidly changing and there are new pressures on parents and teenagers from social media, advertising and technology. Parents and teenagers have little influence on the world around them and they can only deal with it as it is, not as they would like it to be. Parents can only fight their small corner. Parenting is a full- time responsibility, but most parents have lots of other responsibilities as well as lots of problems of their own. Building teenagers into successful adults requires patience, commitment and some luck as well. We knew we were forgiven for our many parenting mistakes when during a heart to heart family discussion our adult children said "I always knew that you cared and you did your best" and "No matter how awful I was I knew that you loved me" Parents can only hope that in the years to come when their teenagers look back on their upbringing, they say – "You were 'Good Enough' !".

Index

Cannabis 185, 189, 194-197
CBT 161, 185
Cerebellum 133
Chlamydia 239
Cocaine 56, 194-197
Communication 29-30, 68, 105-108, 110, 113, 126, 141, 191, 193, 208, 210, 235, 258, 261, 303, 310, 351
Confidence 27, 61, 71, 73, 85, 88, 93-94, 97-98, 117, 119-126, 150, 173, 176-177, 229-231, 248, 263, 304
Conflict 17, 28, 64, 108-109, 146, 165-170, 332, 341-342
Consent 236-237, 285-286, 290, 294, 324, 329
Consequences 65, 95, 97, 109-113, 115, 117-118, 167, 169, 191-192, 229, 234, 260-261, 304, 306, 340-341, 354-355, 358, 361
Coping skills 64, 104, 115, 192, 226
Cortisol 53, 153
Criticism 24, 86, 88, 120, 125, 147, 150, 191, 210, 233, 333, 347
Cyberbullying 173-174, 176, 178, 248, 350
Defiance 147, 165-170
Depression 25-29,35-36, 39, 52-56, 74, 84, 119, 131, 173, 180-189, 197-198, 255, 270, 280, 291, 309, 319, 326, 335, 352
Diet 45, 64, 114, 159-160, 184, 202, 208, 210, 212
Difficult conversations 190-193
Direction 34, 62, 75, 124, 255
Discipline 17, 27-30, 109-113, 115, 174, 176, 361
Discos 297
Dopamine 55-57, 133, 138, 182, 197, 295, 344
Drugs 34-35, 58-59, 63, 143, 190, 194-201, 237, 297, 301, 310, 358
Eating problems and disorders 202-215
Ecstasy 194-198
Electroconvulsive therapy ECT 186
Emotional control 103, 115
Emotional resilience 65
Empathy 55, 116, 119, 158, 175-176, 210, 267, 325
Enabling style 17, 25-27, 62
Epinephrine *see Adrenaline*
Examinations 33-34, 76-78, 88-90, 93, 154, 216-227
Exercise 45, 64, 67, 72, 95, 103, 122, 149, 159-161, 184, 202-203, 206, 222, 255, 266, 269, 315, 351

Permissive style *see Indulgent style*
Phobias 155, 162
Pornography 56, 233, 243, 285-296, 325
Power struggles 28, 169
Practical skills 47, 63, 77, 125
Praise 28, 66, 75, 88, 90, 92-93, 108, 113, 115, 117-118, 120, 124, 167, 183, 261, 304, 340-341
Pre-frontal cortex 133, 158
Pregnancy 48, 233, 237-239, 344
Principles 73
Priorities 32, 50, 60, 64, 86-87, 93-94, 96, 116, 124, 218-219
Privileges 111-112, 114-118, 166, 271, 339, 354
Problem-solving skills 108, 116, 168, 185, 267-268
Progesterone 44, 52, 237
PTSD 155
Puberty 44-46, 49, 52, 58, 138, 150, 203, 231-232, 332, 334
Pubic lice (Pthirus pubis) 240
Recreation *see Leisure and Relaxation*
Relationships 33-34, 55, 68-69, 77, 102, 105, 126, 181, 190-200, 228-242, 258, 266-267, 269, 289-290, 293-295, 303, 310, 327-329, 333-335, 340, 349, 351, 355, 358, 362
Relaxation 54, 95, 148, 158-161, 184-185, 220-222, 266, 272, 282
Resilience 39, 61, 65, 73, 97, 115, 176, 365
Respect 29, 59, 97, 103, 113-114, 119, 125, 150, 167, 169, 174-176, 234-235, 259-260, 294, 304-306, 312, 329, 339-340, 342, 354
Rights 103, 113-119, 125, 176, 358
Role modelling 47, 59, 64, 73, 84, 102-104, 113, 119, 122, 174, 190, 208, 228, 233, 270, 281, 334, 358
Saying no 125, 290, 306
Schools 24, 29, 32-33, 38-39, 41-42, 66, 69, 76, 80, 90, 92-93, 137, 174, 176-178, 216-218, 220, 226, 233, 310, 319-320, 325, 329, 334
Seasonal affective disorder SAD 35, 182
Self-esteem 25, 27-28, 30-31, 45, 84-85, 113, 119-127, 173, 181, 203, 208, 229-231, 234, 241, 260, 263, 266, 290, 318, 326, 338, 350
Self-harm 38, 41-42, 173, 181, 261, 307-322, 326
Sensible drinking guidelines 142-143
Serotonin 54, 182, 197
Sex 33, 47, 52-53, 138, 231, 233-234, 236, 287-295, 332

CPSIA information can be obtained
at www.ICGtesting.com
Printed in the USA
BVHW041320090719
552958BV00016B/589/P

9 780244 759858